New York
From the Air

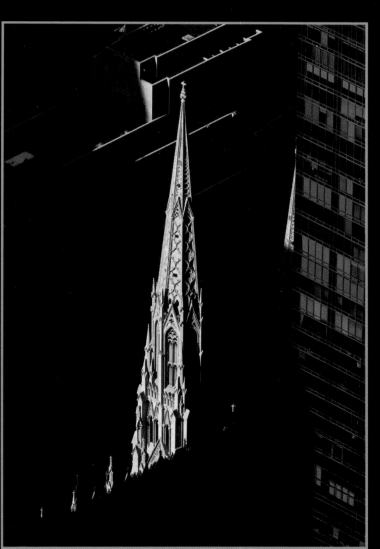

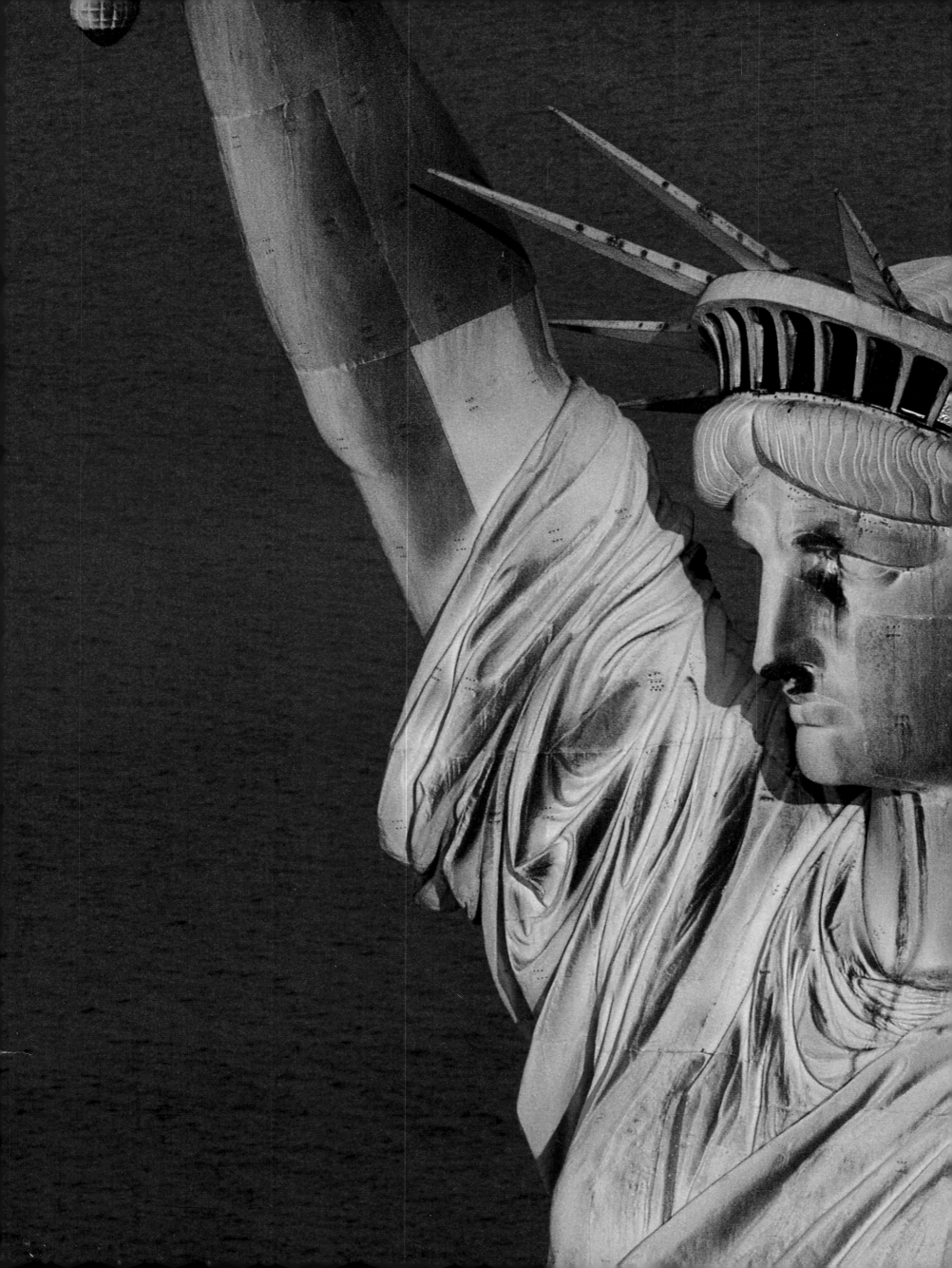

YANN ARTHUS-BERTRAND

New York

From the Air

AN ARCHITECTURAL HERITAGE

TEXT BY JOHN TAURANAC

HARRY N. ABRAMS, INC., PUBLISHERS

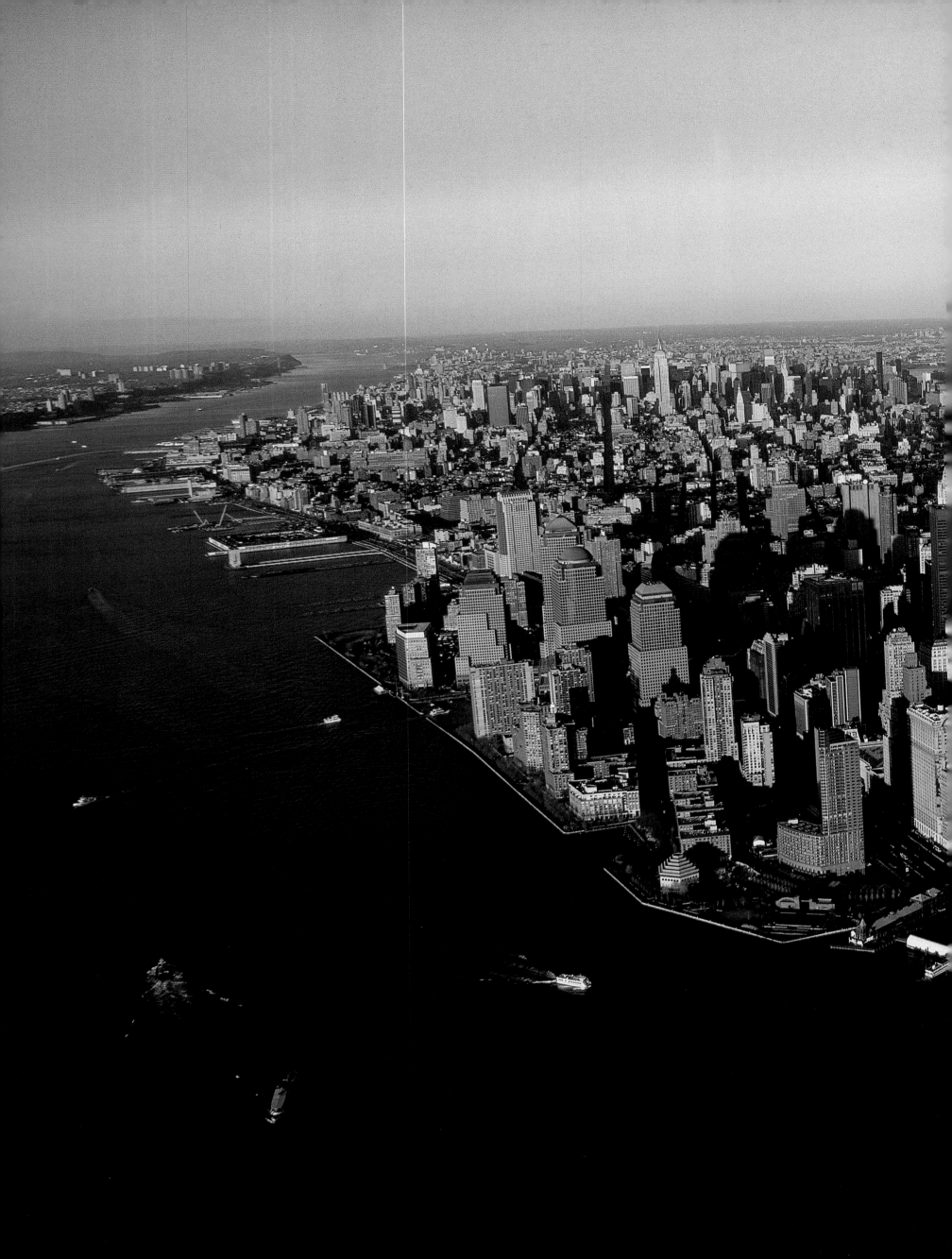

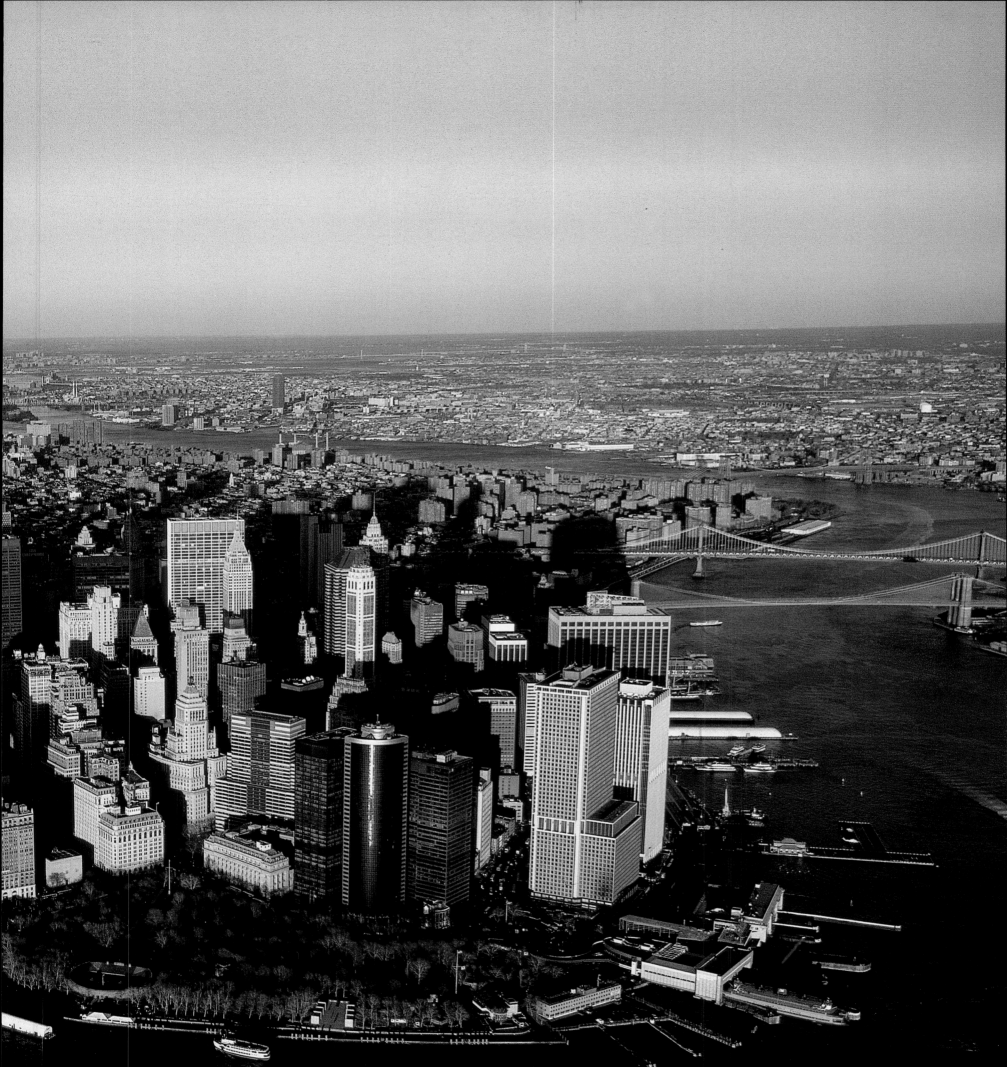

Project Manager, English-language edition:
Susan Richmond
Editor, English-language edition: David Savage
Jacket design, English-language edition:
Michael Walsh and Arlene Lee
Design Coordinator, English-language edition:
Tina Thompson
Map design: Christine V. Edwards

Library of Congress Cataloging-in-Publication Data
Arthus-Bertrand, Yann.
　[New York vu d'en haut. English]
　New York from the air : an architectural heritage /
[photographs by] Yann Arthus-Bertrand ; text by
John Tauranac.— Rev. ed.
　　　p. cm.
Includes index.
　ISBN 0-8109-4577-0
　1. New York (N.Y.)—Aerial photographs.　2. New
York (N.Y.)—Buildings, structures, etc.—Aerial
photographs.　I. Tauranac, John, 1939–　II. Title.

F128.37.A68 2003
917.47'1'00222—dc21
　　　　　　　　　　　　　　　　　2002155255

Printed and bound in France
10 9 8 7 6 5 4 3 2 1

Harry N. Abrams, Inc.
100 Fifth Avenue
New York, N.Y. 10011
www.abramsbooks.com

Abrams is a subsidiary of
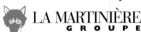
LA MARTINIÈRE
G R O U P E

FRONTISPIECE: STATUE OF LIBERTY, IN NEW YORK HARBOR

The Statue of Liberty, facing the harbor through which so many immigrants and visitors have passed since she was officially unveiled in 1886, is arguably the most famous statue in the world. Officially called *Liberty Enlightening the World*, the 151-foot-high colossus raises her torch of freedom while holding a tablet with the date of the Declaration of Independence. Beside her sandaled feet are broken shackles, yet another symbol of freedom for the "huddled masses yearning to breathe free," as the poet Emma Lazarus wrote.

The statue was a gift from the people of France to the people of the United States. There was only one stipulation with the gift—the people of the United States had to underwrite the cost of the base. July 4, 1876, the propitious date originally scheduled for the consecration of the statue, came and went, and it wasn't until Joseph Pulitzer started raising funds through his newspapers that contributions came trickling in.

The statue, by the French sculptor Frédéric-Auguste Bartholdi, holds within her copper-repoussé skin the secret of how, for over a century, she withstood the rigors of the winds that whistle across the harbor. A skeleton of iron not unlike the Eiffel Tower supports the statue. It is, in fact, an Eiffel tower, designed by the brilliant French engineer Gustave Eiffel.

The statue suffered the effects of time and weather despite this, and another enormous fund-raising effort was initiated for the restoration. The statue's skin was completely restored, the iron skeleton was reconfigured and strengthened, and a new torch was installed.

OVERLEAF: MANHATTAN ISLAND VIEW LOOKING NORTH

Manhattanites frequently forget that their home is an island, their city an archipelago. If not for the waterways surrounding Manhattan, however, the city probably would not have developed into the seat of a mighty metropolis. The fact that Manhattan is hemmed in by water is one reason why the city did not readily spread out, like other cities, but instead spread up, creating in its upward sprawl its most famous feature: its skyline. In 1906 H. G. Wells described Manhattan's skyline as "the strangest crown that ever a city wore."

Despite what Manhattanites might think, Manhattan is not a world unto itself. Ferries and helicopters link the island with its neighbors, as do four automobile tunnels, two rail tunnels, twelve subway tunnels, and eighteen bridges. The three bridges you see on your right are the Brooklyn, Manhattan, and Williamsburg.

The city has a natural deepwater harbor for Atlantic shipping and a back door to its waterways via Long Island Sound, which leads to the East River on your right; the Hudson River is on your left. The Hudson offered a path to the Hudson River Valley and, after 1825, to the Midwest via the Erie Canal. The East River, which in geological terms is actually a tidal strait, has strong tidal currents that made it the city's primary docking area in the days of sail; until the end of the nineteenth century, it was where the biggest ships docked.

INTRODUCTION

I am not a photographer of cities. I would even go so far as to say that the city seems to me to be a "mistake" opposed to the happiness of mankind. To this radical judgment, however, I would make two exceptions: Venice and New York. Two cities with very different faces but where, strangely, I feel at ease, in harmony.

But here we speak only of New York. So many cultures are mixed together in this city, so many strangers cohabit here, that no matter how much of a stranger you may be, you become a New Yorker as well. You merge with the movement, a constantly boiling mixture that is completely coherent in every way and has been for a long time.

With the terrorist attacks on September 11, 2001, and the destruction of the city's two tallest buildings, New Yorkers lost a bit of their identity. Yet despite its wounds, New York is striving to heal itself. Although an exact rebuilding of the World Trade Center is improbable, reconstruction is certain, not only to revive that part of the city but also to pay homage to the thousands of Americans and foreigners who perished there. While waiting to see what the new face of New York will be, we can continue to contemplate this city and dream of all manner of architectural feats, mythical and vertiginous.

Yann Arthus-Bertrand

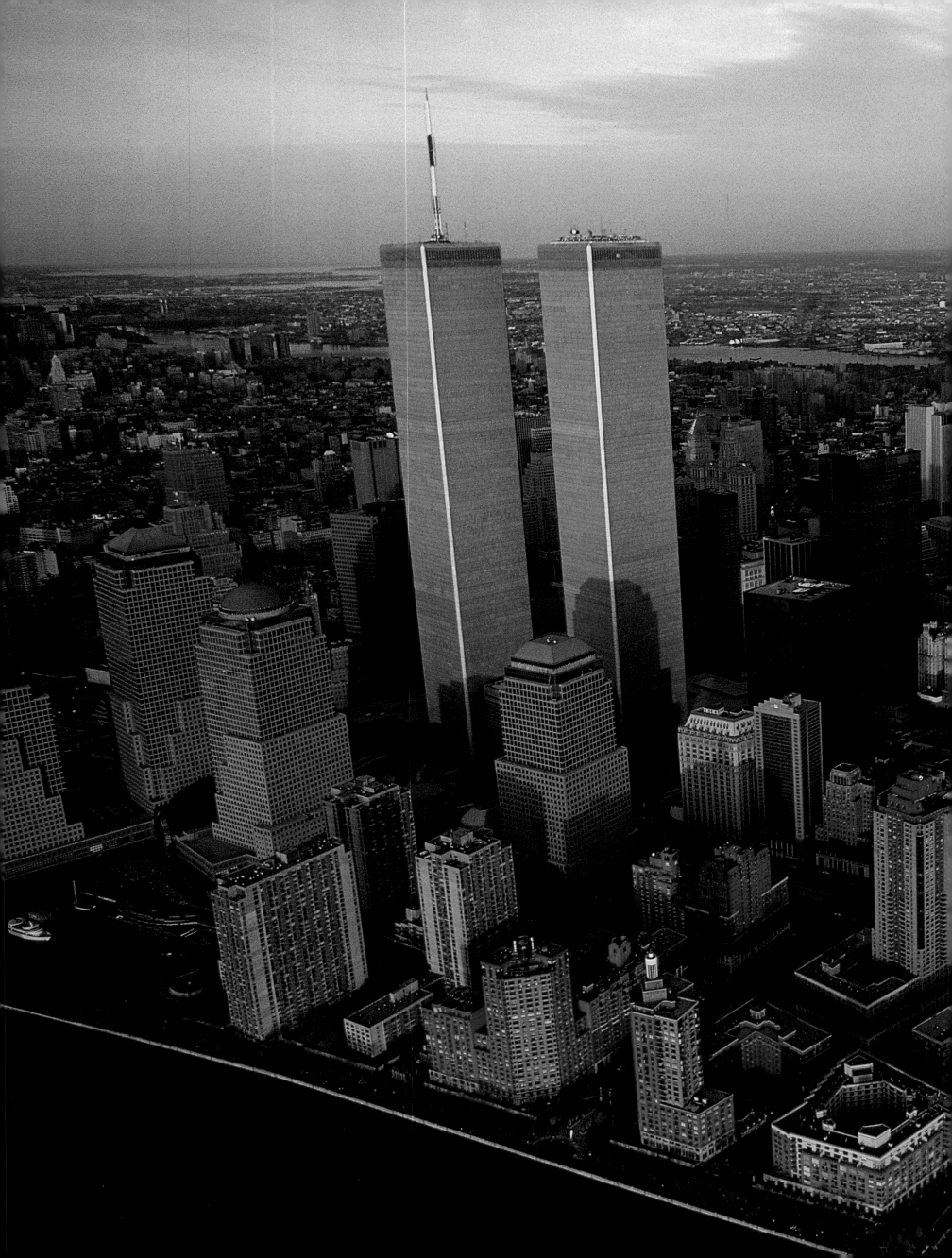

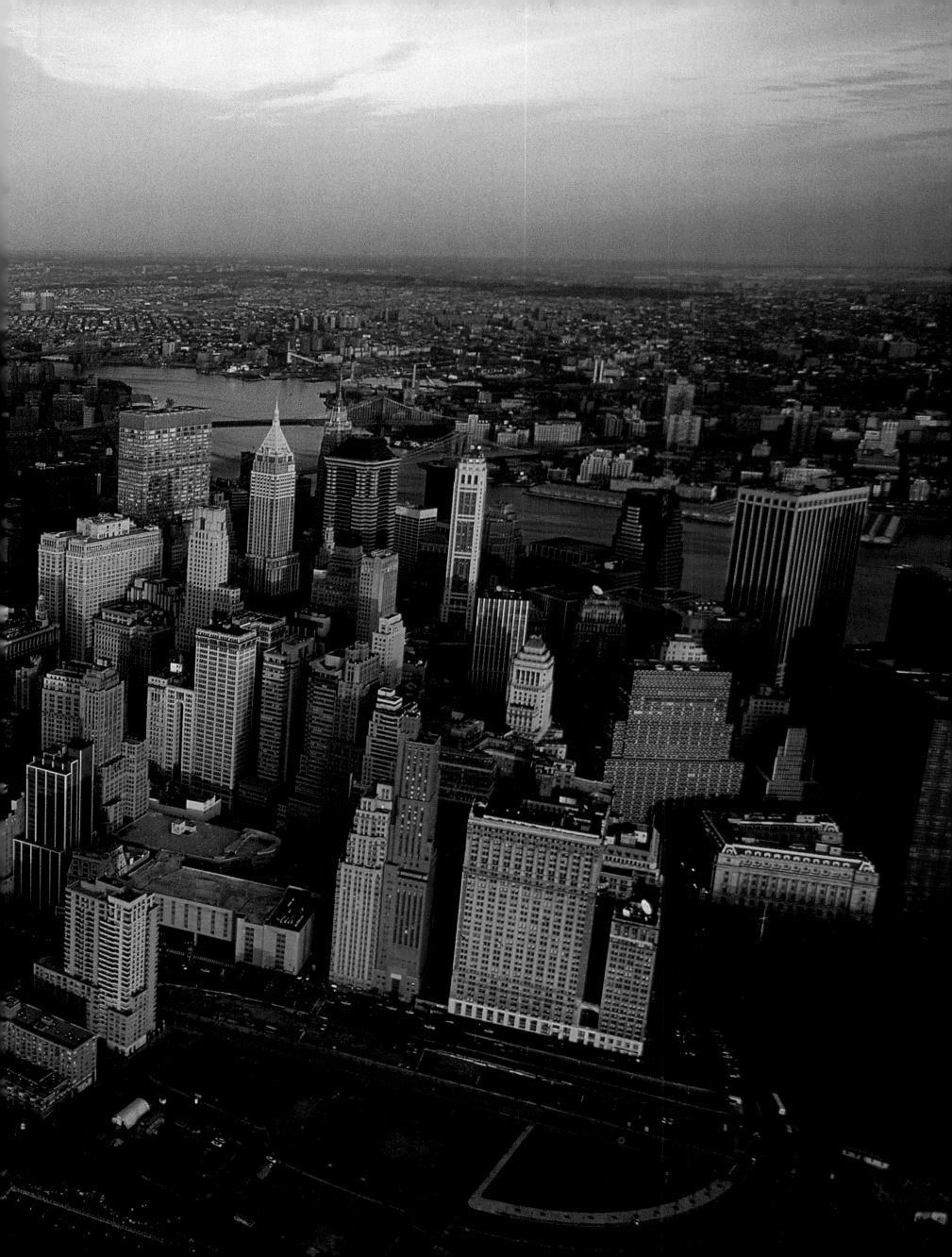

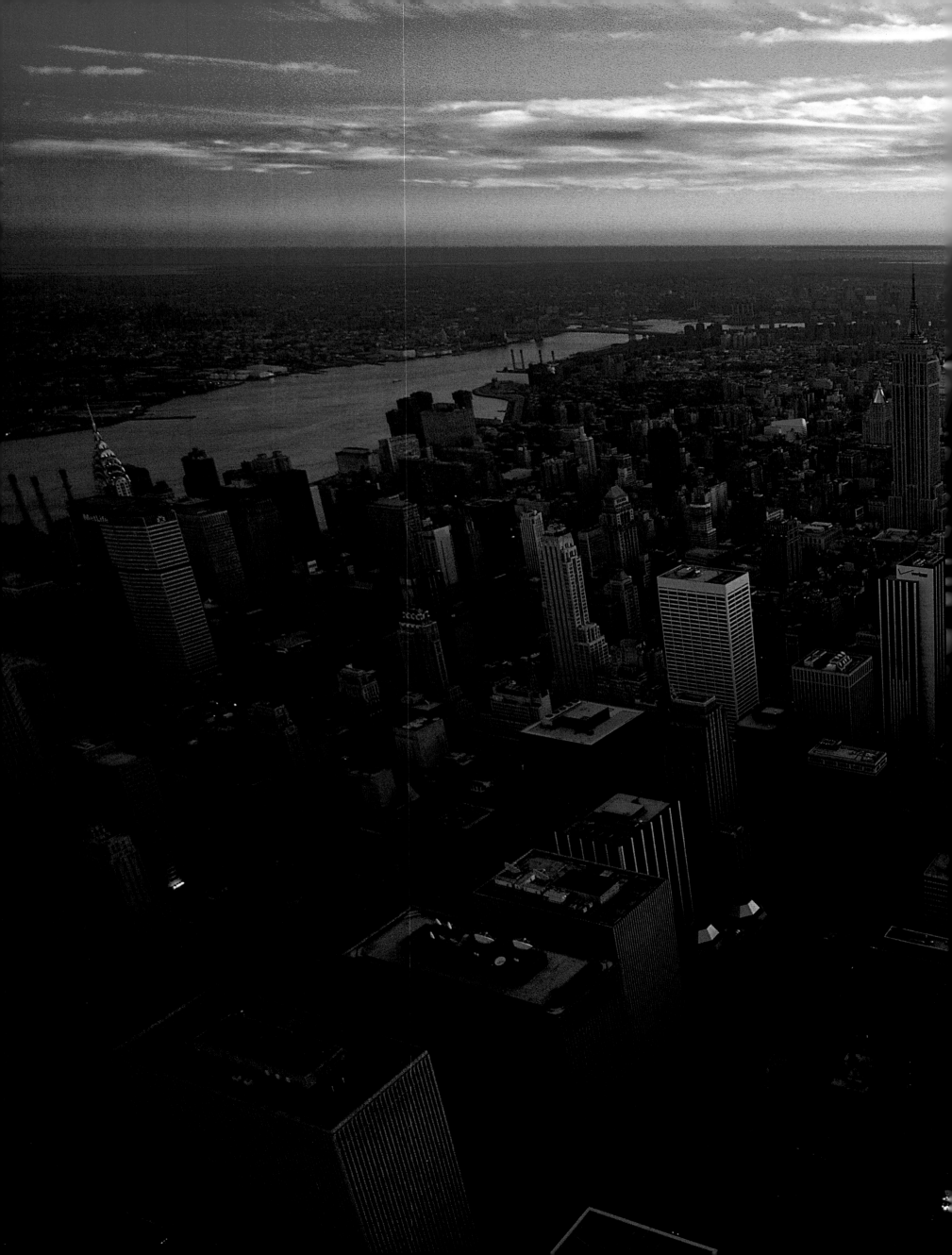

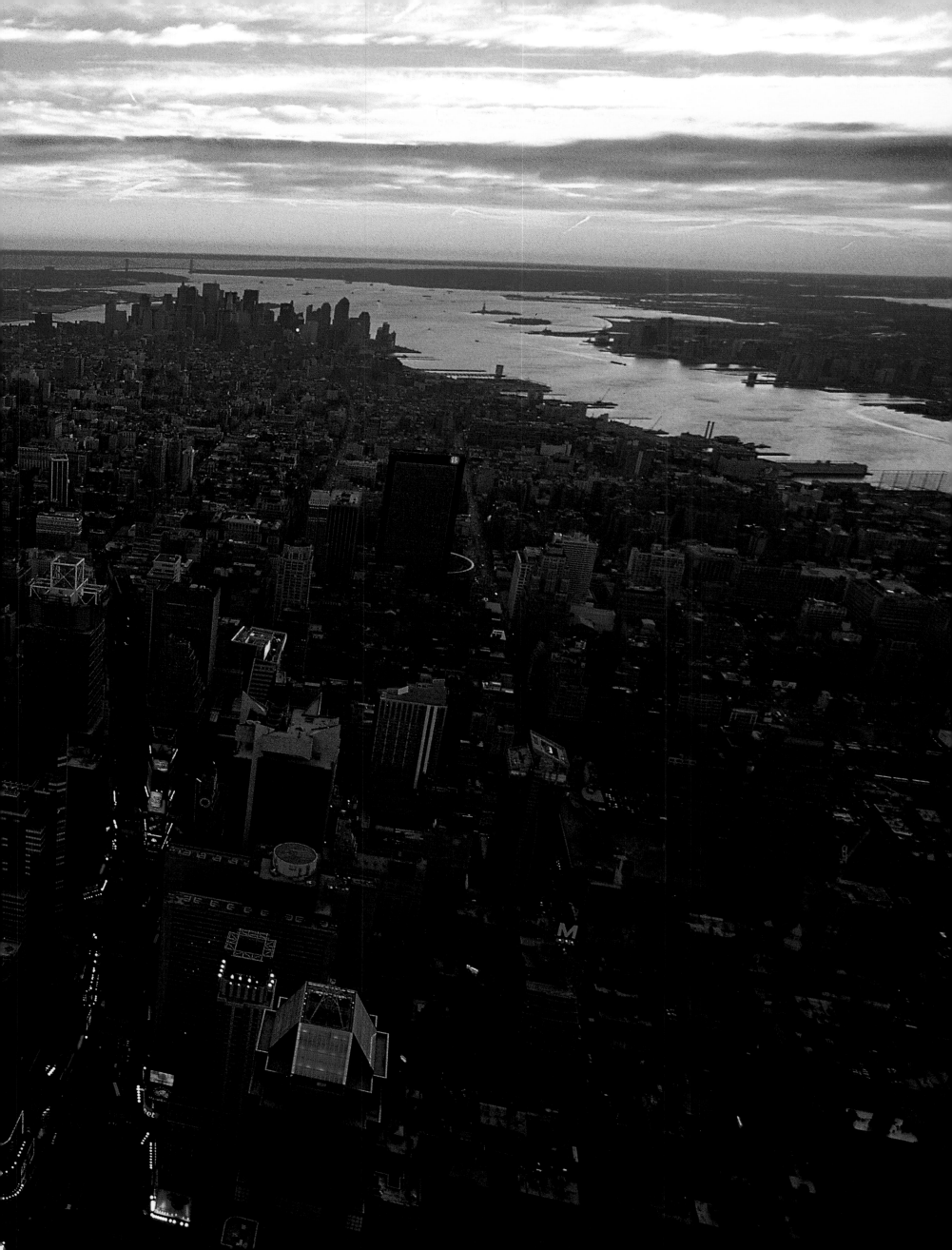

New York is known for holding more world records for the tallest structures than any other city in the world.

In this view looking south from Midtown are two record-holding suspension bridges across the East River linking Manhattan with Brooklyn: the Williamsburg Bridge (1903) and the Brooklyn Bridge (1886). Also visible is the Verrazano-Narrows Bridge (1964), the suspension bridge linking Brooklyn with Staten Island that spans the Narrows.

Buildings that have held the blue ribbon for world's tallest include the Chrysler Building (1930), the Empire State Building (1931), the Metropolitan Life Tower (1909), and the Woolworth Building (1913).

New York also had the distinction of holding another kind of record—the tallest building ever torn down, the Singer Tower (1908–1970), which had been the world's tallest when it was first built. Now the city holds an even sadder distinction—the two tallest buildings ever destroyed.

In the shadow in center stage stands the building that for more than forty years was the tallest structure in nineteenth-century New York, the steeple of Trinity Church on Broadway at the head of Wall Street. Visitors would climb to the top and comment on how small—how antlike—the pedestrians seemed below.

By the beginning of the twentieth century, Trinity's steeple was already overshadowed by some of the buildings in this view. By 1916 the buildings were even taller, their shadows longer. Although it was not quite the wall of skyscrapers we see now, the area at that time included one forty-story building and one thirty-three-story building, two with twenty-three stories, and three with twenty-one. They all rose straight up from the building line, obscuring the sun from the streets below. In their shadows the City wrote a zoning law that stipulated that buildings could only rise a certain multiple of the width of the street they faced, above which setbacks or towers had to be constructed to allow sunlight to reach the streets below. Legislators and developers alike had concluded that without such a law the city would be cast in darkness.

Seventy Pine Street was one of the last entries in the frenzied real-estate boom that started in the 1920s. Like other buildings that opened in the 1930s after the stock market crash, 70 Pine had difficulty renting its offices, even though it combined the panache of a chic Art Deco facade with a height of 965 feet, making it Lower Manhattan's tallest building.

The management sought to attract tenants by giving the building a slightly tonier address than 70 Pine Street. A bridge was built to connect it with the building at 60 Wall Street, and 70 Pine was dubbed 60 Wall Tower. (With the demolition of 60 Wall Street, the bridge came down; the new brickwork that patched up the south wall of 70 Pine is clearly visible from the street.) The building boasted a marvelous observation area, but it never caught the public's fancy.

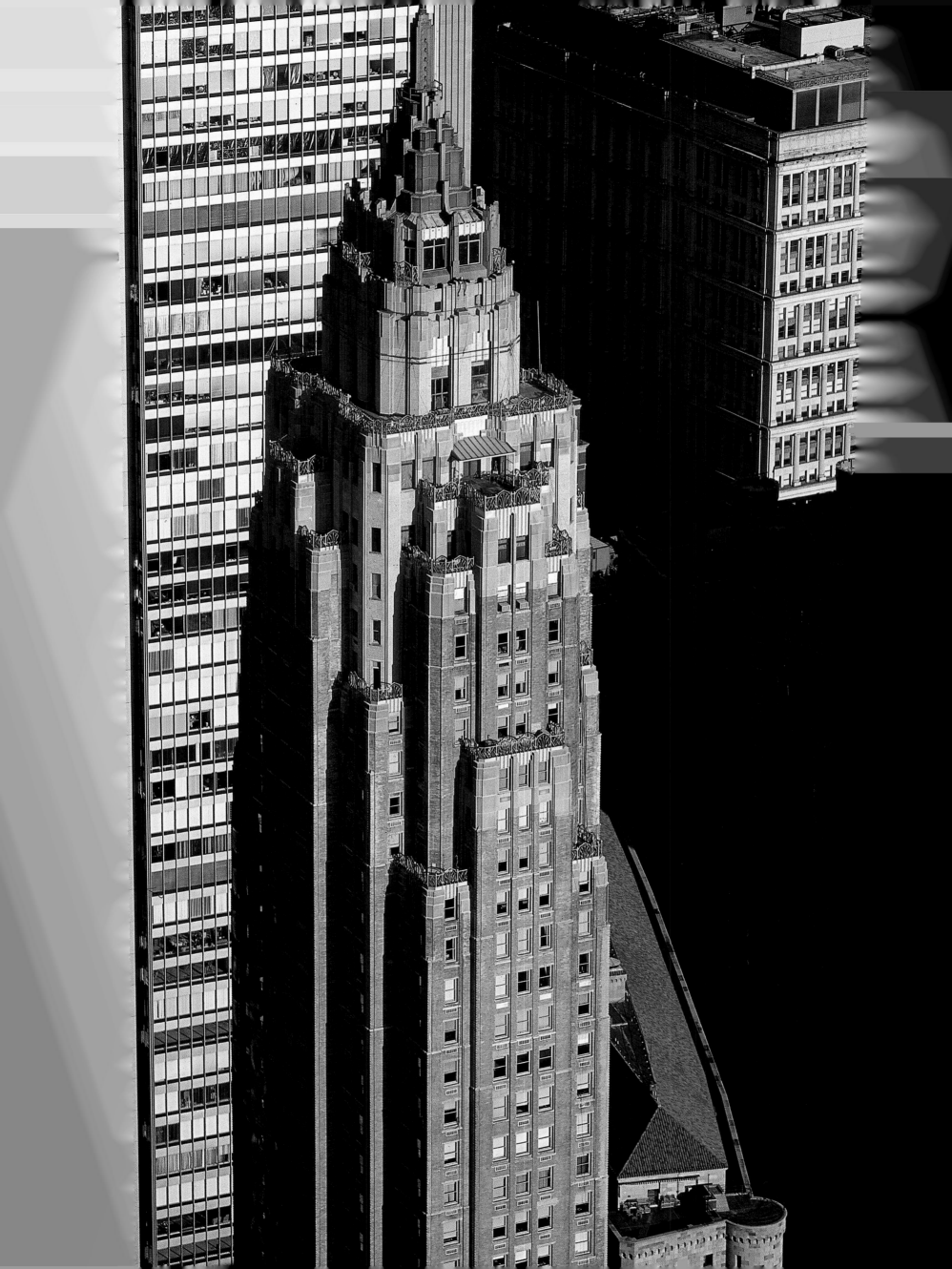

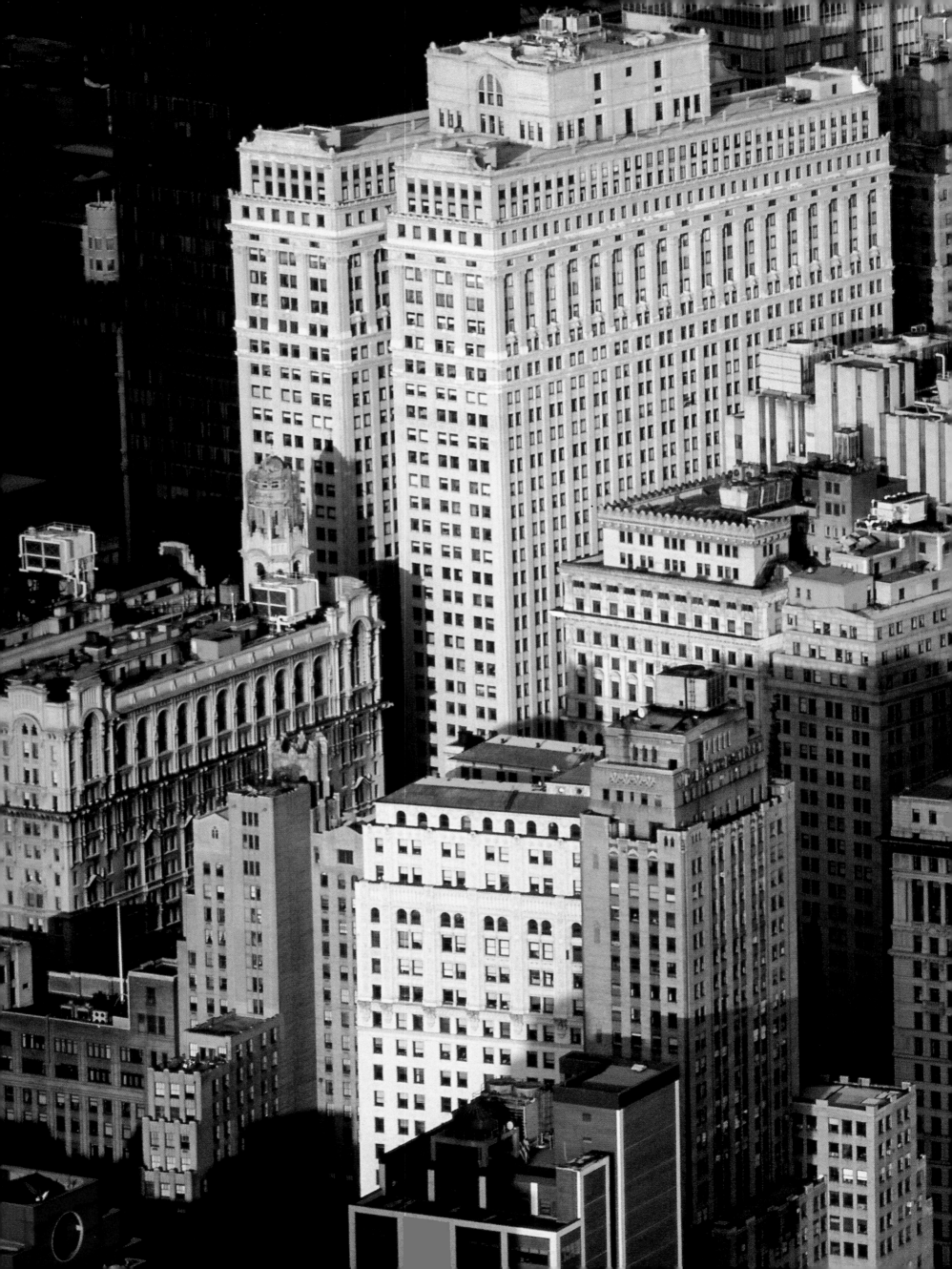

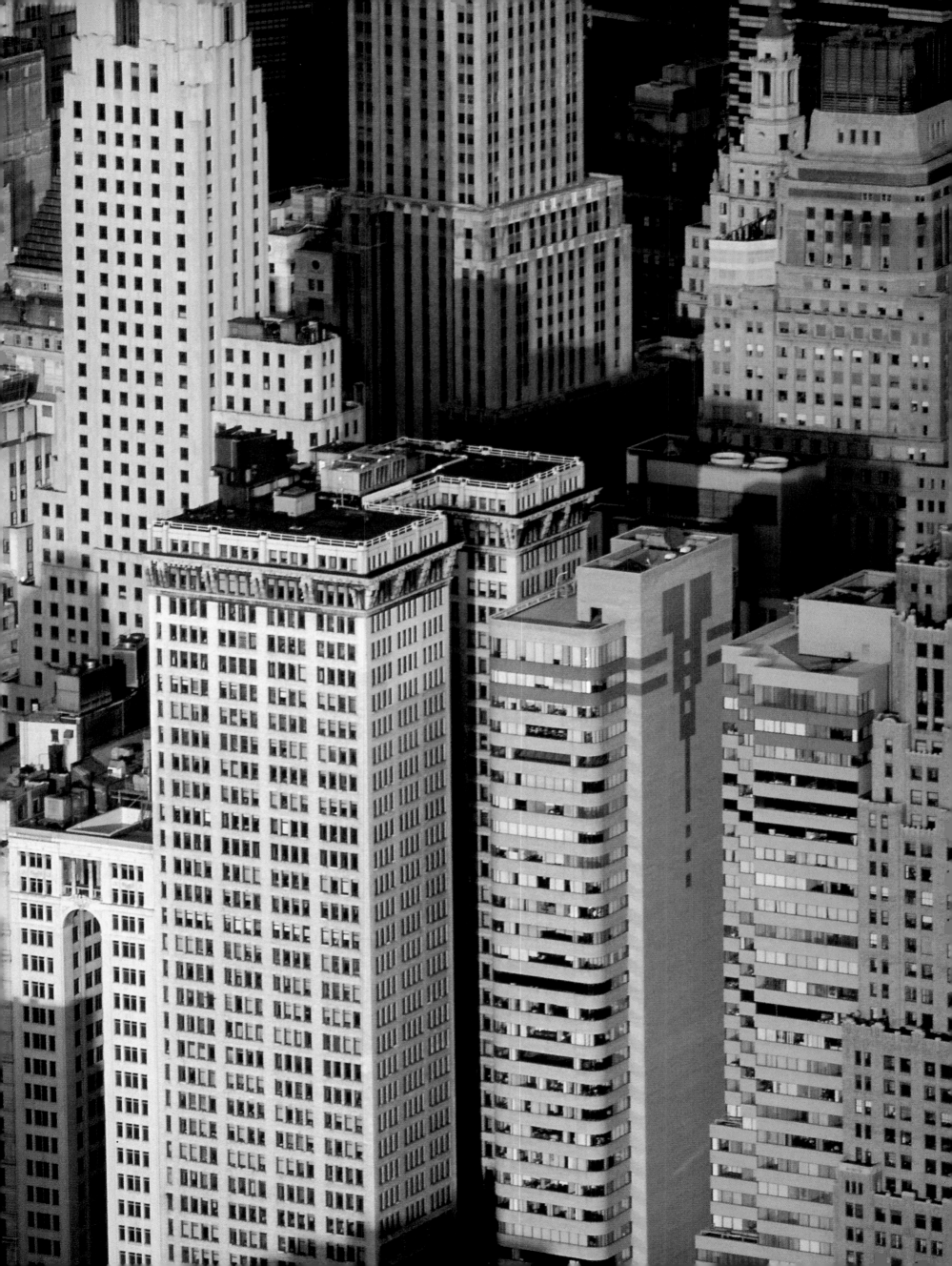

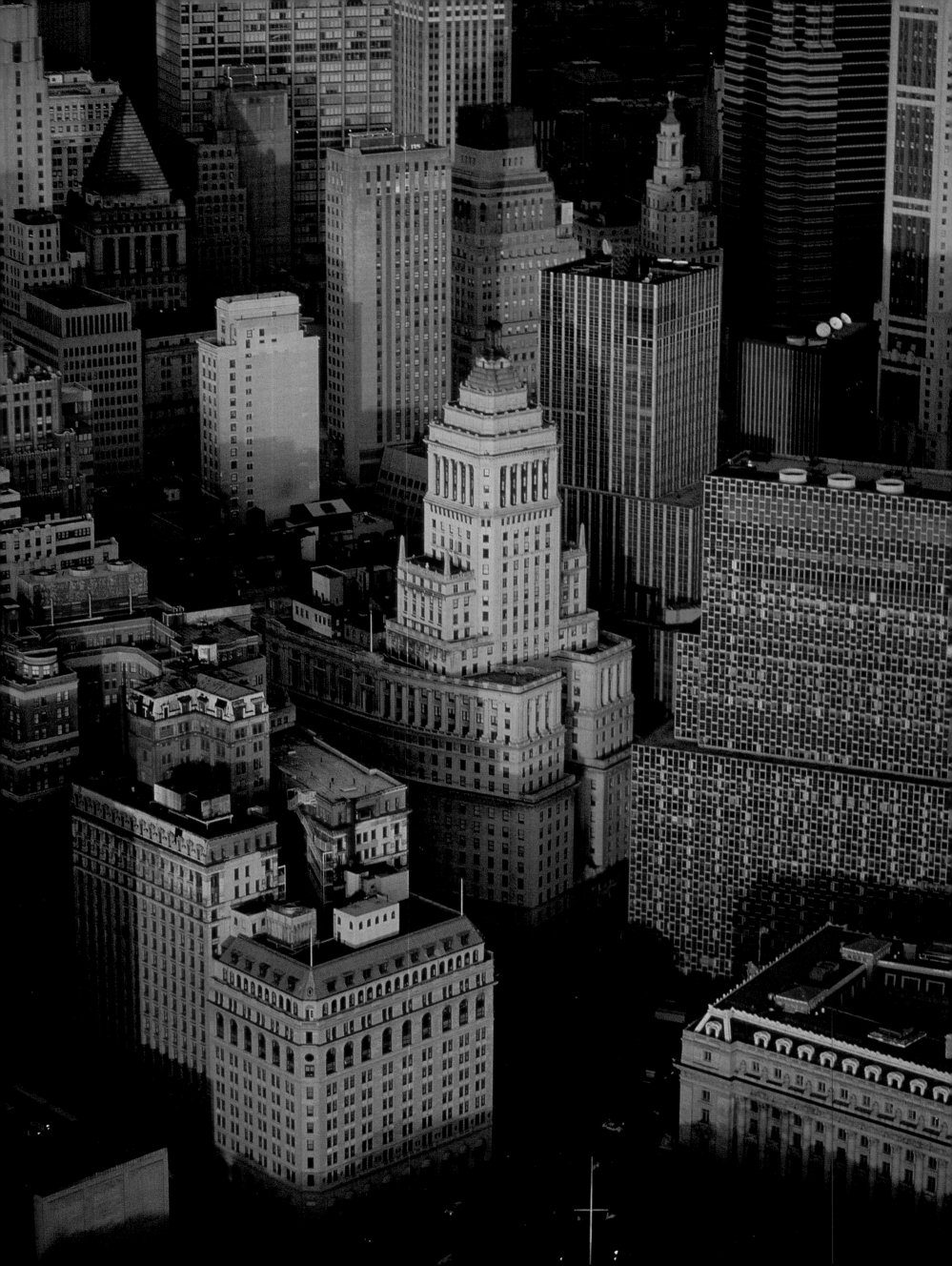

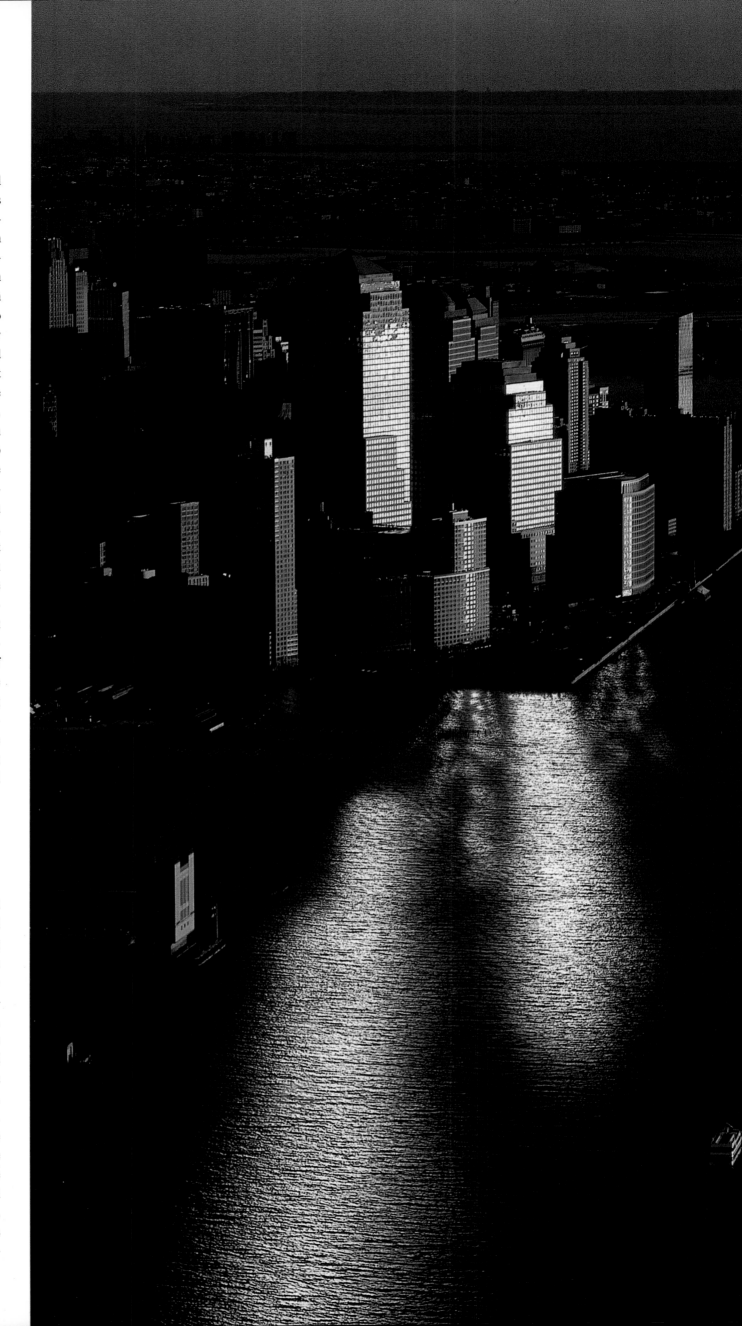

A whole catalogue of commercial building styles is laid out before us here. From bottom right going counter-clockwise is the former U.S. Custom House (1907), a Beaux-Arts extravaganza designed by Cass Gilbert, which now houses the National Museum of the American Indian. Next, Two Broadway (1958), designed by Emery Roth & Sons in a style best described as "Commercial Modern." Top right is Wall Street Tower at 20 Exchange Place (1931), in the Art Moderne style. To its left, the Postmodern J. P. Morgan Building (1988) at 60 Wall Street. Top center is 40 Wall Street (1929), whose style merges neoclassicism with functionalism. Next, One Chase Manhattan Plaza (1963), designed by Skidmore, Owings & Merrill in the Modernist style. The Art Moderne building with chamfered corners at the top left is One Wall Street (1931). Originally the Irving Trust Company, it is now the Bank of New York. The neoclassical building to its right with the pyramidal roof is Bankers Trust. Bottom left is One Broadway, the most venerable building in sight—built as the Washington Building in 1884, it was given a new facade in the Renaissance style in 1922. In the center is the neoclassical Standard Oil Building (1922) at 26 Broadway.

The architect Cesar Pelli designed four office buildings for the World Financial Center. Seen here glittering in the setting sun are the American Express and Merrill Lynch headquarters. The idea for the development—built on landfill in the Hudson River, known as Battery Park City—was sparked by a very sensible idea: instead of carting away the excavation from the World Trade Center construction, use it for landfill right across the street. Money would be saved in haulage fees, and a new development site would be created in Manhattan where none had been before. The magic spell was broken on September 11, 2001, when the World Trade Center was destroyed and many neighboring buildings were damaged.

The skyscraper housing New York's newest hotel and condominium apartments is The Ritz-Carlton New York, Battery Park. The hotel, a proud heir to the Ritz name, occupies the lower fourteen floors, with condominiums under its management on floors 15–39. Standing at the southern tip of Manhattan, you are offered commanding views of the city to the north and east and panoramic views of the harbor to the south and west.

This is one of the most exclusive hotels to open in New York in recent years. For instance, in a first-class hotel restaurant you might be accustomed to having a sommelier recommend a Château Margaux or Lynch-Bages. But when was the last time Evian or Perrier was recommended as your water of choice? In this dining room, a water specialist, trained at a Swiss hotel school, will do just that. For the average New Yorker though, tap water—straight from the Croton Reservoir—is perfectly acceptable.

The late 1920s saw a rush to construct buildings that dramatically changed the face of the city.

Forty Wall Street rose to a height of seventy-two stories (927 feet), and in summer 1929 construction stopped, with the title of world's tallest building seemingly secured. Walter P. Chrysler, not to be outdone, ordered construction to continue on his building, and soon the Chrysler Building was the world's tallest. For one brief shining moment, however, 40 Wall had reigned supreme.

The building was erected in the then record time of eleven months by Starrett Bros. & Eken. With that on their résumé, the construction company won the bid on the Empire State Building.

The 1.3-million-square-foot 40 Wall has been refurbished under its new owner, Donald Trump. Unfortunately, there are no plans to reopen the lookout that was housed within the pyramidal top.

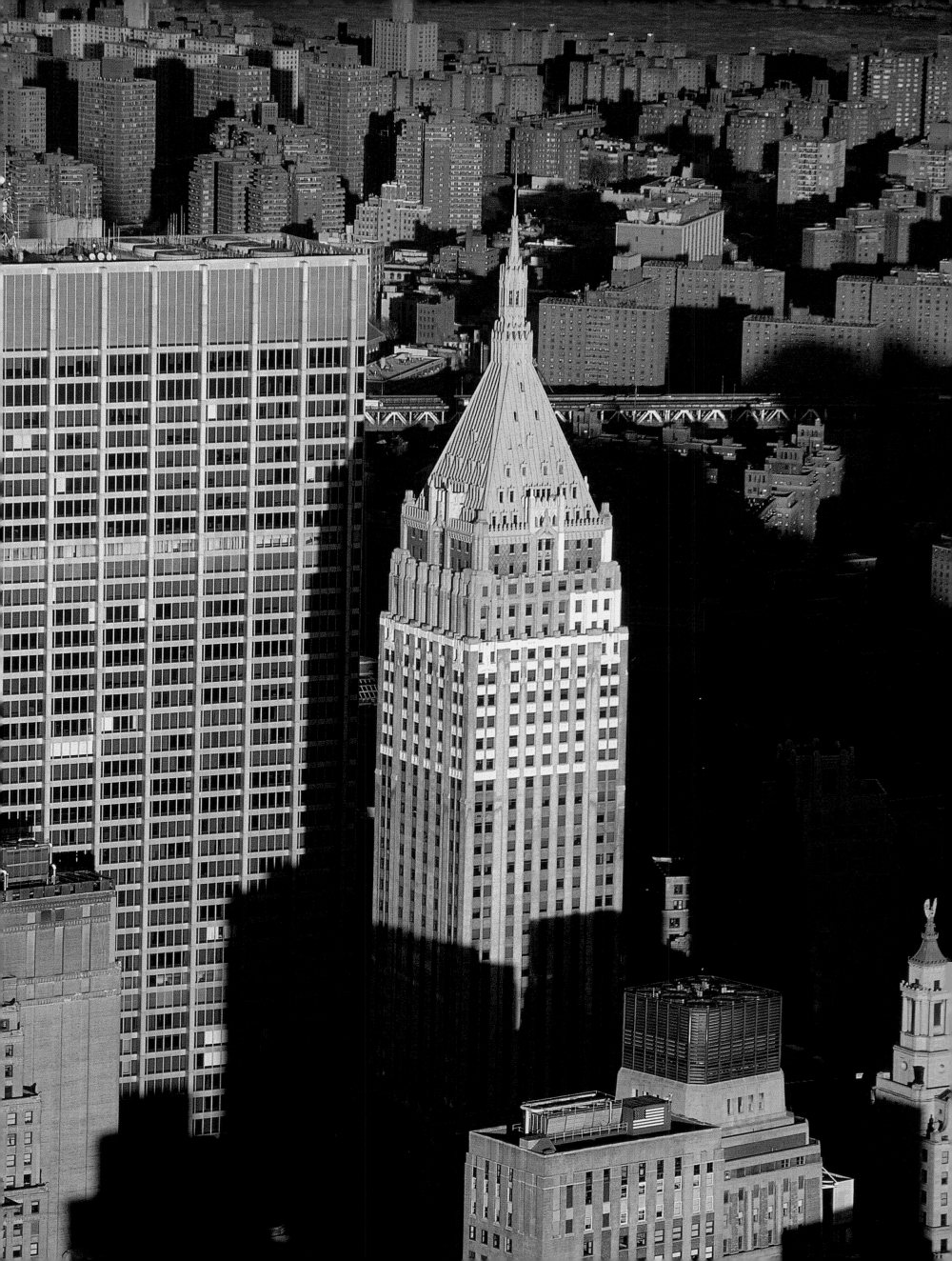

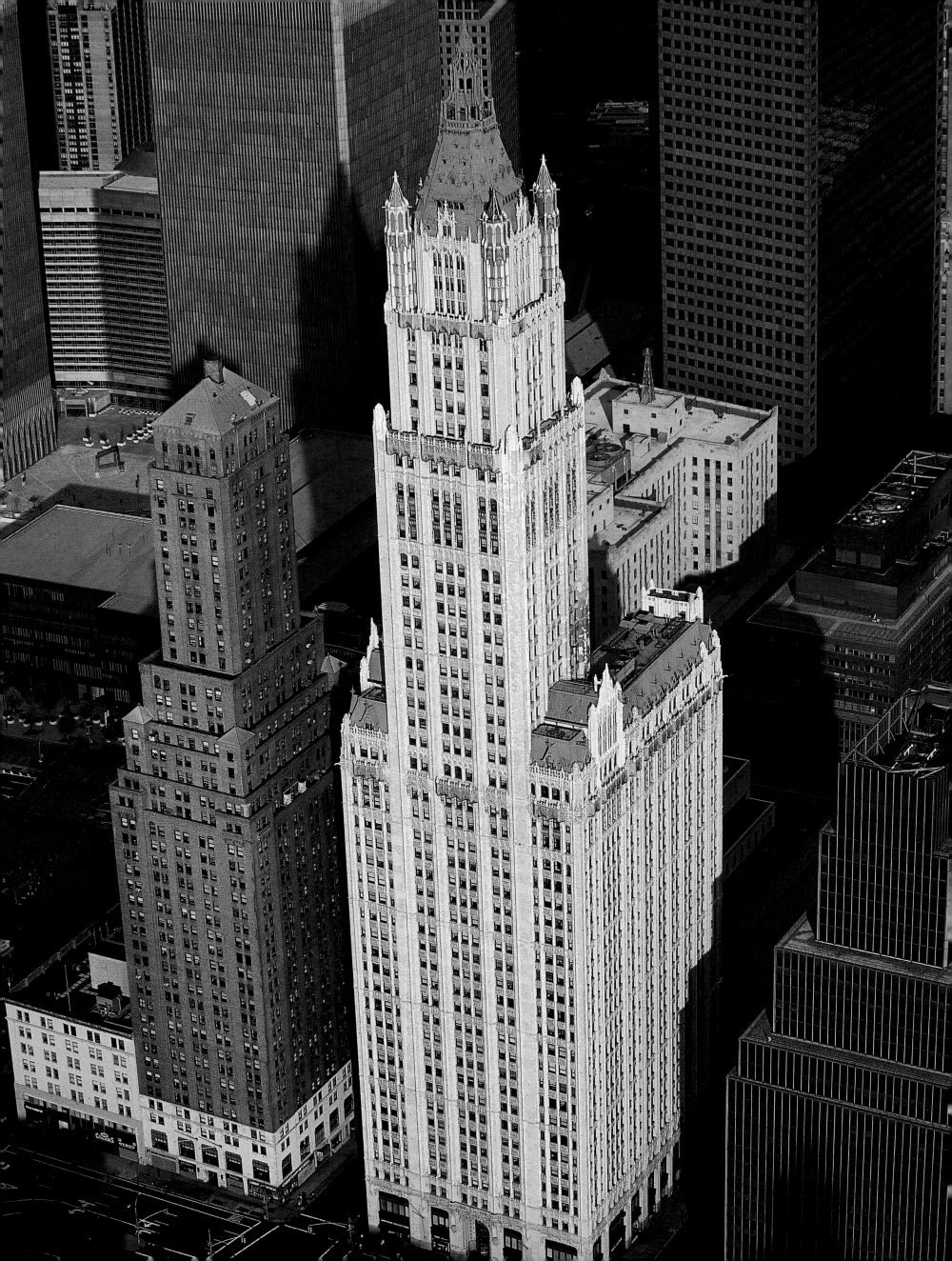

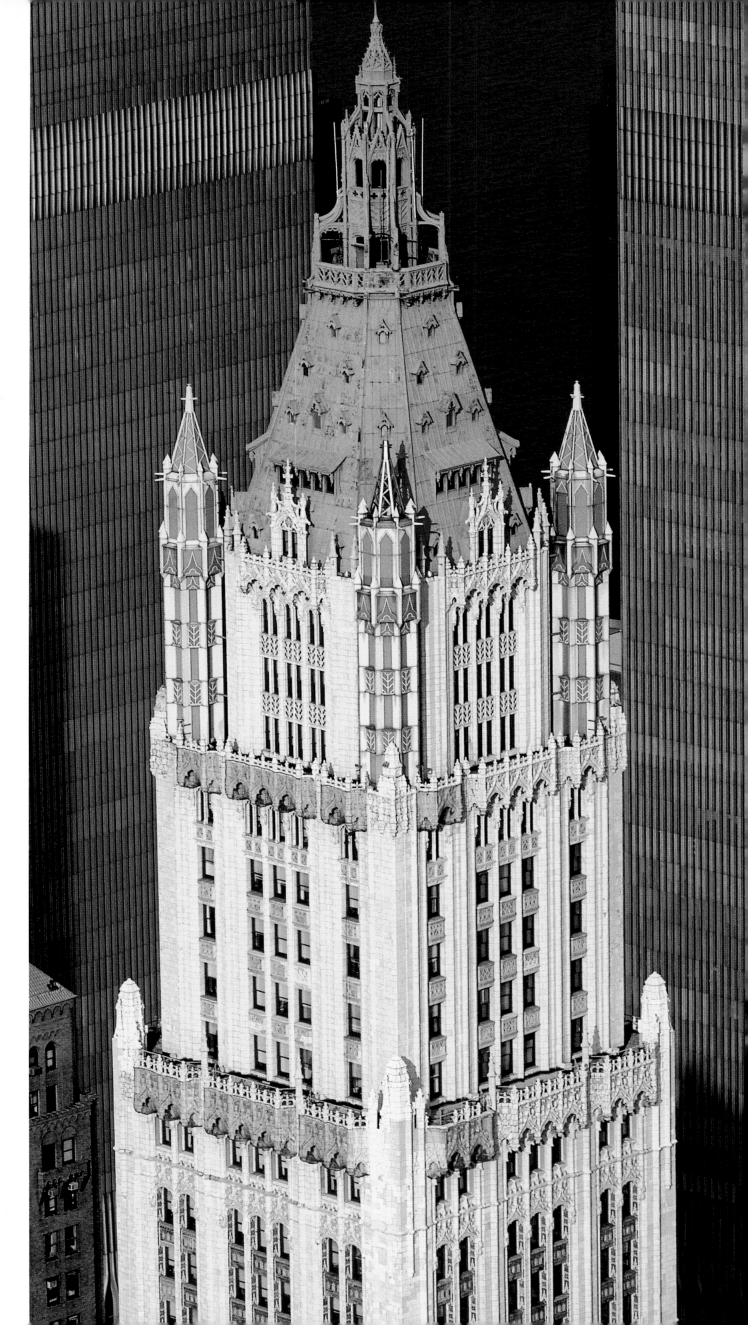

WOOLWORTH BUILDING, 233 BROADWAY, BETWEEN BARCLAY STREET AND PARK PLACE
VIEW LOOKING SOUTHEAST

In 1913 the Woolworth Building was dubbed the "Cathedral of Commerce" by the Episcopal bishop of New York at the consecration-of-the-house dinner. The Gothic style indeed lent the building an ecclesiastical air, and the sobriquet has remained to this day.

Frank W. Woolworth, whose chain of five-and-ten-cent stores had become worldwide by 1910, had two requirements for the design: he told the architect Cass Gilbert that he wanted his new corporate headquarters to resemble London's Houses of Parliament and that he did not care how tall the building was—as long as it was the tallest.

Woolworth wanted the biggest advertising billboard in town, and he got it. Every major newspaper ran a story on the building when it opened, every guidebook to the city was updated to include it, and every tour guide and civic booster pointed it out.

The building is undeniably one of the masterpieces of early-twentieth-century skyscraper architecture, a building that was the embodiment of Louis Sullivan's idea of the "great soaring thing." It is still in the guidebooks, still pointed out by guides, and still a favorite of New Yorkers. In a recent poll taken by the local chapter of the American Institute of Architects that asked members to name their favorite New York buildings, the Woolworth Building ranked eighth.

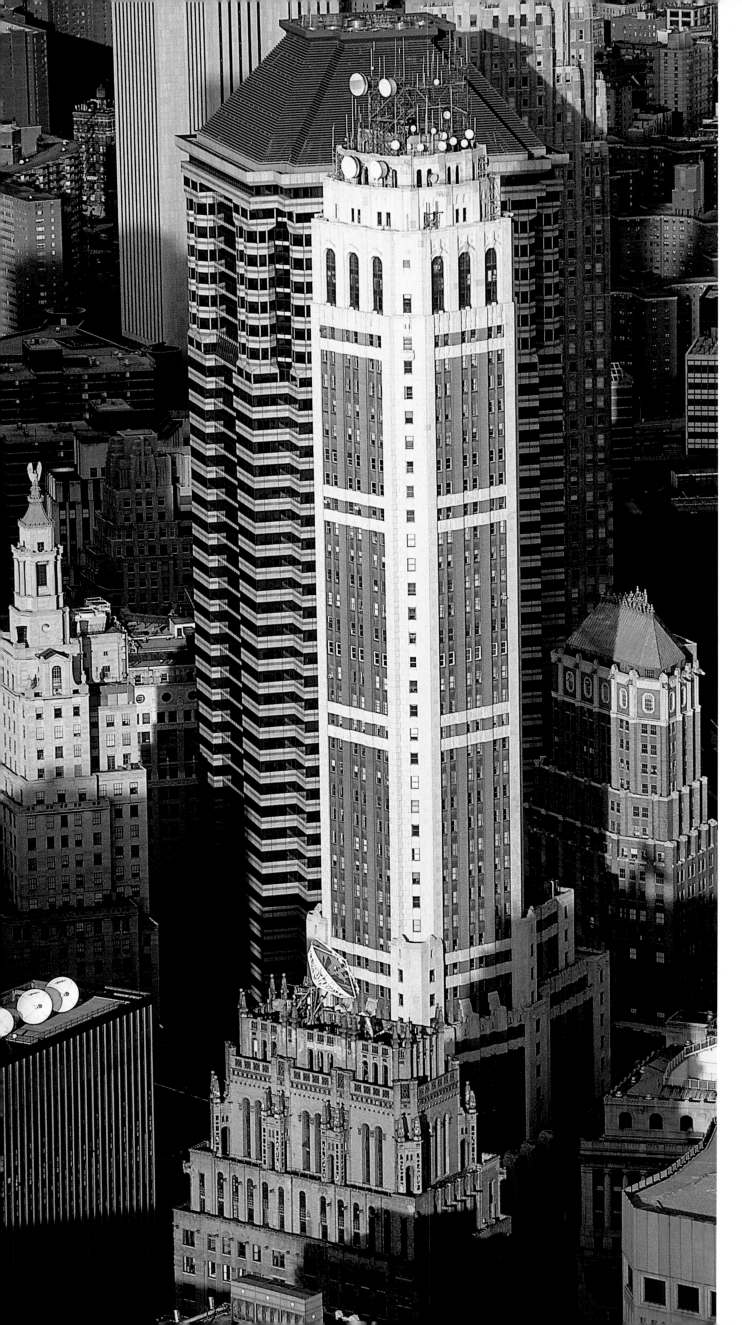

This building now bears a name that may have greater cachet than its simple address, but it belies the building's precise whereabouts a block away from Wall Street.

With its fifty-four stories and 760-foot height, 20 Exchange Place was heralded as "almost as high as the Woolworth Building" when it opened in 1931, a strange claim to fame because several buildings had already eclipsed the height of the Woolworth Building. The style of this dramatic Art Moderne tower emphasizes its height: it has corners that are gently chamfered, with vertical rectangular panels that become shorter the higher they climb. The base of the tower sits on a peculiar trapezoidal plot, but the architects Cross & Cross successfully made the transition from an awkward site to an especially graceful building.

A forest of neoclassical obelisks atop 67 Broad Street contrasts with the starkness of the entrance to this office building, one of dozens of buildings erected by Abraham E. Lefcourt in the 1920s. But unlike most of his buildings—the Lefcourt Colonial (see pages 54–55), the Lefcourt National, the Lefcourt State, the Lefcourt Normandie, the Lefcourt Manhattan—this one does not have his name on it.

In 1927 International Telephone & Telegraph signed a twenty-one-year lease on about 120,000 square feet of space. Lefcourt asked Ely Jacques Kahn, of Buchman & Kahn, to design the building, and the work was supervised by Louis S. Weeks, the architect for the corporation.

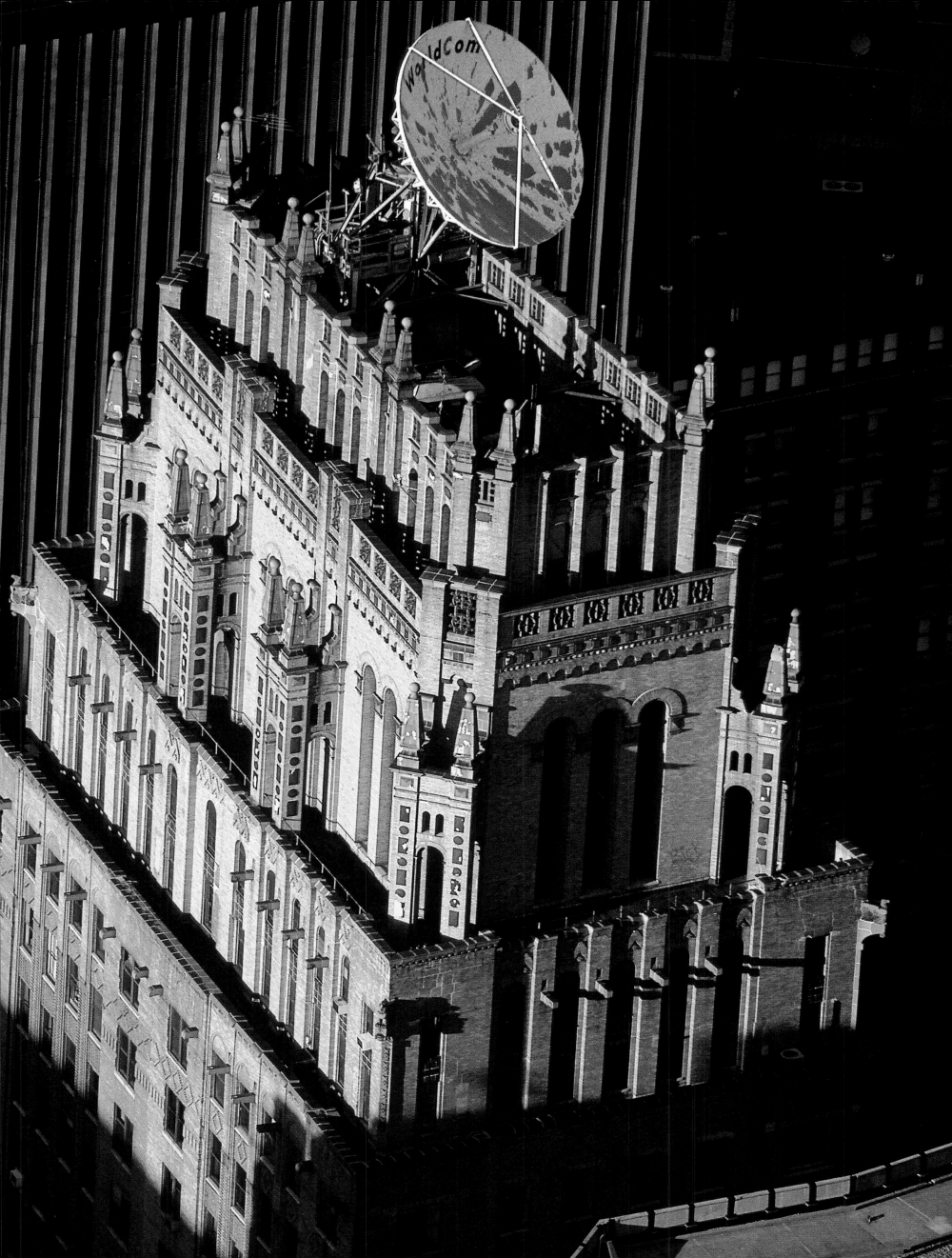

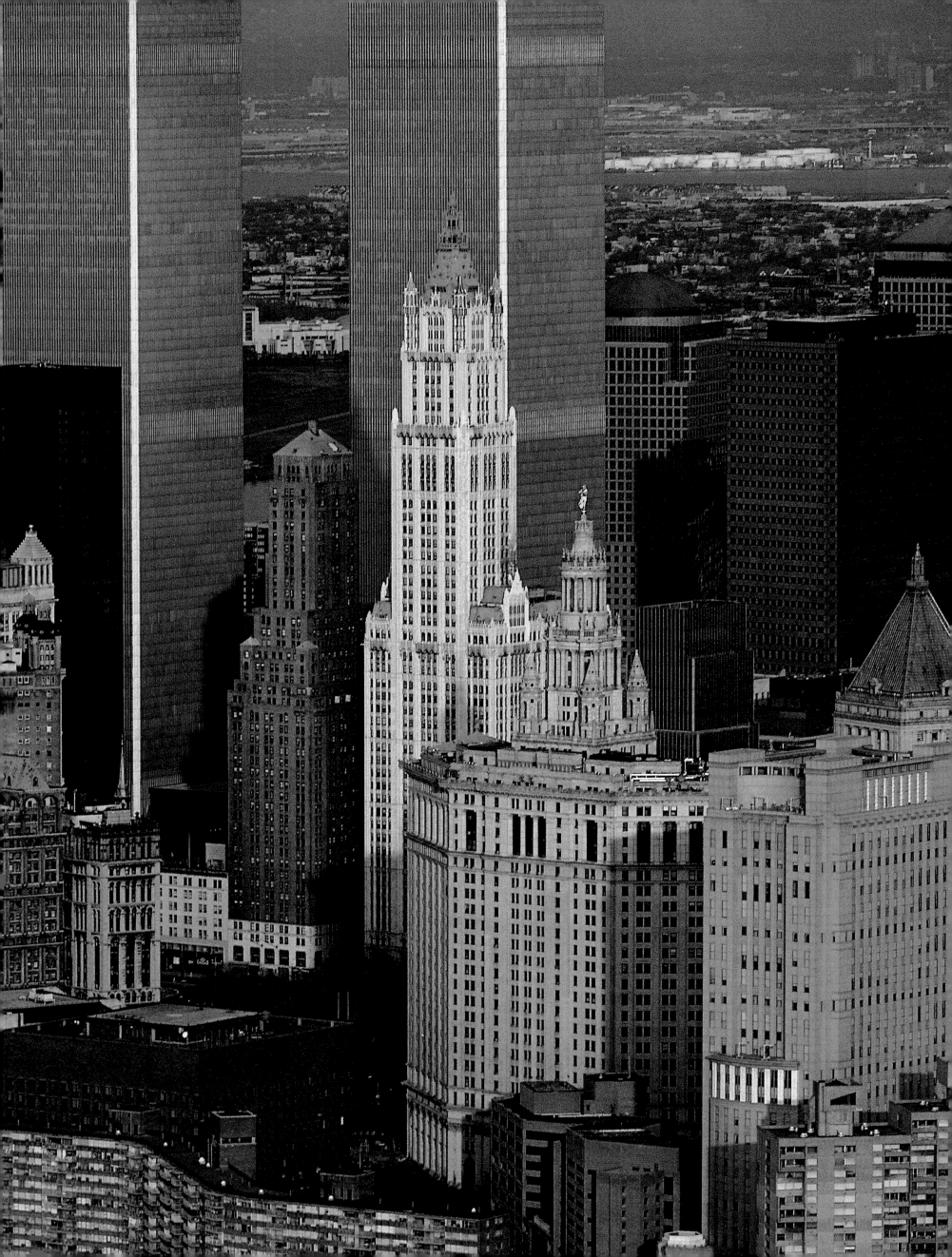

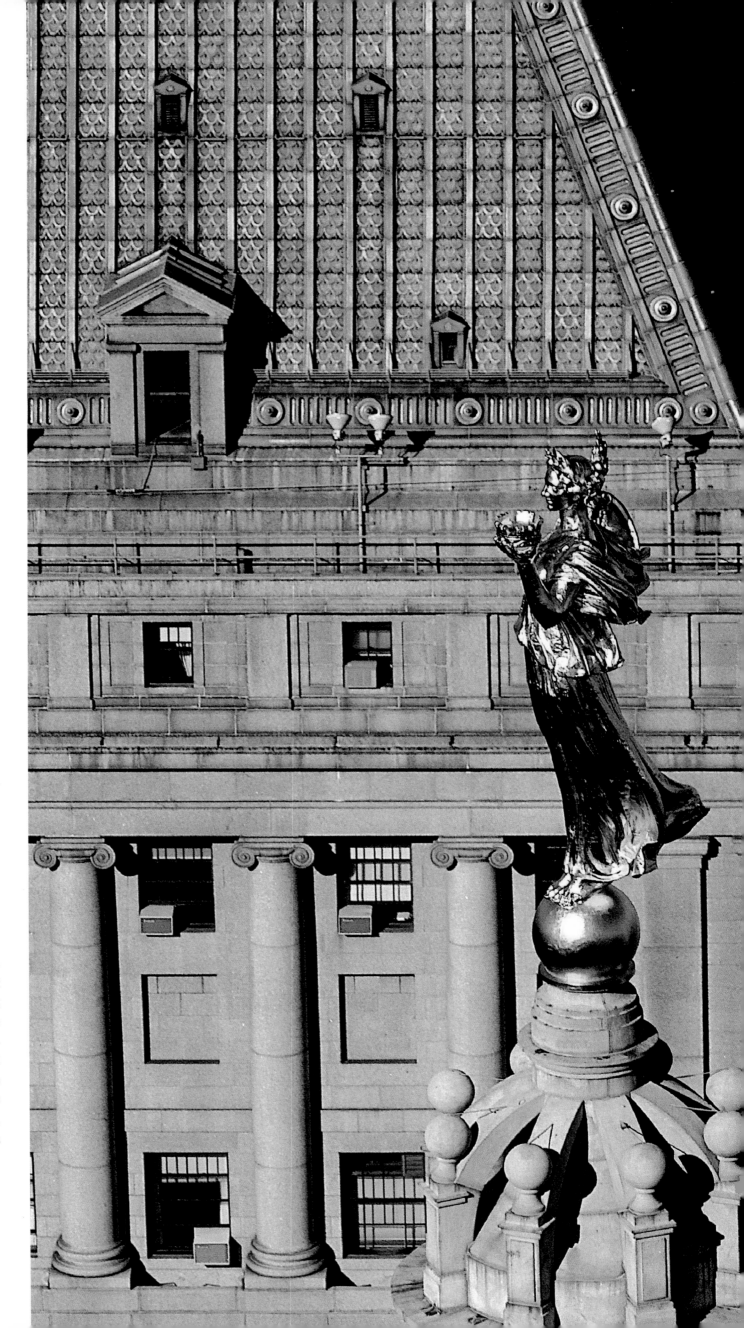

OPPOSITE: **WOOLWORTH BUILDING**
IN CENTER
VIEW LOOKING SOUTHWEST

Ｎew York is a hodgepodge of neighborhoods and districts, a fact seldom more evident than in views such as this.

At the bottom of the photograph are some of the most recent Chinatown apartment houses. The next layer of buildings represents the southern tier of the Civic Center: the cube with the helicopter landing pad is Police Headquarters, and the low-lying building with the horizontal banding to its right is a jail. The tower looming above is the Municipal Building, and to its right are the two federal courthouses. The next tier of buildings, with the Woolworth Building in the center and the Transportation Building to its left, are private-sector office buildings. Beyond lies the World Trade Center.

RIGHT: **FEDERAL COURTHOUSE ON**
FOLEY SQUARE; MUNICIPAL
BUILDING IN FOREGROUND,
AT CHAMBERS AND CENTRE STREET
VIEW LOOKING NORTH

Ａdolph A. Weinman's gilded statue *Civic Fame* tops the forty-story, 550-foot-high Municipal Building. The 1914 building brought under one roof the sprawling bureaucratic apparatus of the City of Greater New York (the statue's left hand holds a crown with five turrets to symbolize the five boroughs). When people say they were married at City Hall, they usually mean this building's "chapel."

Cass Gilbert designed this U.S. courthouse in the federal government's neoclassical style, but extra height was needed for more space. So Gilbert created a neoclassical temple as the base, and then added a twenty-five-story tower, complete with loggias and urns and pilasters, bursting through the temple's roof. This view shows the intricate details on the pyramidal roof, all variations on a classical theme, or a "Fantasy on a Double Triptych."

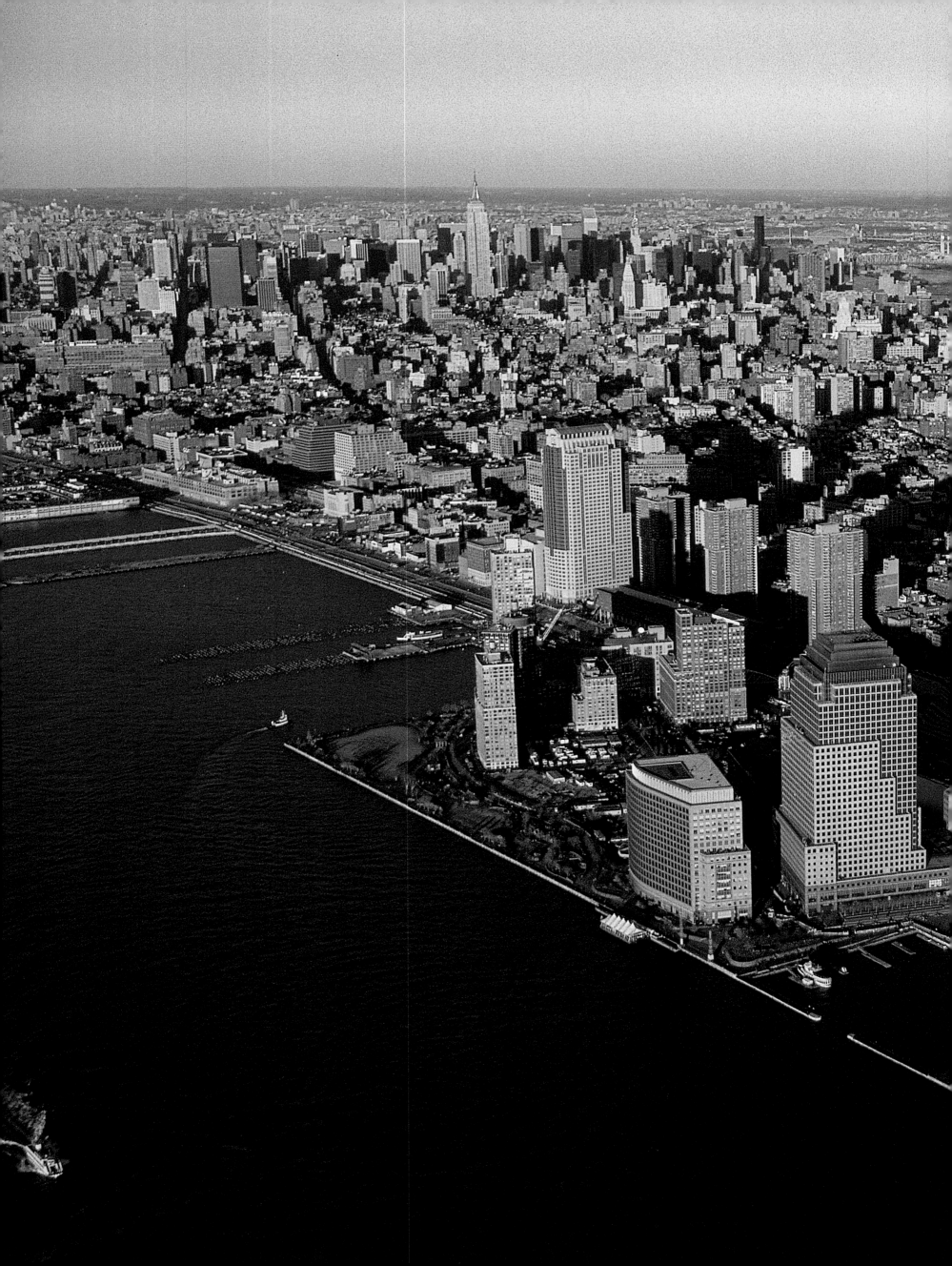

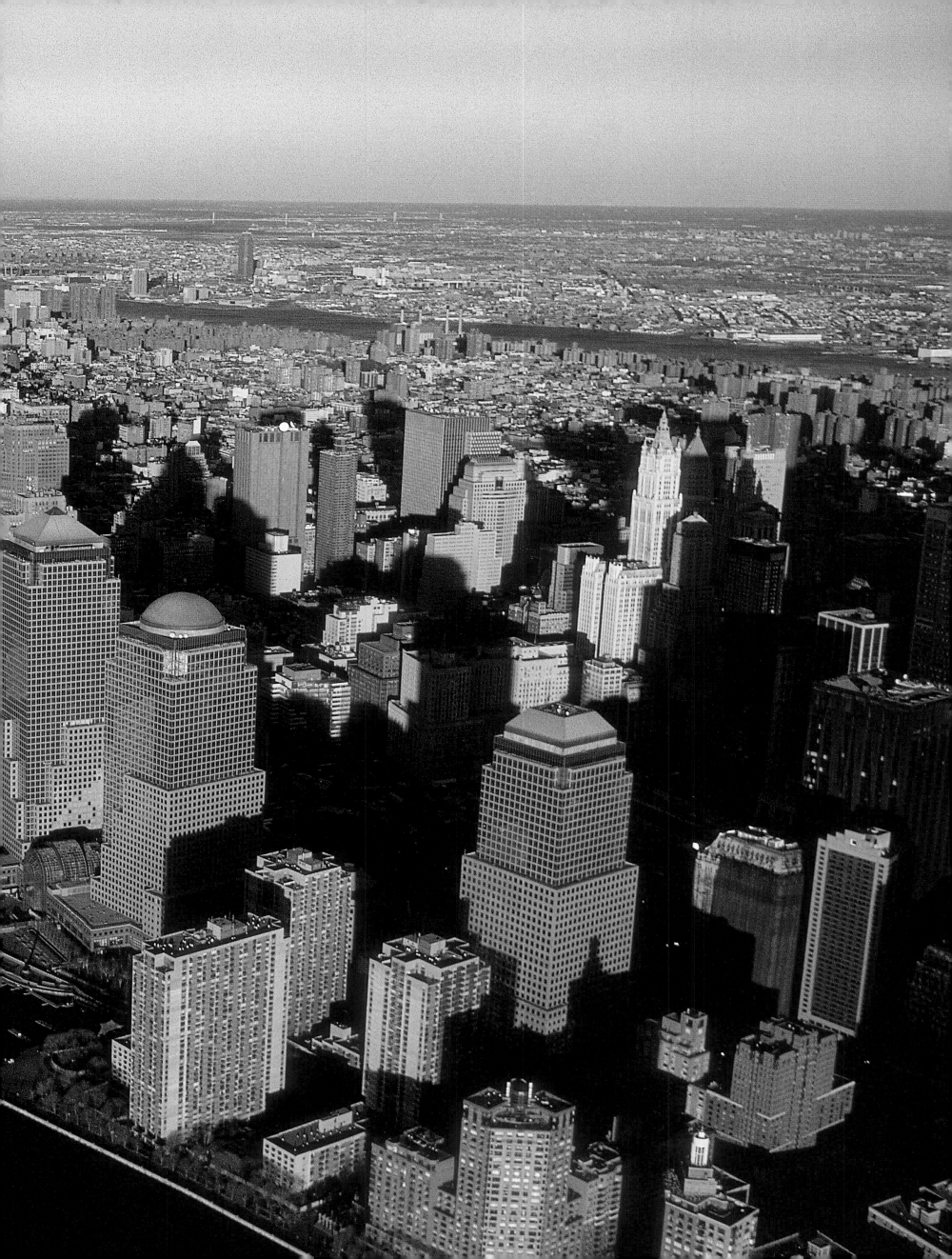

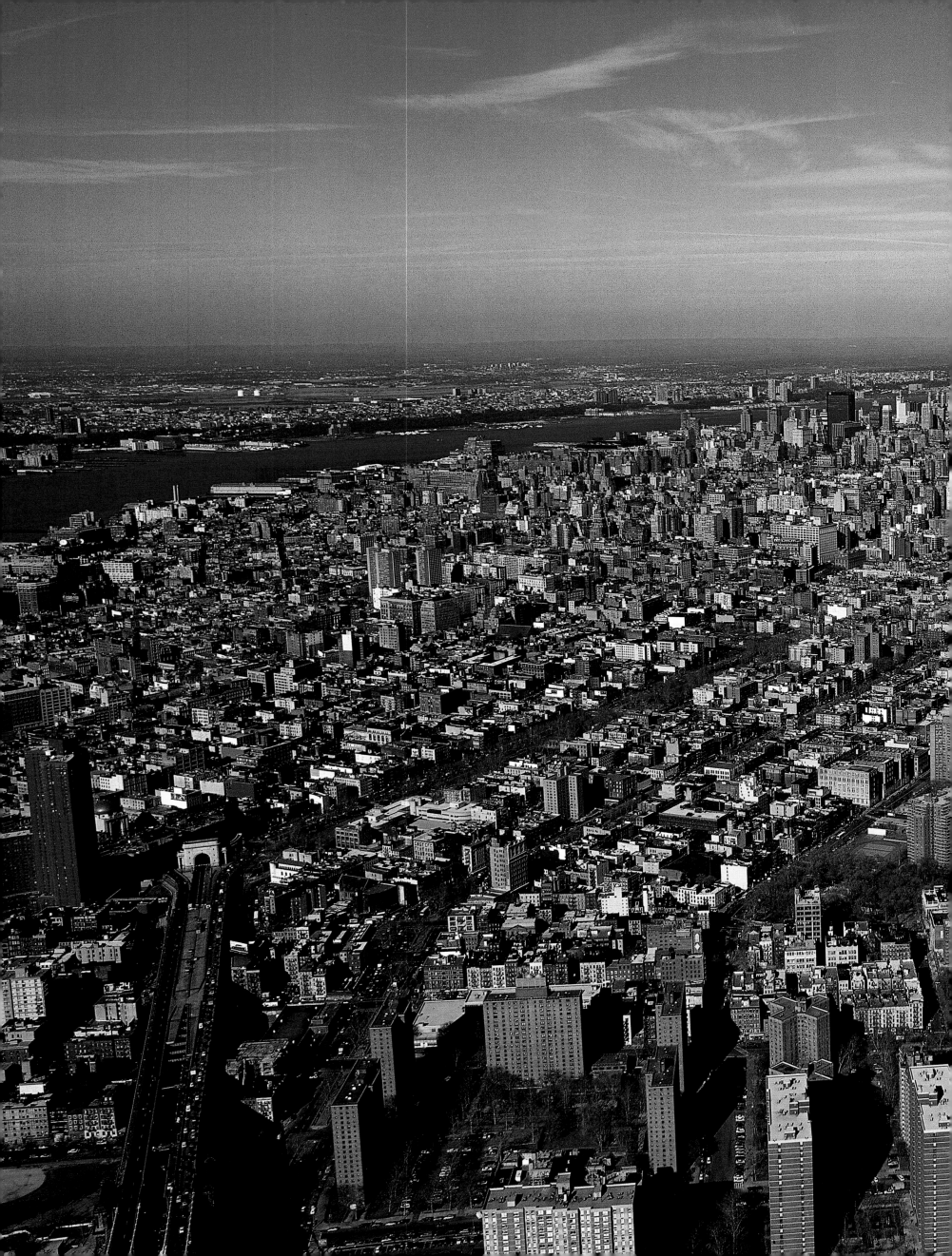

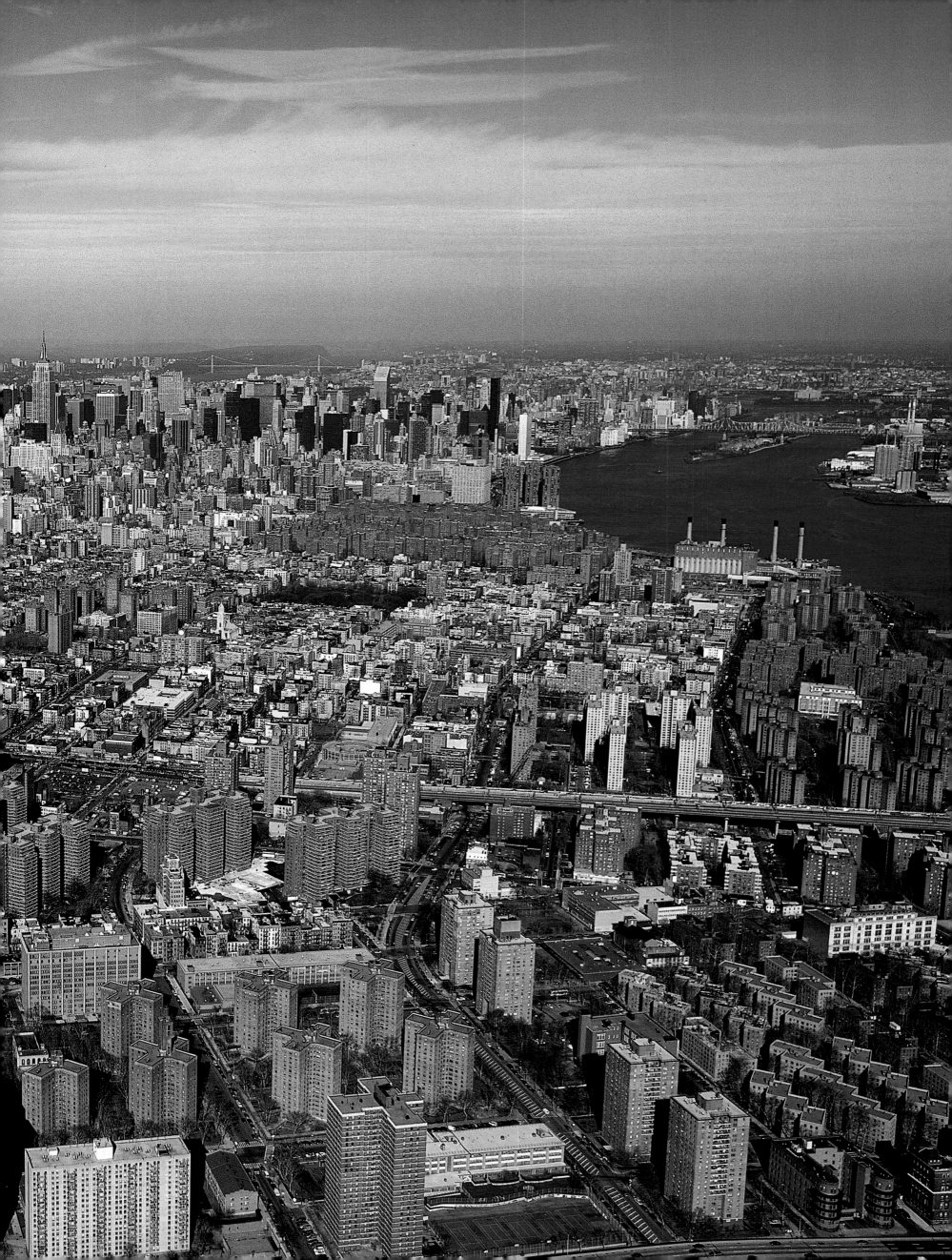

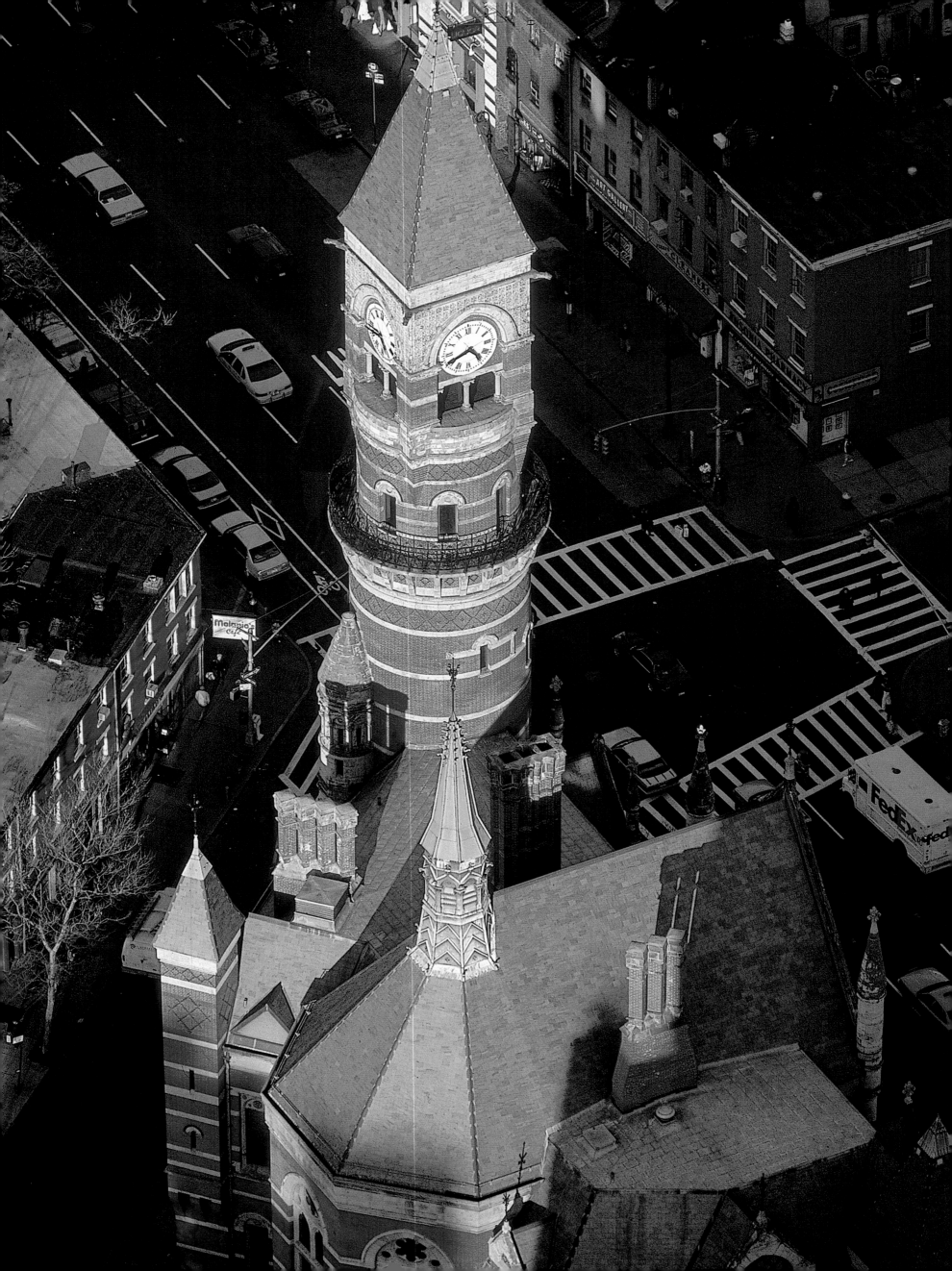

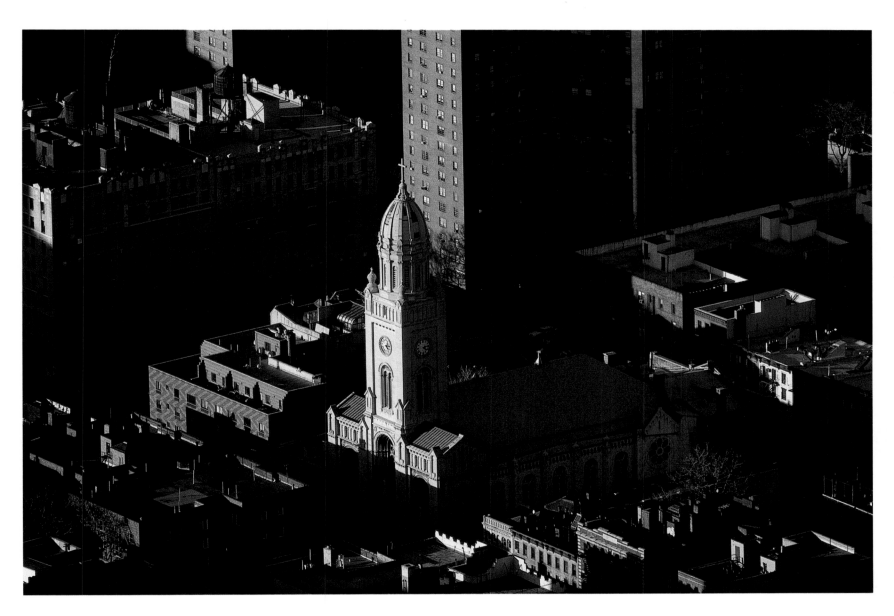

**OPPOSITE: JEFFERSON MARKET LIBRARY,
425 SIXTH AVENUE, AT 10TH STREET
VIEW LOOKING NORTHEAST**

This building was a wonderful architectural anachronism when it was built as the Jefferson Market Courthouse in 1877. Designed as part of a larger complex in the Victorian Gothic style by Frederick Clarke Withers and Calvert Vaux, this romantic evocation of medieval times has served various and mostly mundane roles. Built to house a fire tower, courthouse, jail, and market, by the mid–twentieth century most of the original complex had been torn down. The future of the building was uncertain, until local preservationists prevailed upon the municipal government to metamorphose it into a public library in 1967.

**PAGES 26-27: LOWER MANHATTAN
VIEW LOOKING NORTHWEST**

This scene, seemingly so serene was on September 11, 2001, and for months thereafter, one of sheer horror. The shadows cast by Battery Park City and the World Financial Center in the foreground fill the void where once had stood two of the world's tallest buildings—the World Trade Center Towers—both destroyed in the terrorist attack.

**PREVIOUS SPREAD: LOWER EAST SIDE
VIEW LOOKING NORTHWEST**

The Lower East Side, home to different waves of immigrants over the past 150 years, has lost the distinctive character firstly of Eastern

Europeans, of African-Americans who settled here in the early twentieth century, and of Hispanics who populated the neighborhood after World War II. Today a growing number of Asians are moving here beyond Chinatown, where they first settled over a century ago.

The triumphal arch seen on the left is the monumental entry to the Manhattan Bridge across the East River, and is hardly ever noticed by drivers and passengers speeding through it. The other ramp, on the far right, leads from Delancey Street to the Williamsburg Bridge.

Flanking Roosevelt Island in the East River is the Queensboro Bridge, also known as the 59th Street Bridge, and popularized in the song of that title by Simon and Garfunkel. In the distance, bridging the Hudson River, is the George Washington Bridge, which the architect Le Corbusier described simply as "the most beautiful bridge in the world."

**ABOVE: MOST HOLY REDEEMER CATHOLIC CHURCH,
173 EAST THIRD STREET, BETWEEN AVENUE A AND B
VIEW LOOKING NORTHWEST**

The Most Holy Redeemer Catholic Church has been one of the great visual landmarks of the Lower East Side since it was built in the late nineteenth century when this neighborhood was predominantly made up of German immigrants. Most of them were Lutheran, but this church was built by the Roman Catholic community and it remains as such. Its construction was a true act of faith, showing that the spirit can overcome the hardships of living in downtrodden tenements. The church's architectural style is not easy to pinpoint, and some historians might simply call it eclectic. In 1890 it was described as Byzantine but today as "Romanesque Baroque."

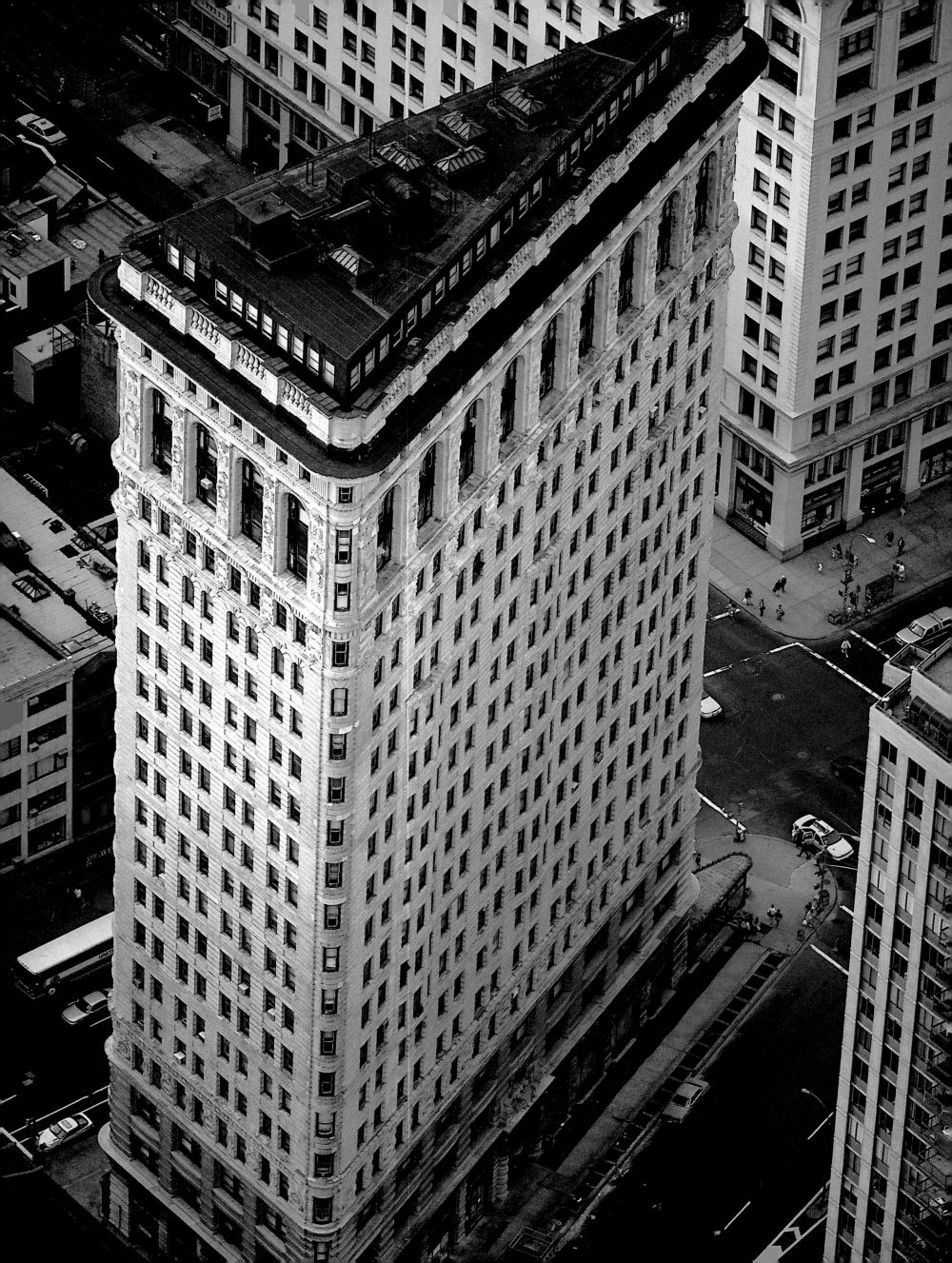

FLATIRON BUILDING, FIFTH AVENUE TO BROADWAY, 22ND TO 23RD STREET

The Flatiron Building, which commands the dramatic setting at the juncture of Broadway and Fifth Avenue, cuts its way through the right-angled gridiron of Manhattan's streets like the prow of a great ship. Due to its triangular shape, its heavily draped neo-Renaissance style, and the fact that it was the tallest building in the neighborhood, the building captured the imagination of citizens and visitors alike and served as a symbol of the dramatic new age of skyscrapers.

Contrary to popular belief, however, the Flatiron Building was not the world's tallest building when it was built in 1902—it wasn't even New York's tallest building—nor was it the city's first steel-framed skyscraper. The building's sole claim to fame in the record books is that it was arguably the subject of more postcards than any other building in the city in the first decade of the twentieth century.

The building was dubbed the Flatiron because of the triangular plot upon which it was built. It did not seem to bother anyone that a "flatiron" is an isosceles triangle, whereas the building's plot is a right triangle, and the name has stuck.

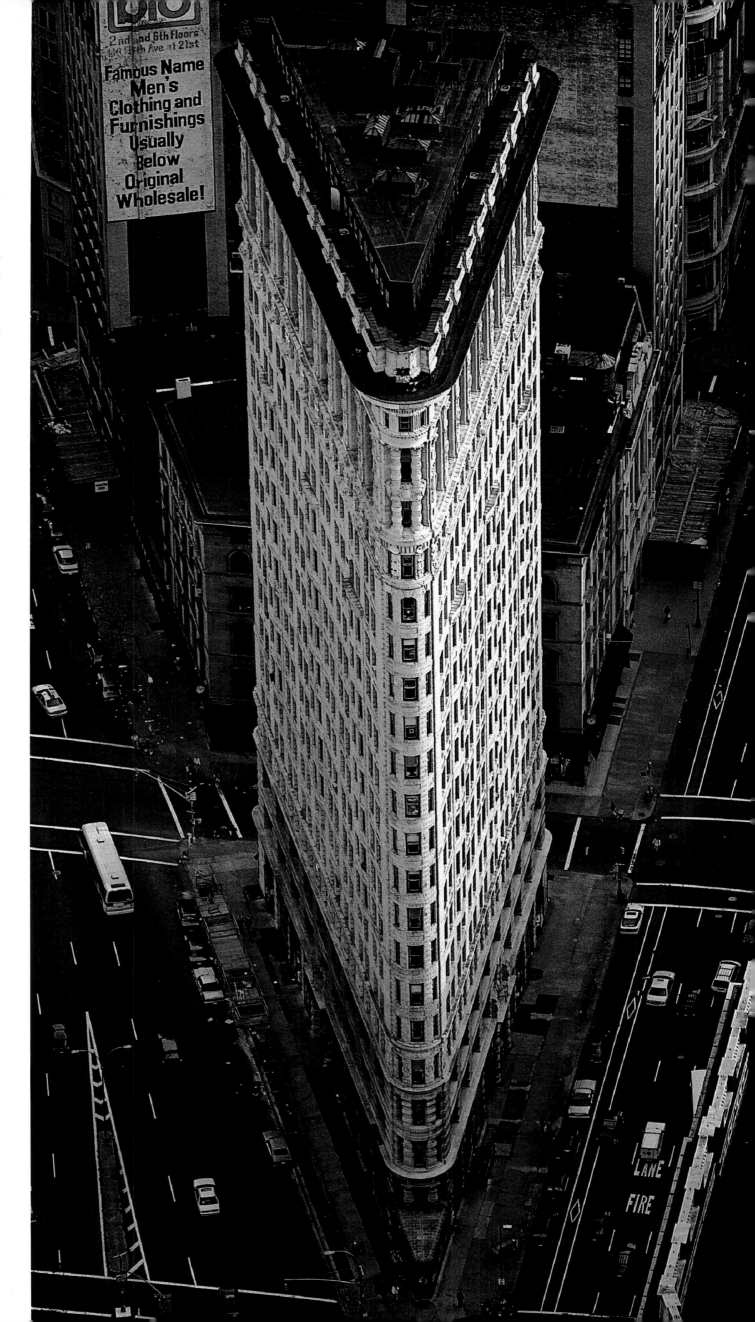

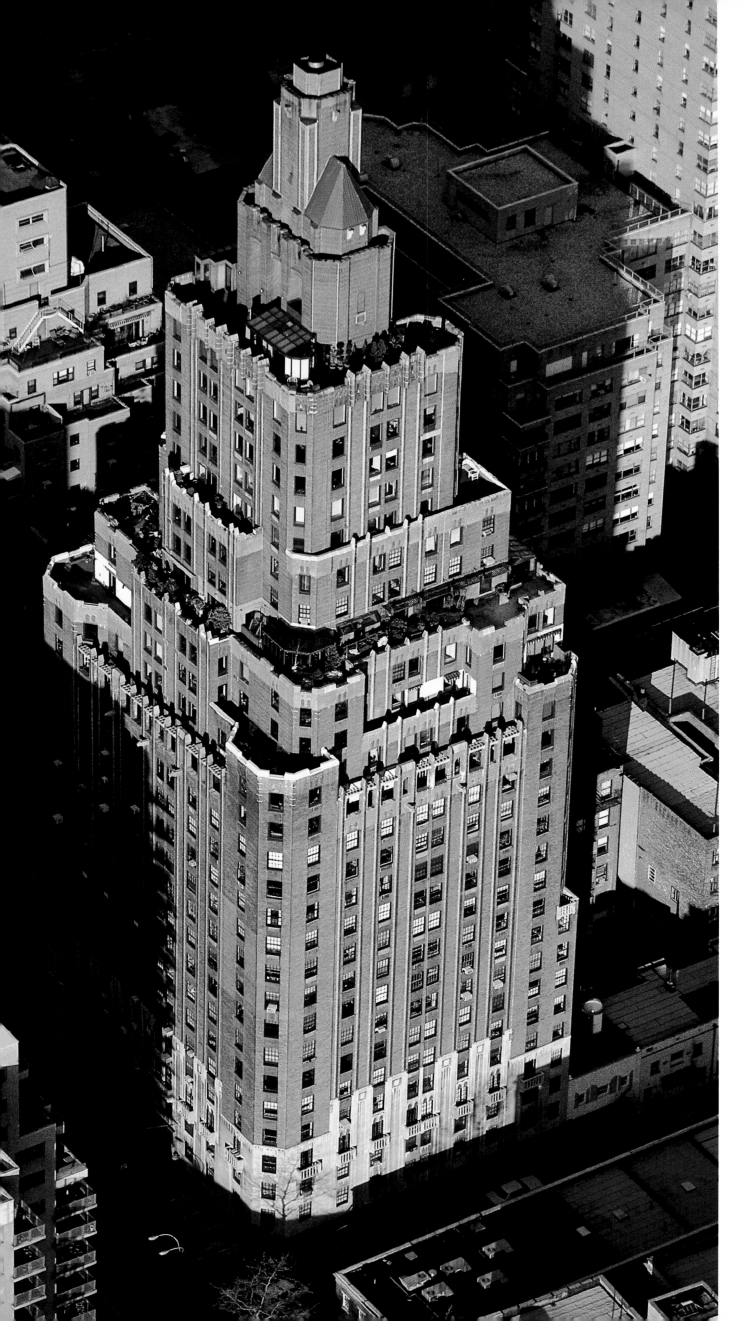

The assumption is that Greenwich Village is filled with writers and artists and rebels with or without causes, but Greenwich Village wears many hats. It has its share of people in the creative arts, but you will also find bankers, advertising executives, Wall Street traders, and just plain folk who like the ambience of the place. And that's what makes it interesting.

The spirit of Greenwich Village might dwell in a garret, but most people prefer the creature comforts, and apartment houses such as the twenty-seven-story One Fifth Avenue provide them and then some.

The low buildings in shadow in the bottom right show the scale that is perhaps more the image of Greenwich Village. Originally stables for the residents of Washington Square, they have been converted into charming mews houses, many of them home to New York University faculty.

New York buildings frequently have their most interesting decorative details out of sight of the average pedestrian, and 40 Fifth Avenue is indicative of this phenomenon. Only a pigeon ordinarily sees the balustrades and finials that decorate this building's setbacks, or can appreciate the neo–English Baroque folly that masks what otherwise would be a humble water tower.

The building's most famous tenant might have been Judge Joseph Force Crater, the Tammany-appointed judge who climbed into a taxicab one August evening in 1930 never to be seen again. He had moved into a two-bedroom apartment here with his wife when the building opened in 1927. They paid $14,000; by the mid-1980s, asking prices for two-bedroom apartments started at $325,000.

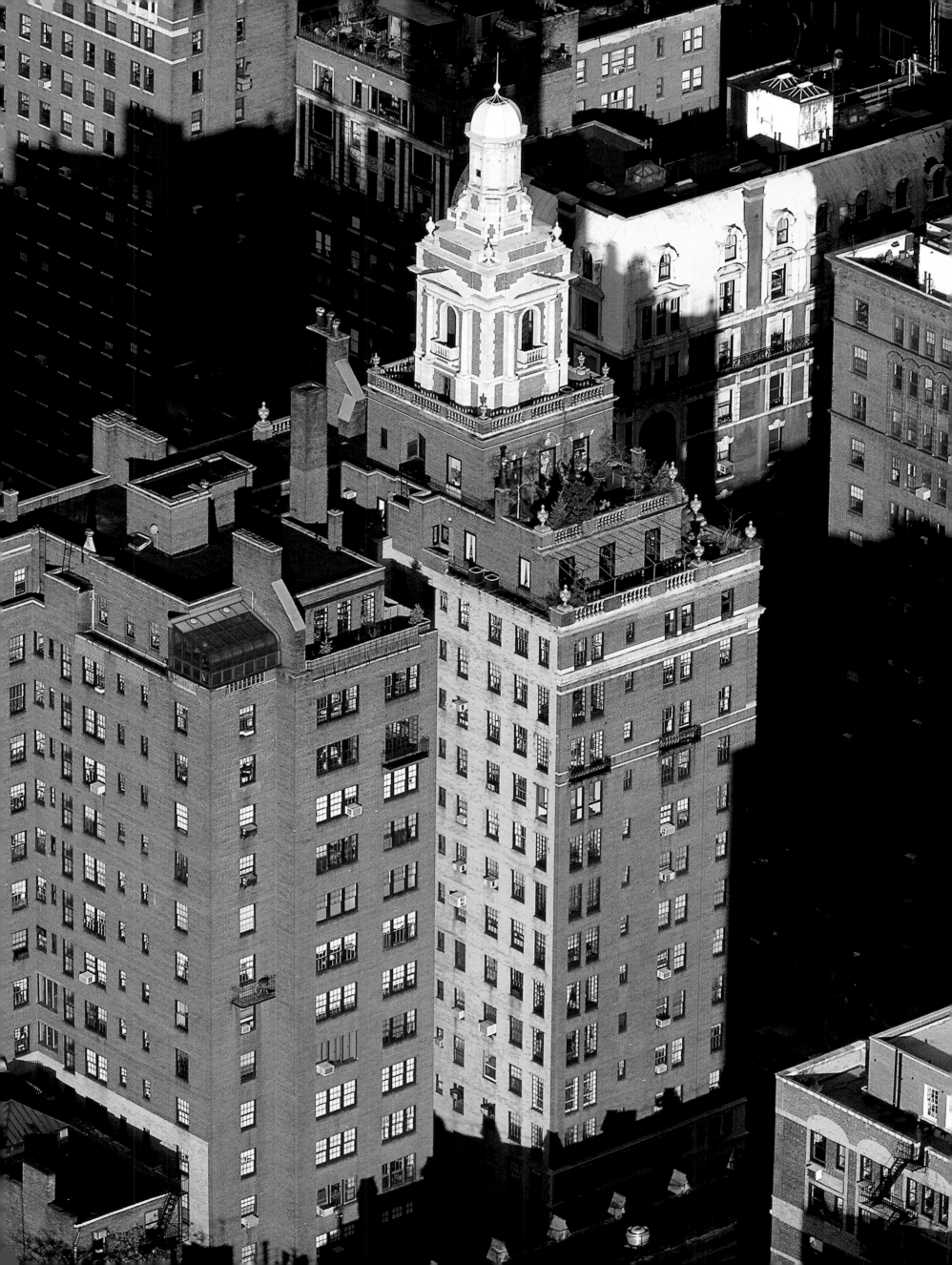

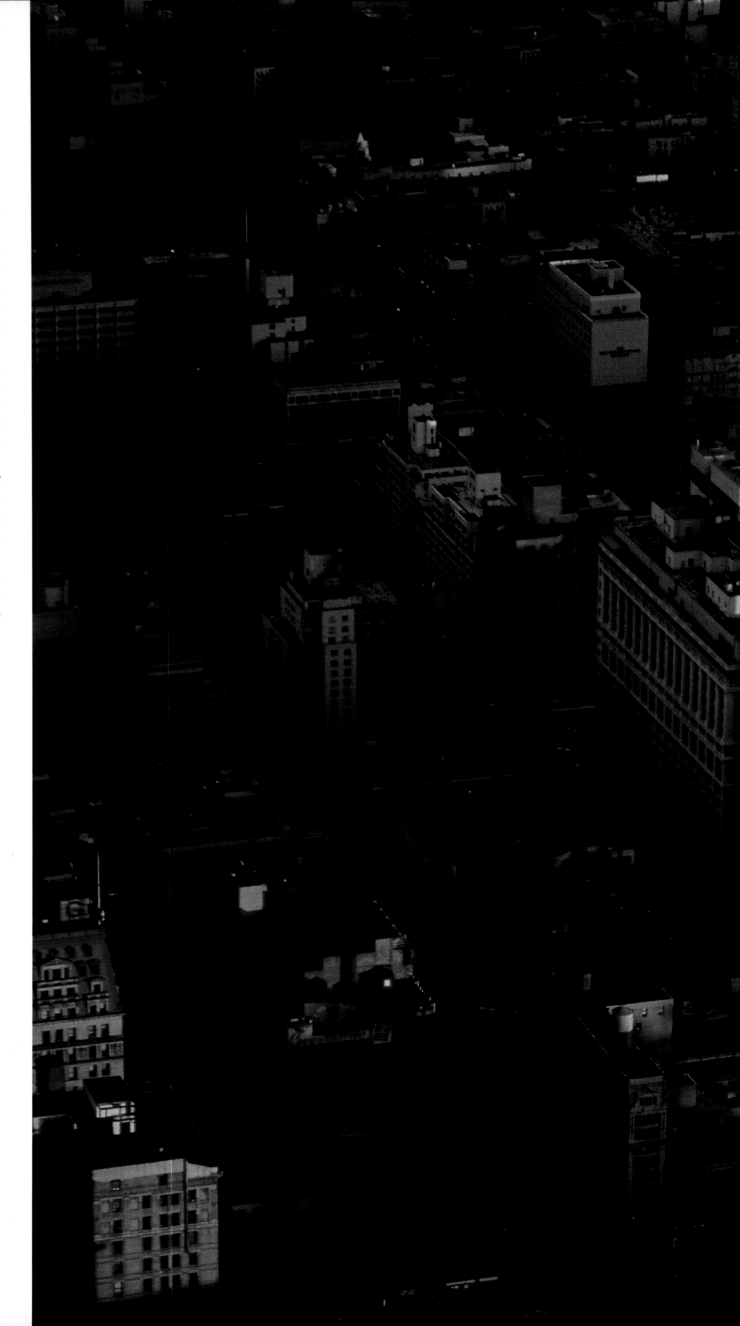

Dominating this view is the 531-foot-high Consolidated Edison Tower, designed by Warren & Wetmore in 1926 as an addition to the earlier building by Henry J. Hardenbergh. Although the lantern-topped crown has a mausoleum-like quality, its design is also quite joyous. The company, known locally as Con Ed, supplies the city with its electricity. Con Ed was one of the first companies in New York to light the top of its building, advertising not just itself, but its product.

The four towers are Zeckendorf Towers, the residential part of a mixed-use venture occupying the block between 14th and 15th Street, between Union Square East and Irving Place. The architects Davis, Brody & Associates added pyramidal tops to the towers, perhaps paying homage to their neighbor.

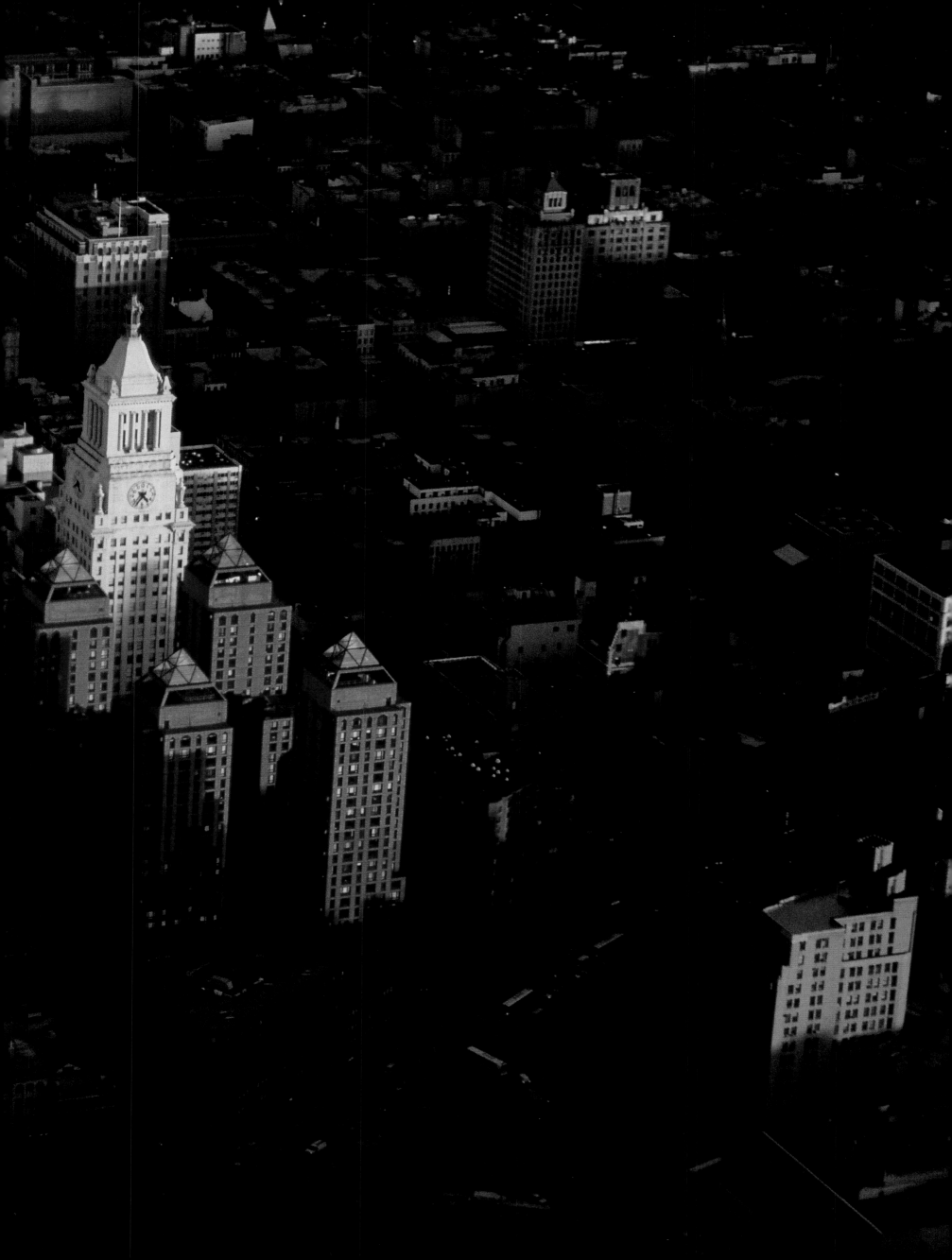

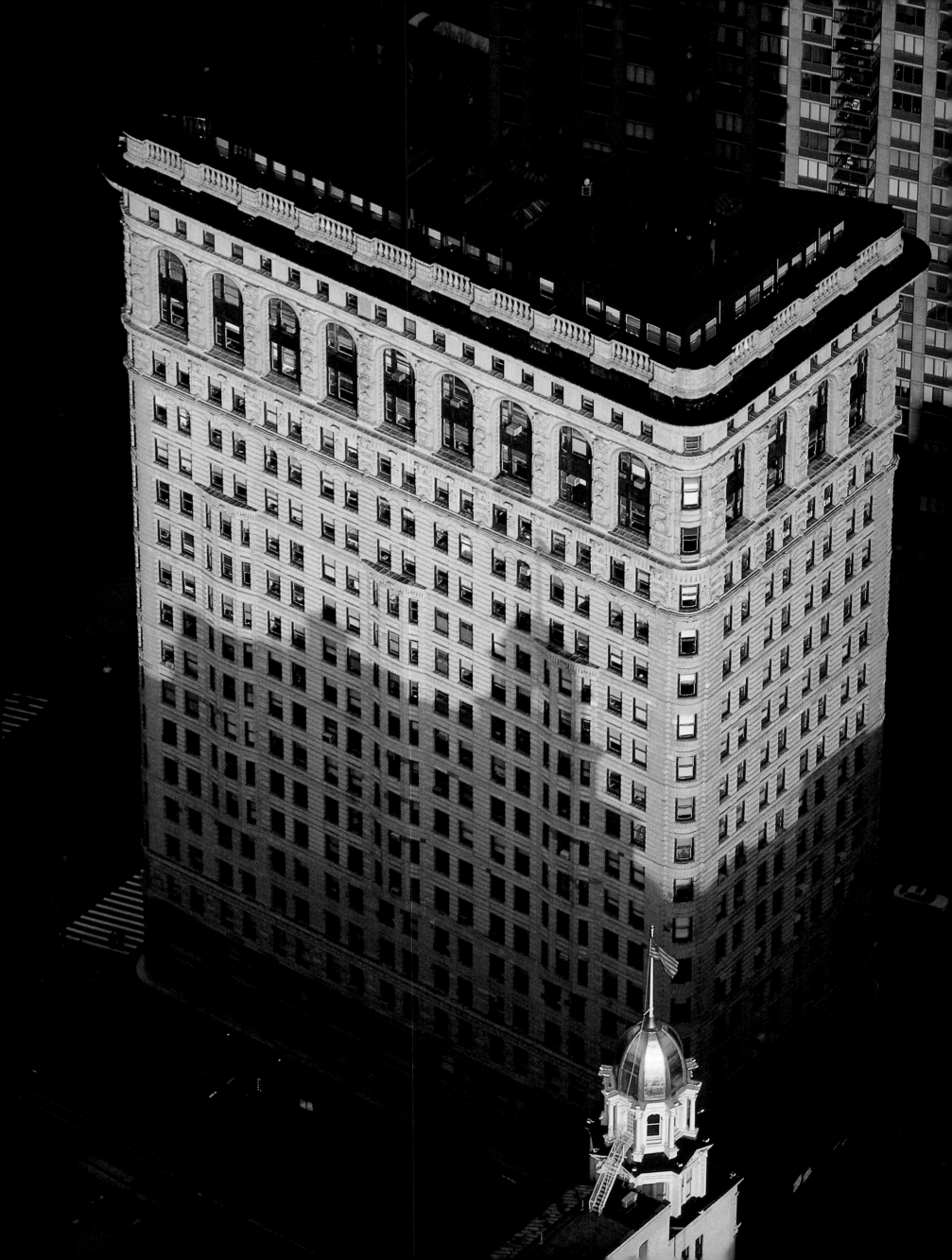

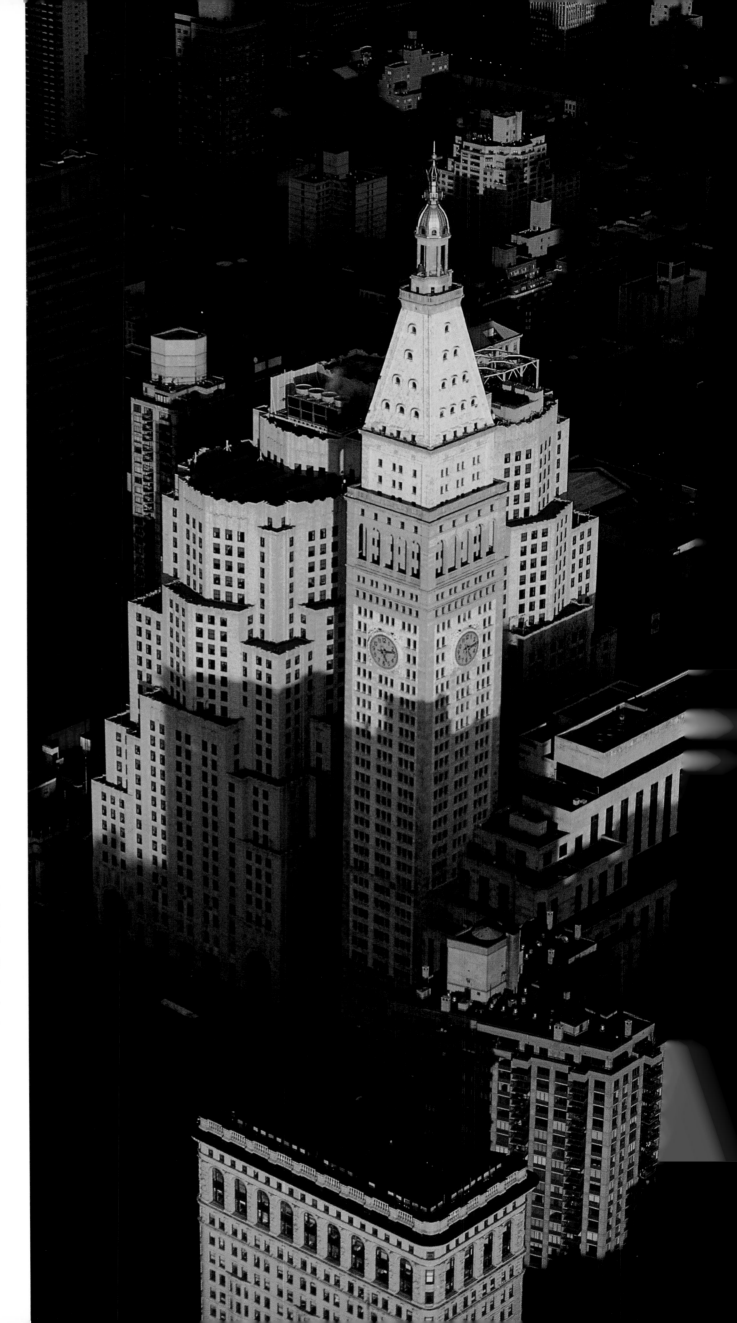

OPPOSITE: **FLATIRON BUILDING,
FIFTH AVENUE TO BROADWAY,
22ND TO 23RD STREET**

For caption, see page 33.

RIGHT: **METROPOLITAN LIFE TOWER,
ONE MADISON AVENUE,
AT 24TH STREET
VIEW LOOKING NORTHEAST**

Commanding center stage is the Metropolitan Life Tower, an astigmatic vision of the campanile of St. Mark's in Venice. At 700 feet, this was the world's tallest building in 1909, and the one that Woolworth wanted to best.

In the spirit that bigger is better, the building's boosters described the clocks that are set into each of the four facades as bigger than London's Big Ben. Each dial is twenty-six and a half feet in diameter, with numerals five feet high and a minute hand that is seventeen feet long and weighs 1,000 pounds.

The observation gallery cost a hefty fifty cents to visit in 1911. The gallery was reached first by elevator to the forty-fourth floor, then by steps the rest of the way—buildings are not designed this way today because it denies accessibility to the handicapped. The booklet given to visitors claimed that from the highest lookout on the fiftieth floor, 660 feet up, "the homes of over one-sixteenth of the entire population of the United States" were visible. With the present population of Metropolitan New York at more than eighteen million, a claim could be made that one can today view the homes of about one thirty-second of the population. The drawback is that the roughly twenty-seven taller buildings erected since the tower's construction now seriously block the view.

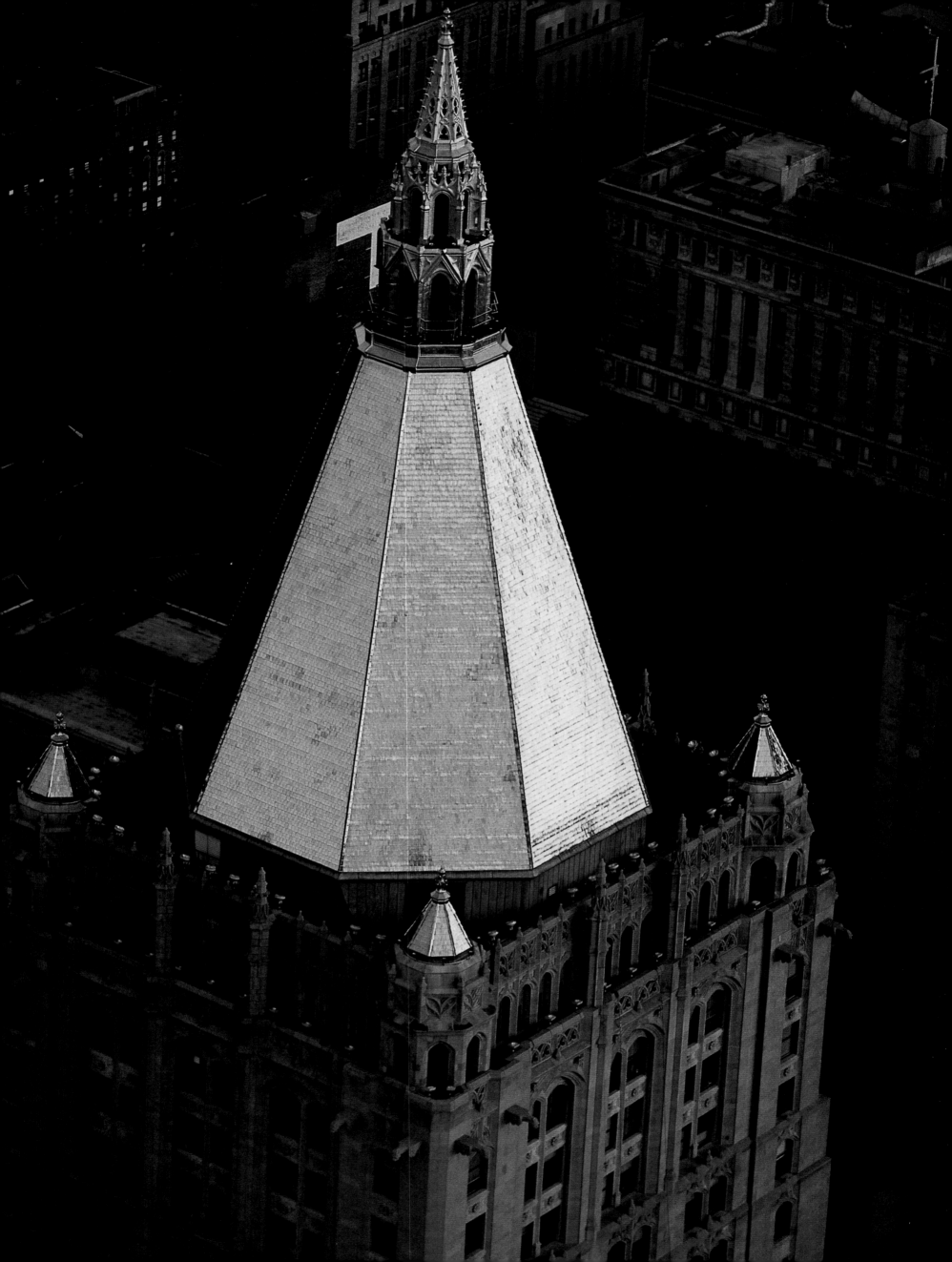

NEW YORK LIFE INSURANCE BUILDING, 51 MADISON AVENUE, BETWEEN 26TH AND 27TH STREET VIEW LOOKING SOUTHEAST

New York Life is housed in a strange pastiche of Gothic- and Renaissance-inspired motifs, as in a Loire Valley château. Pure twentieth-century technology created the building, of course, a fact that is inescapable when you realize that it is 617 feet high and, unlike towers of old, is filled with workers on thirty-three floors of office space on over 1.2 million square feet.

Designed by Cass Gilbert and opened for business in 1928, the building has a distinctive roofline, a feature found in many of Gilbert's works. This roof is gilded, but the gilt regularly flakes off. It settles somewhere, perhaps lending some credence to the notion that the streets are paved with gold.

The insurance company uses its building as a symbol of strength in advertisements in print and on television. One commercial presents photographs that purport to show its construction, but some of the shots are actually of the Empire State Building and other buildings.

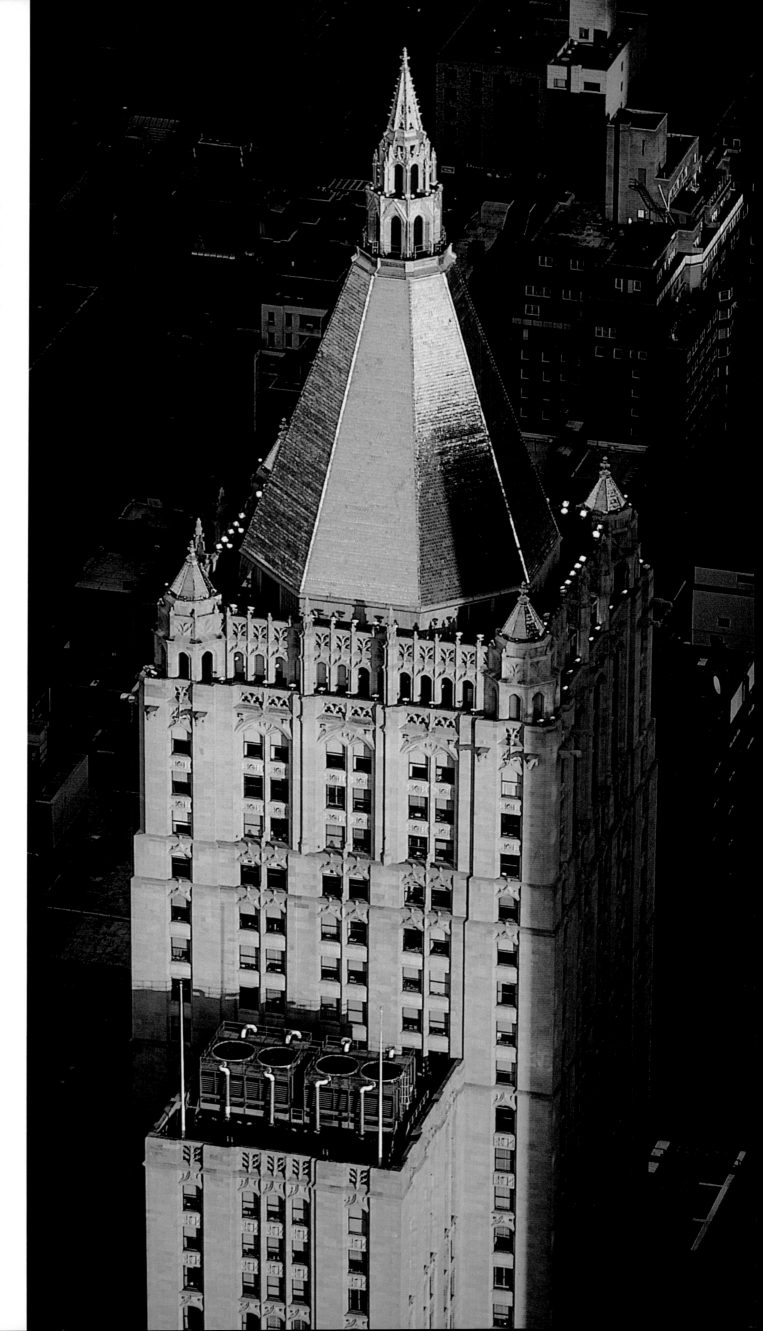

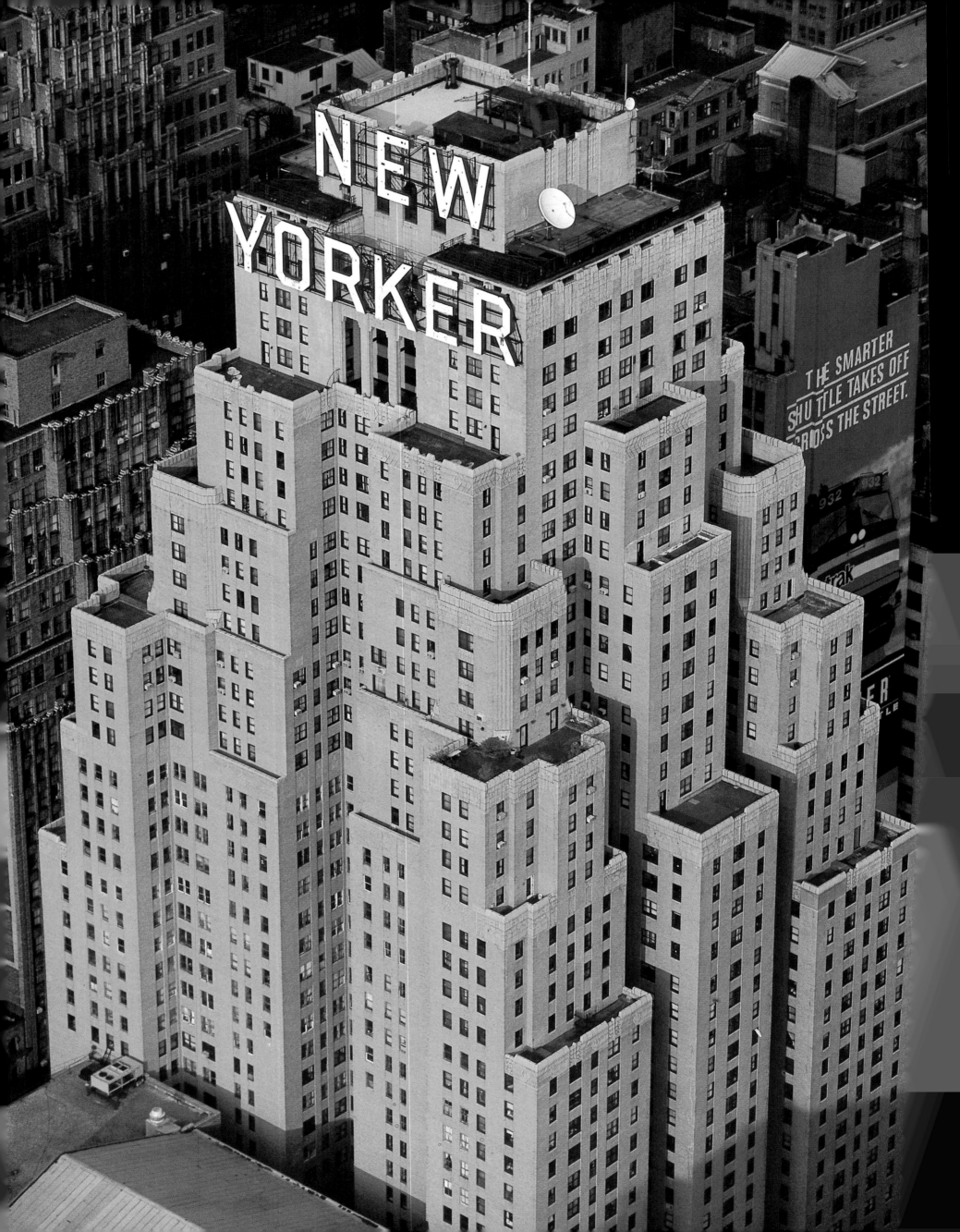

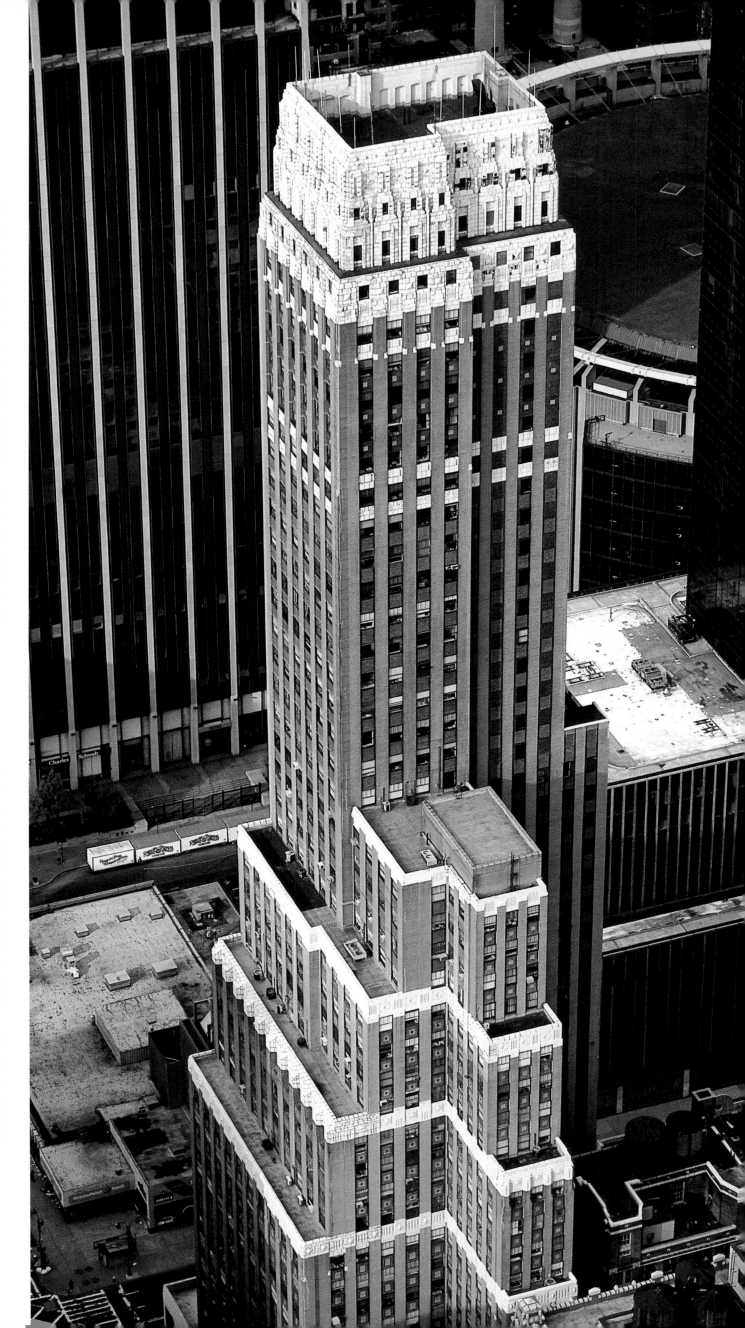

The forty-three-story New Yorker Hotel opened in 1930. All of the hotel's 2,500 rooms had windows, both bathtubs and showers, and radios when radios were still novelties. Dancing took place nightly in the Terrace Restaurant "made famous in millions of homes," according to the manager, "through the nation-wide radio hook-up . . . [of] one of New York's greatest syncopated orchestras." The main dining room had walls of Persian walnut inlaid with solid bronze, and the hotel's barbershop had forty-two chairs and twenty manicurists.

But the hotel was west of Eighth Avenue when hardly any other hotel was west of Seventh, and most were east of Sixth. Although it is still operating, the hotel never lived up to its potential, lending credence to the real-estate cliché "Location, location, location."

The Nelson Tower is hardly a building that the average New Yorker knows by name, and it is certainly not a building that the average guide points to with pride. The Nelson Tower opened in 1931 and was designed by H. Craig Severance, who designed 40 Wall Street. It is forty-six stories, or 560 feet, tall. If the Nelson Tower were in Cincinnati, Ohio, it would be a marvel of the city, only eight feet shorter than the Carew Tower, Cincinnati's tallest building; in New York, however, it escapes notice.

The office building to the left is Two Penn Plaza; the round building is the city's third Madison Square Garden (the original was catercorner to Madison Square, hence its name; the second was on Eighth Avenue between 48th and 49th Street).

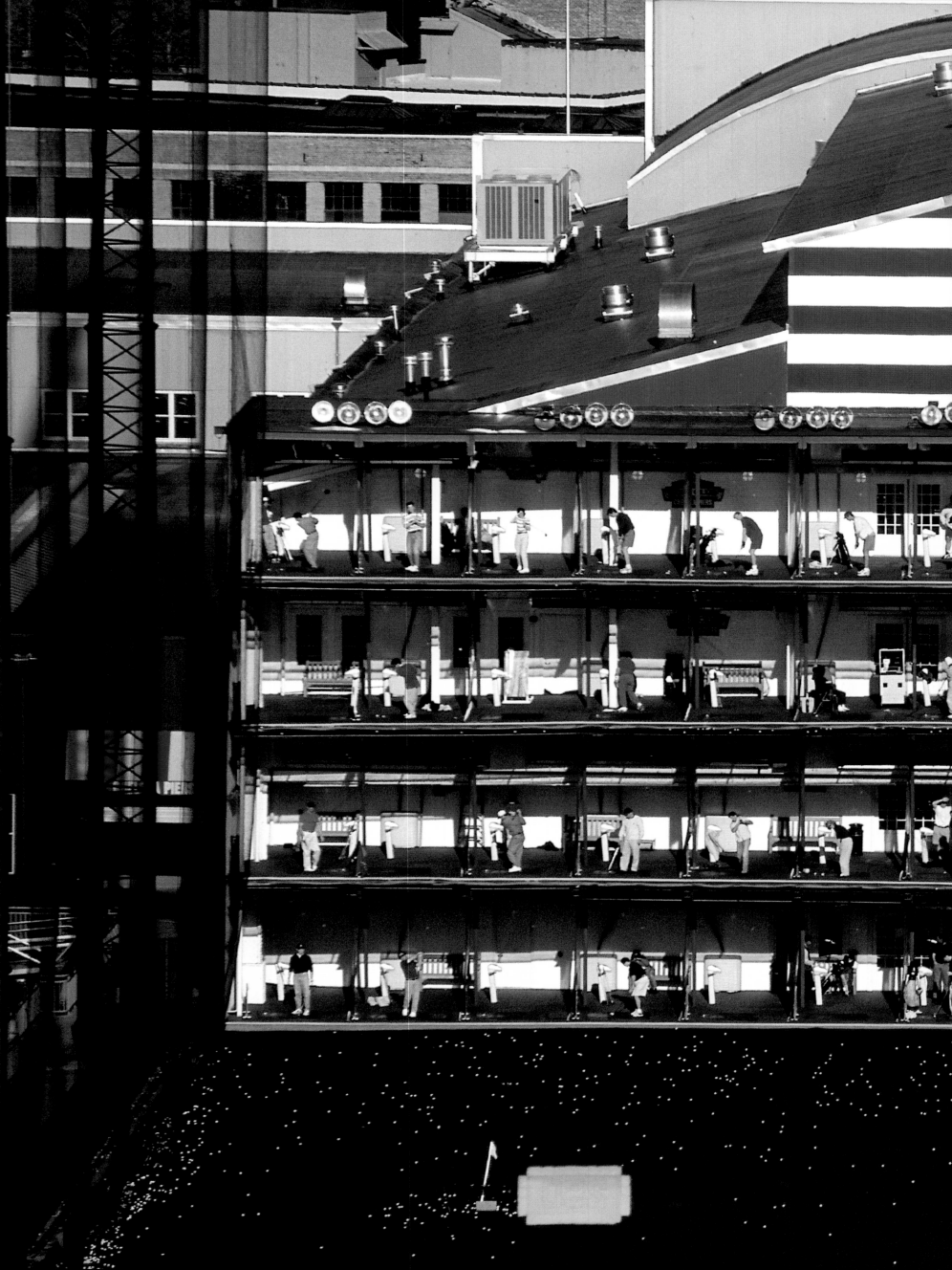

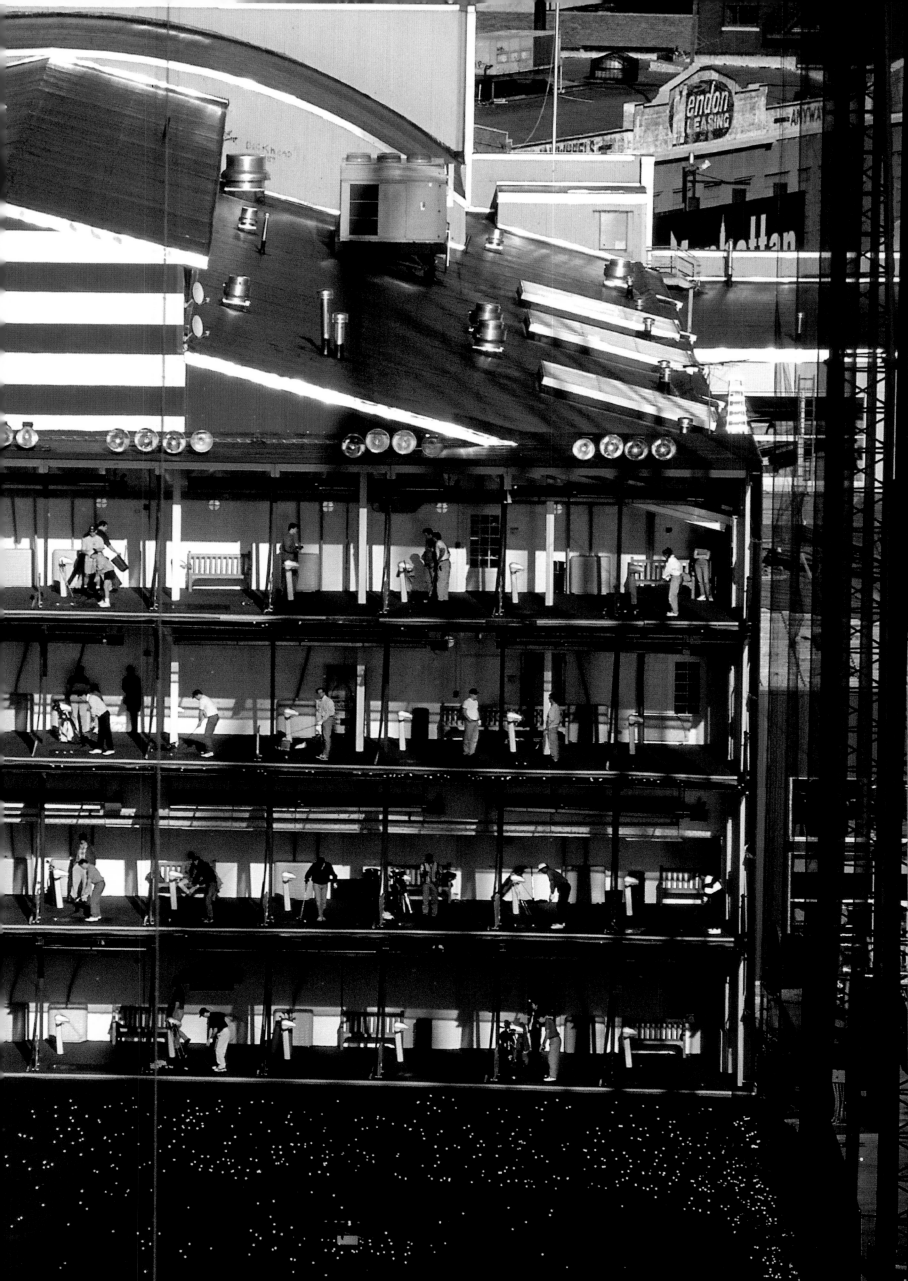

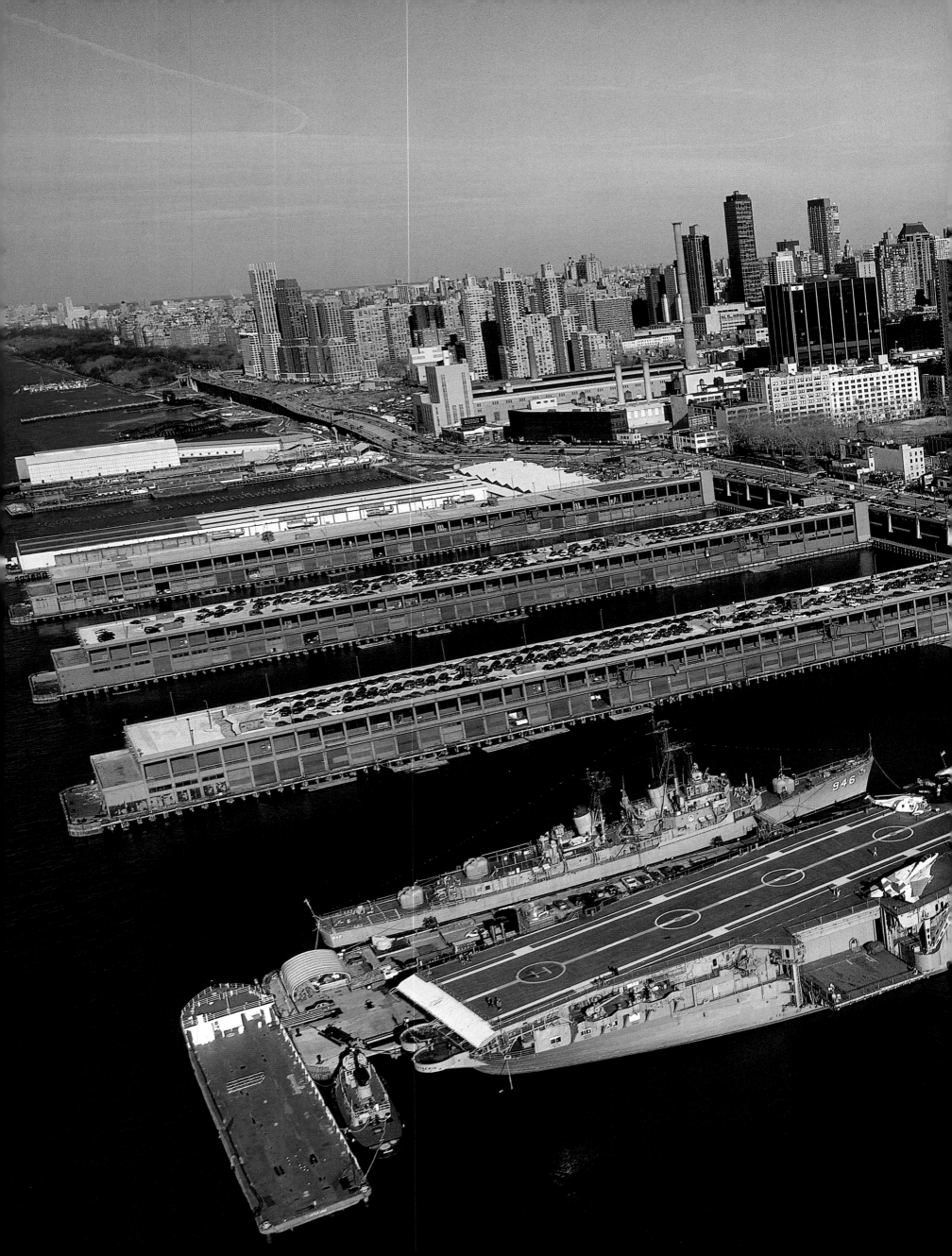

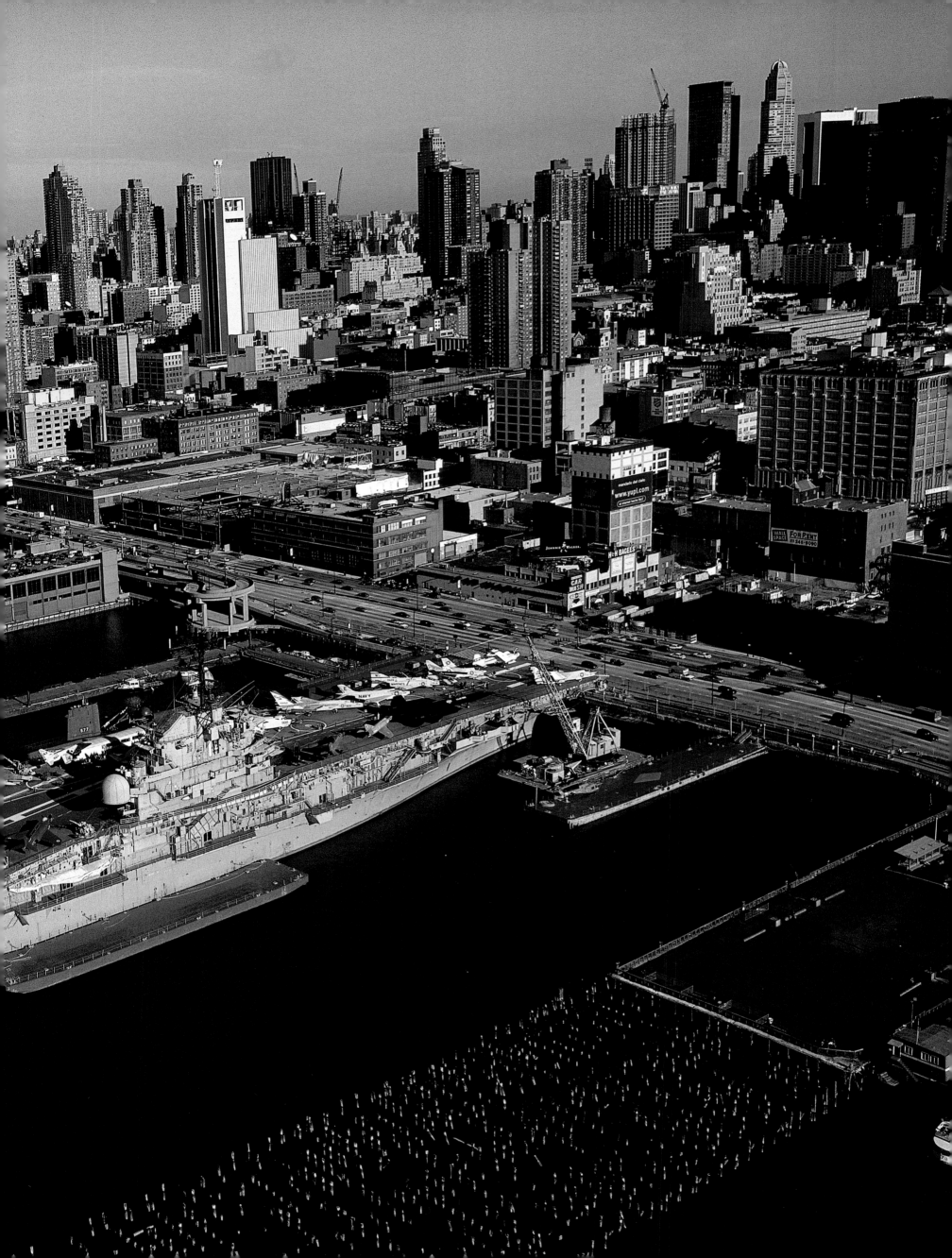

The golf-driving range at Chelsea Piers is a bizarre scene, a stage set showing a slice of the urban athletic life. The idea for today's Chelsea Piers was brilliant: take some derelict old piers on the edge of Manhattan and turn them into a sports complex offering activities from figure skating to bowling, from rock climbing to basketball.

In the first few decades of the twentieth century, the scene here had a different rhythm. Instead of hearing the click of golf club hitting golf ball you heard the call of "All ashore going ashore," and the splash of hawser hitting water as the coal-powered engines started up. The great passenger steamships on the North Atlantic run all berthed here. The *Titanic*, of course, never made it to her berth at Pier 59 just down the block at 19th Street.

If you ask the average New Yorker to name the city's national historic monuments, you would probably hear Federal Hall and Grant's Tomb. Odds are that they would not mention the 42,000-ton U.S.S. *Intrepid*, the aircraft carrier at the heart of the Intrepid Sea-Air-Space Museum. But there, moored at Pier 86 at the west end of 46th Street, is this national treasure and historic monument.

Perhaps the reason that the *Intrepid* does not loom large in a New Yorker's mental picture of the city is that unlike the average Parisian or Londoner, the average Manhattanite could go for months at a time without seeing the rivers that border their city. And as seldom as they might look at the Hudson River, they might see the *Intrepid* even less.

The piers beyond the *Intrepid* are the passenger ship piers, where cruise liners berth, including the *QE2*, the last of the mighty transatlantic steamers. When the piers are not scheduled for arriving and departing ships, they are frequently used as venues for antique shows and flower shows.

The neighborhood that immediately faces us in the West 40s and 50s was called Hell's Kitchen at the end of the nineteenth century and for most of the twentieth but it is now officially named Clinton. Perhaps because of its new name, but in large measure due to the continually pressing need for housing, this neighborhood is being built up with new high-rise apartment buildings. If it's not being rebuilt, it's being refurbished.

North of Clinton and to the west of Lincoln Center is a whole new residential development, with three new apartment towers just along the river, financed by Donald Trump and named Trump Place.

Opposite: Empire State Building,
350 Fifth Avenue,
between 33rd and 34th Street
View looking northeast

The Empire State Building rises as a sheer tower from a six-story base, a tower that in diminishing jetés reaches the sky 1,250 feet above Fifth Avenue. The building, designed by William Lamb, was built at a record rate of 4.5 floors a week, with the first steel laid on March 17, 1930, to open on May 1, 1931.

The building's first president was Al Smith, the former governor of New York, the "Empire State." The man who installed Smith as president, and the building's primary backer, was John J. Raskob, who had been the chief financial officer of General Motors. When Chrysler's building rose to 1,048 feet, Raskob could not let his competitor best him, so he decided to take his building from the originally announced 1,000 feet to 1,050 feet in order to win the title of world's tallest building. Raskob boasted that all eighty-five floors of his building could be used to full advantage, and that an outdoor promenade for viewing the city would be located on the eighty-sixth floor, an observatory 150 feet higher than Chrysler's.

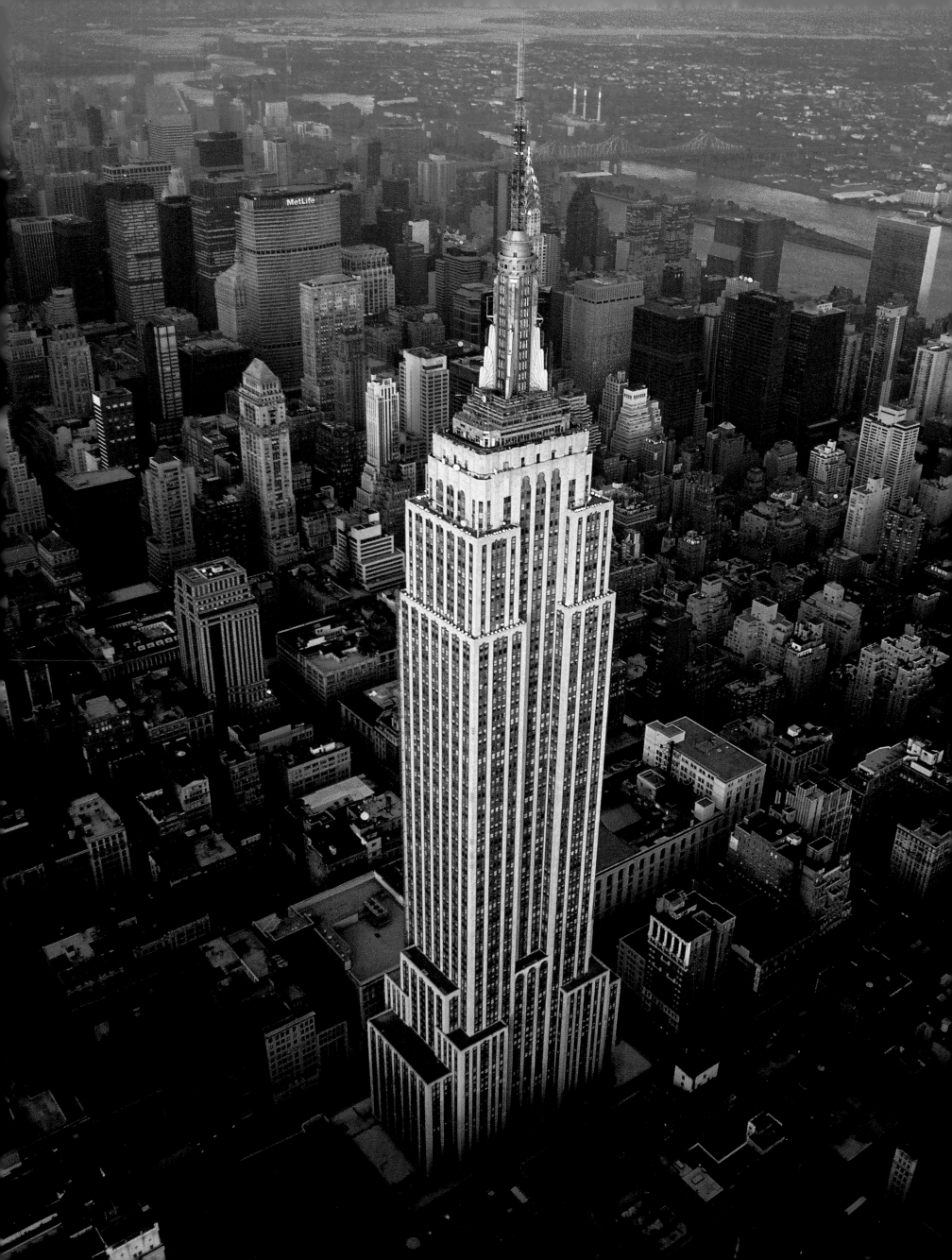

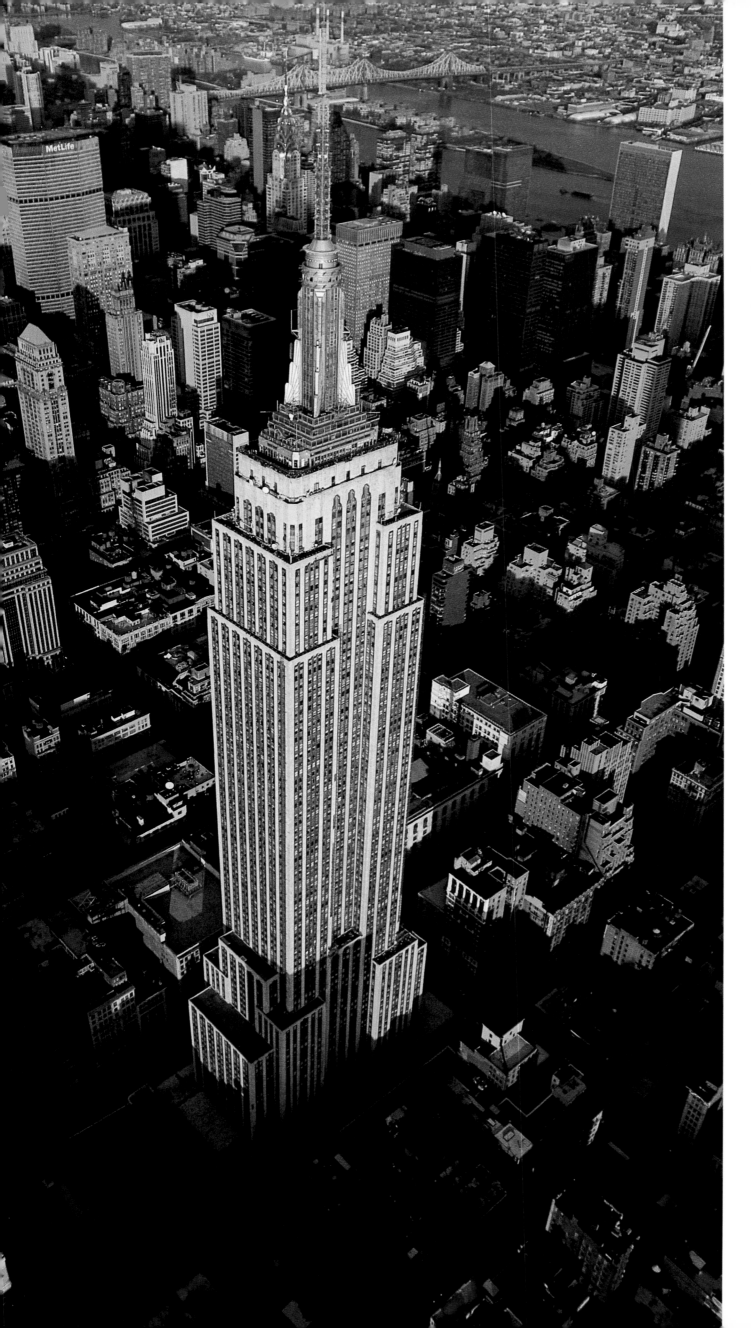

EMPIRE STATE BUILDING, 350 FIFTH AVENUE, BETWEEN 33RD AND 34TH STREET

The 200-foot tower atop the Empire State Building was originally intended as a dirigible mooring mast, one of the looniest building schemes since the Tower of Babel. The planners assumed that dirigible captains would willingly brave the treacherous air currents swirling around the building and navigate their lighter-than-air crafts close enough to the mooring mast to drop a line over the side. The line would then have to be caught, winched in, and the dirigible secured. A gangplank would drop from the passengers' gondola to a parapet ringing the 102nd floor, and supposedly passengers would happily walk the gangplank, 1,250 feet up in the air. Although the plan never worked, the mooring mast gave the building one of the city's most distinctive crowns and provided an enclosed observatory one floor below.

The observatories, however, were an unexpected boon. The building that was planned in the boom of the '20s opened in the bust of the '30s. Tenants were sparse, and it was quickly nicknamed the "Empty State Building." But one of its few lucrative sources was the revenue generated by the observatories.

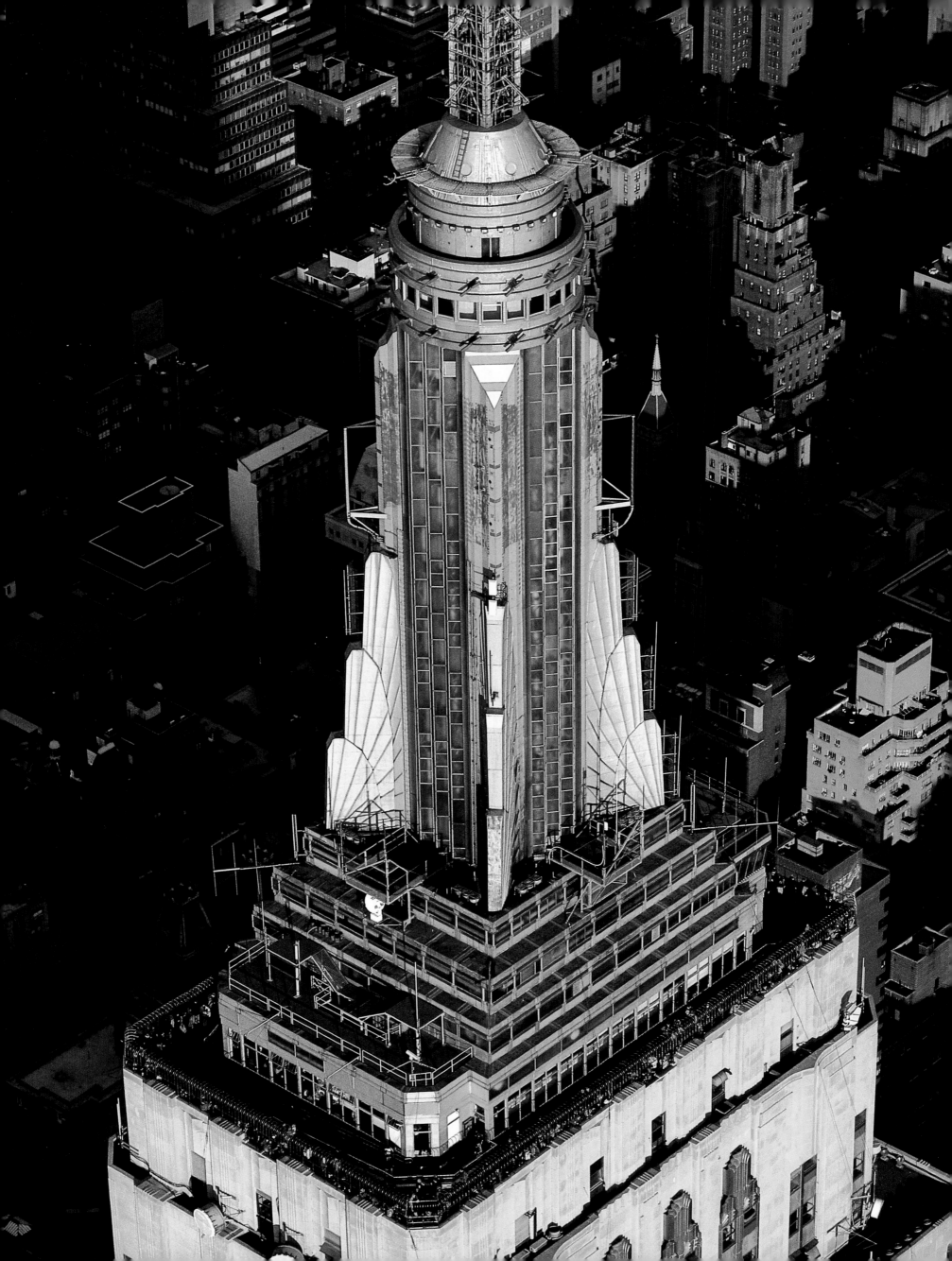

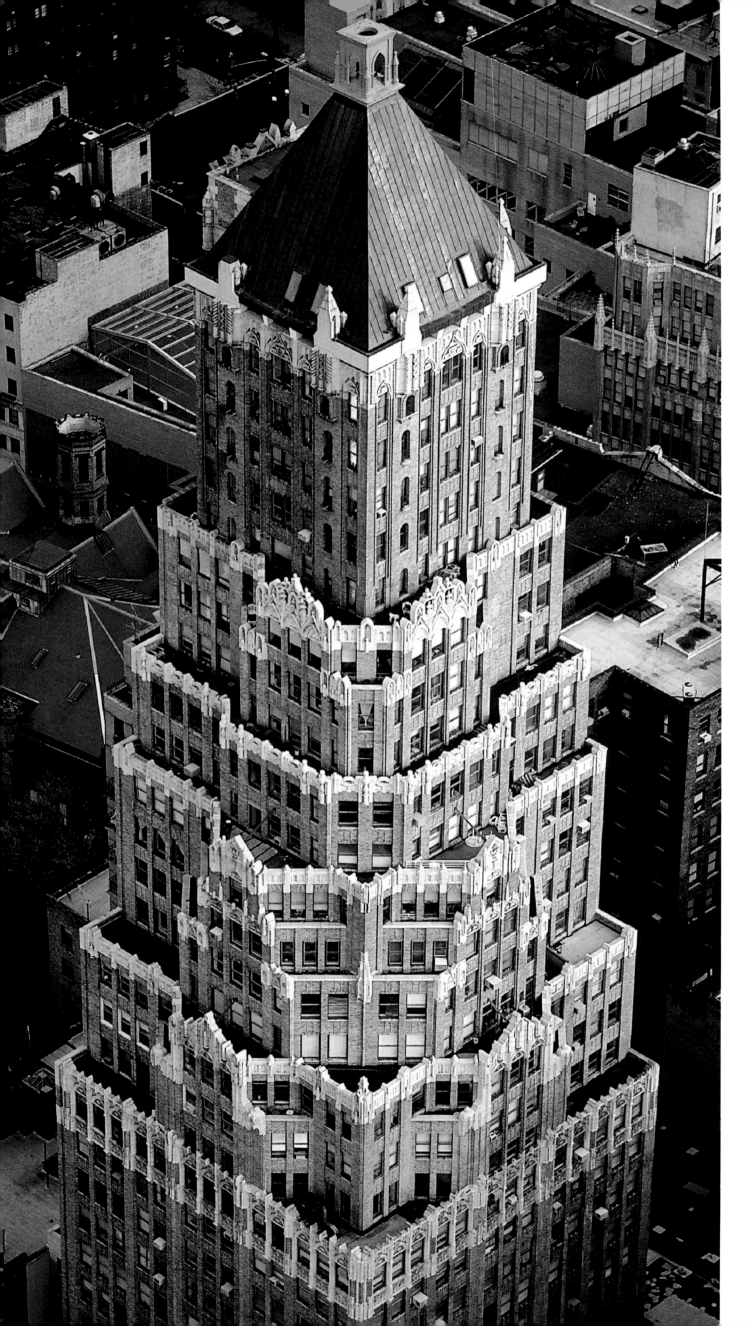

Brooklyn, which was the nation's third-largest city in 1860, saw its identity consumed by the consolidation of the City of Greater New York in 1898, when Brooklyn's role as a city in and of itself was reduced to being only one of five boroughs.

Almost thirty years later, in 1927, Brooklyn's Chamber of Commerce erected this thirty-six-story office building (which now houses apartments) as a show of strength. The architect, A. F. Simberg, here designed what some people declare is the "Woolworth Building of Brooklyn," an appellation that lends an air of second-class status.

This twenty-one-story loft-and-office building opened in 1925, the year that ground was broken for the Eighth Avenue subway line. It is axiomatic that population follows transportation, and with a station planned for 23rd Street, this building was well served by the prescience of its developer.

The building's setbacks are especially dramatic, with parapets that have a hint of the Gothic in a modern idiom. Some of the walls are at acute angles to each other, others at obtuse angles, all with a mind to creating a visual tension on an aesthetic level, while, on a practical level, allowing light to stream into the workplace.

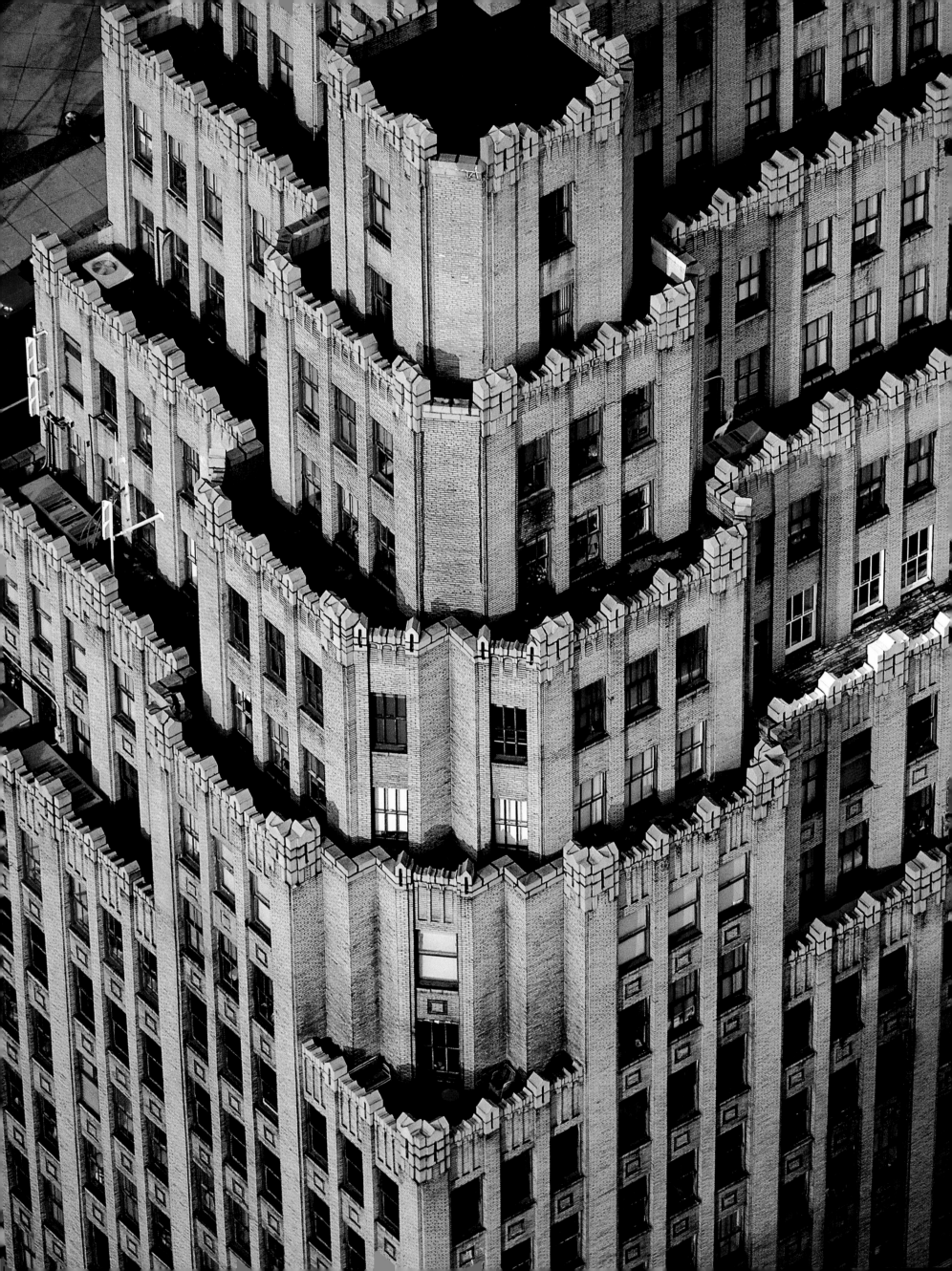

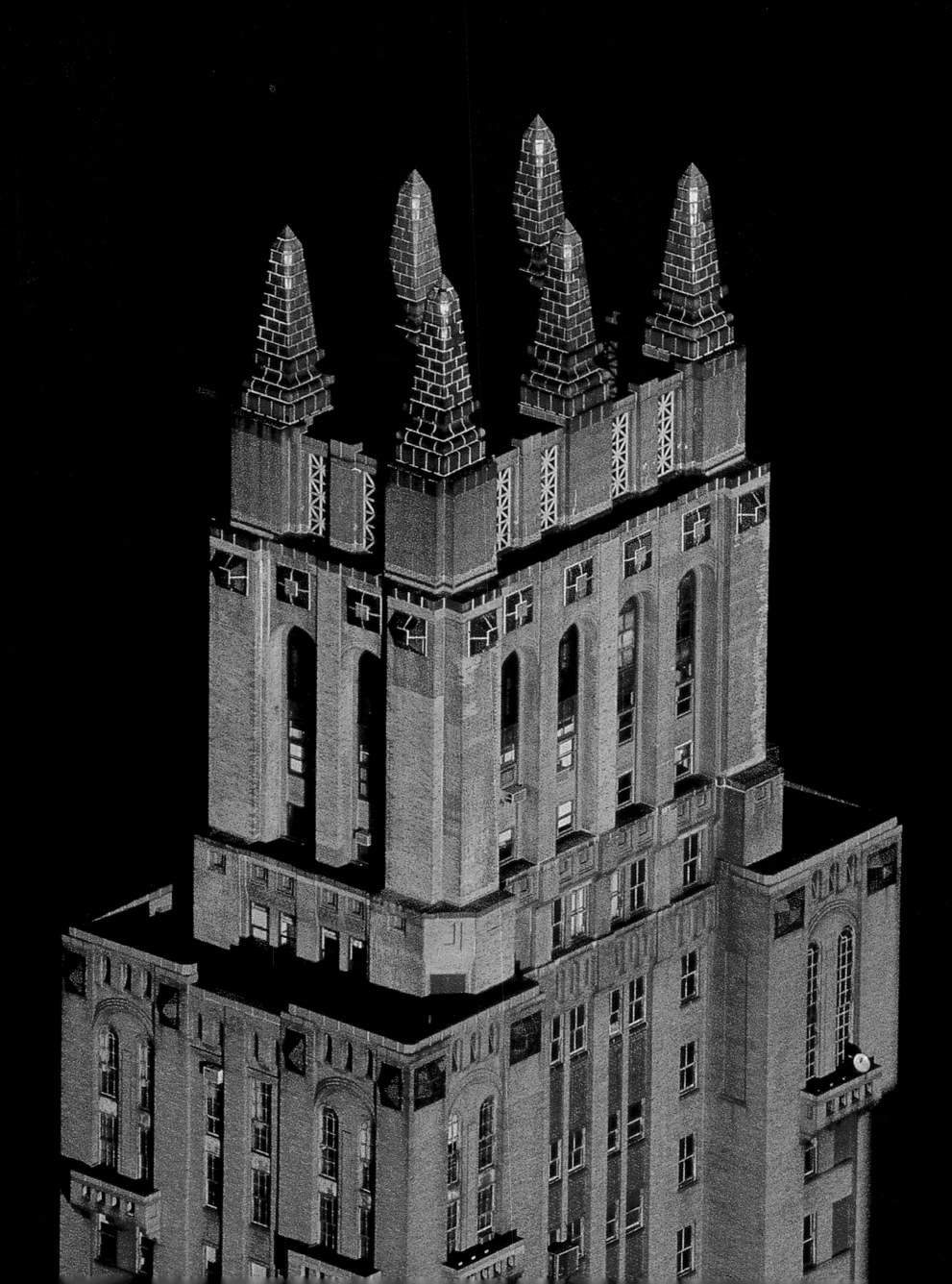

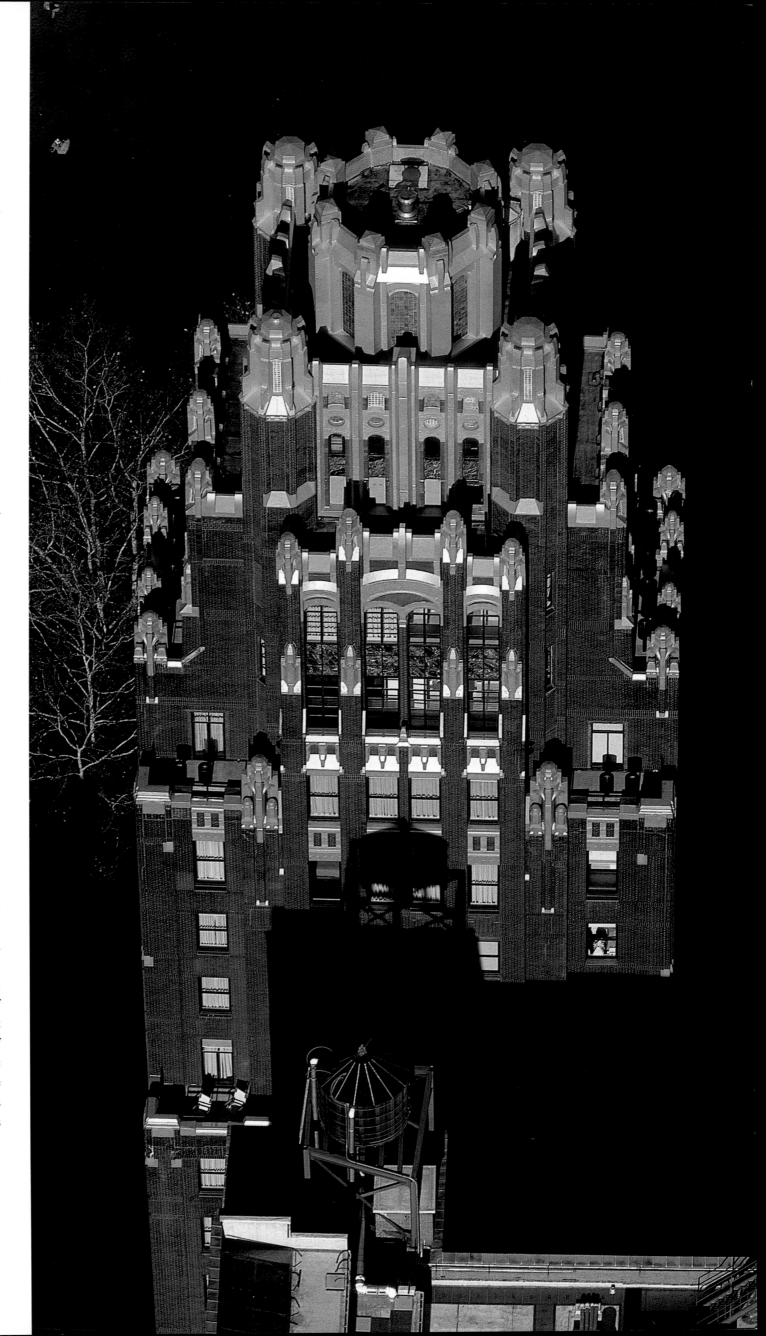

OPPOSITE: **LEFCOURT COLONIAL BUILDING, 295 MADISON AVENUE, AT 40TH STREET**
VIEW LOOKING NORTHWEST

By the time Abraham E. Lefcourt built 295 Madison in 1929, he had already built about forty buildings in New York. He liked to stamp them with his name, and in a flight of fancy he here added "Colonial," which has nothing to do with the building's style.

Lefcourt retained the little-known Charles F. Moyer to design the building, a forty-seven-story tower that sits well east of Madison Avenue. Fully anticipating a neighbor to rise to the building's east, Moyer installed a bank of elevators at the east end of the building, which explains the window-less wall.

Moyer used all the tricks of light and shadow, and the building's appearance changes according to the time of day, making it a constant source of interest and surprise.

RIGHT: **AMERICAN RADIATOR BUILDING, 40 WEST 40TH STREET, BETWEEN FIFTH AND SIXTH AVENUE**
VIEW LOOKING NORTHEAST

Forty West 40th Street was one of the first buildings to show the dramatic possibilities of the 1916 zoning law, which stated that buildings had to be set back above a certain point. However, if built on only twenty-five percent of a site, the building could rise straight up as high as was technologically possible. Raymond Hood's American Radiator Building was the first to combine the two ideas, rising as a pure, unembellished tower from a low base on a midblock site.

Whereas other skyscrapers still looked like overbloated versions of Chartres or the Parthenon, 40 West 40th Street was a cubist's dream of massing in ziggurat forms, a stylistic achievement surpassing the average early 1920s office building. Hood's style would develop still further in his later McGraw-Hill Building.

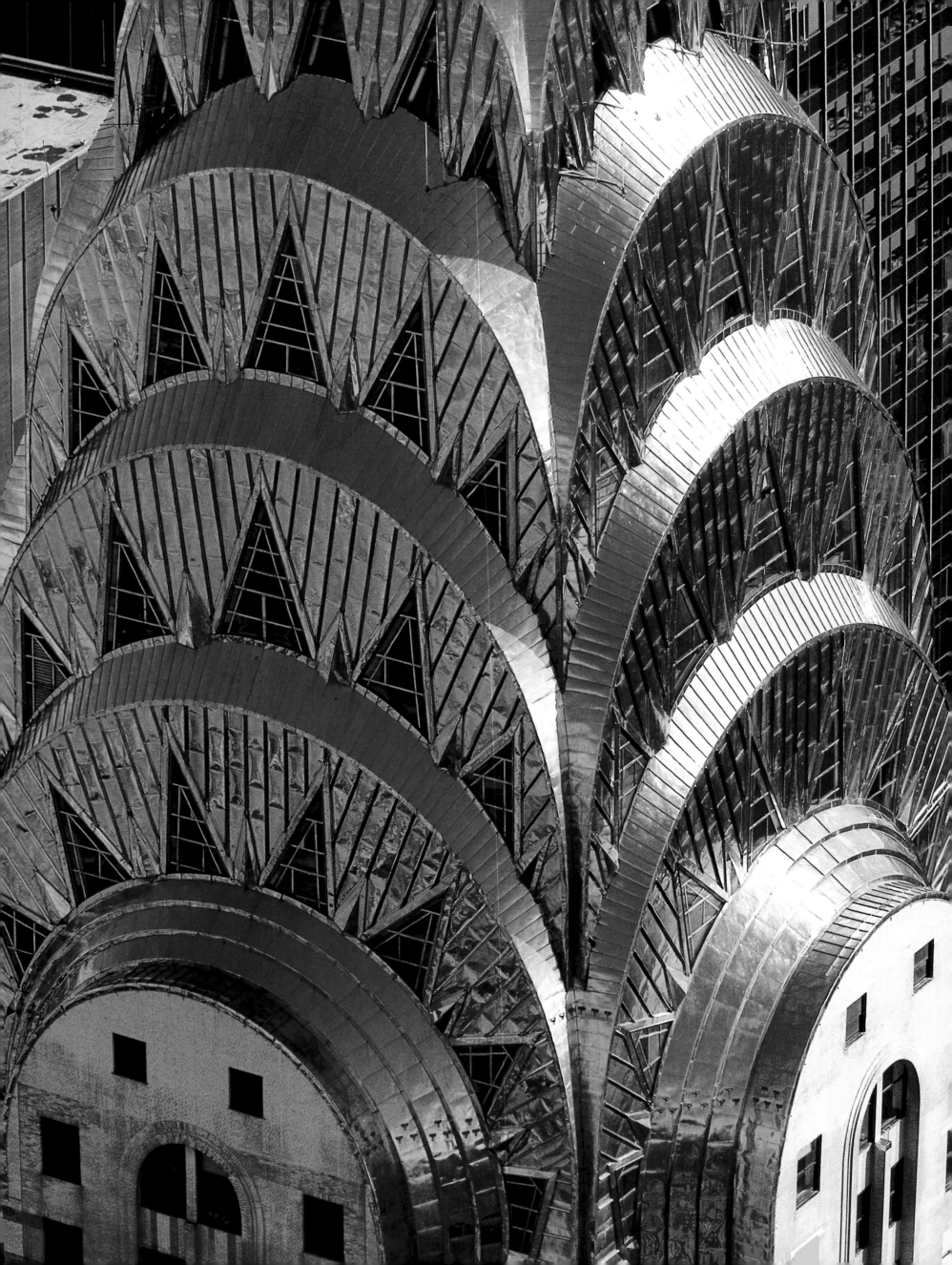

When the Chrysler Building opened in 1930, architectural critics turned up their noses. One newspaper said that its spire gave the appearance of an uplifted swordfish. Another said it was "the height of commercial swank." "A stunt design," said *The New Yorker*, with "no significance as serious design."

So much for what the critics thought. In the same 1997 poll that had the Woolworth Building eighth in popularity among local members of the American Institute of Architects, the Chrysler Building was first. And the professionals are hardly alone in their appreciation of the building. This is undoubtedly the favorite building of New Yorkers.

The spire that offended the critics is one of the leading reasons why people respond so positively to the building. Yet, in the original design Chrysler's building had a dome in the Romanesque style. But the building needed more lift in order to be taller than 40 Wall Street in the race to become the world's tallest building. Chrysler had his architect, William Van Alen, add more revenue-producing floors, and then top the whole thing off with something dramatic. The spire ensured the short-lived victory.

When the building's owners asked the Landmarks Preservation Commission for permission to turn on the lights in the spire's triangular windows, the commission quickly granted the request. Van Alen had originally planned for the windows to be framed by lights, but the installation had never been completed.

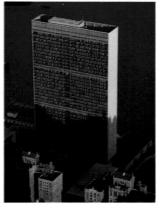

**UNITED NATIONS
SECRETARIAT, EAST OF
FIRST AVENUE,
AT 43RD STREET
VIEW LOOKING
NORTHEAST**

Although New York has always been an international city, the arrival of the United Nations in 1952 made it the international city of the world.

The team of architects that comprised the United Nations Planning Staff was true to the nature of the institution. They represented the United States (Wallace K. Harrison, director, and Max Abramovitz, deputy director), France (Le Corbusier), the Soviet Union, the United Kingdom, Belgium, Canada, China, Sweden, Brazil, Australia, and Uruguay.

The design of the UN combined the International Style's spare design with the style of Le Corbusier's utopian plan called the "radiant city," where tall, freestanding towers and low buildings would stand apart from each other in large, landscaped areas. The Secretariat was not greeted by all with pleasure and was dismissed as being little more than a shoebox stuck on end.

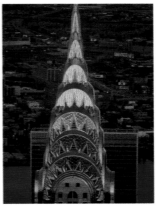

**CHRYSLER BUILDING,
405 LEXINGTON AVENUE,
BETWEEN 42ND AND
43RD STREET**

The spire of the Chrysler Building at night.

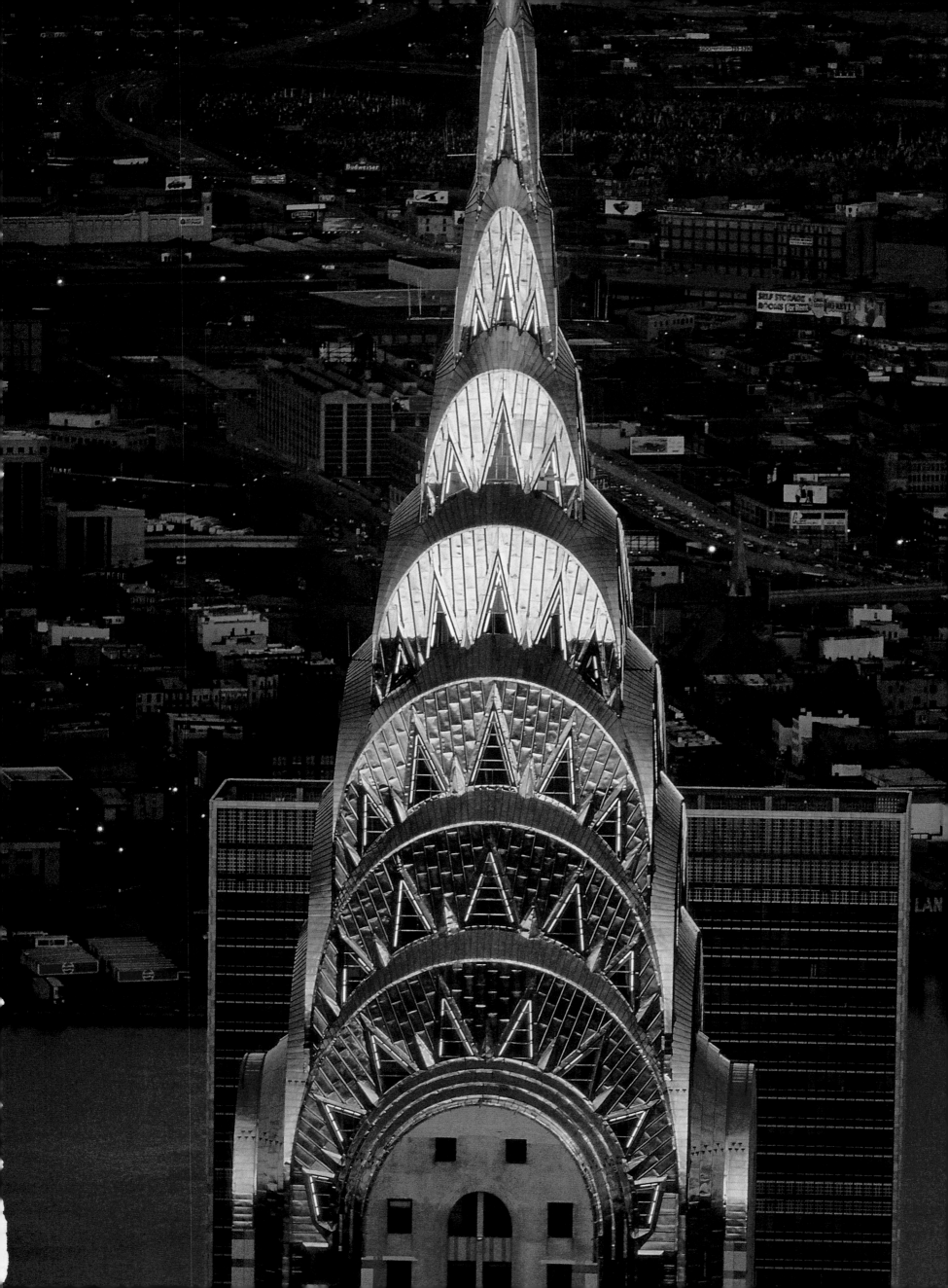

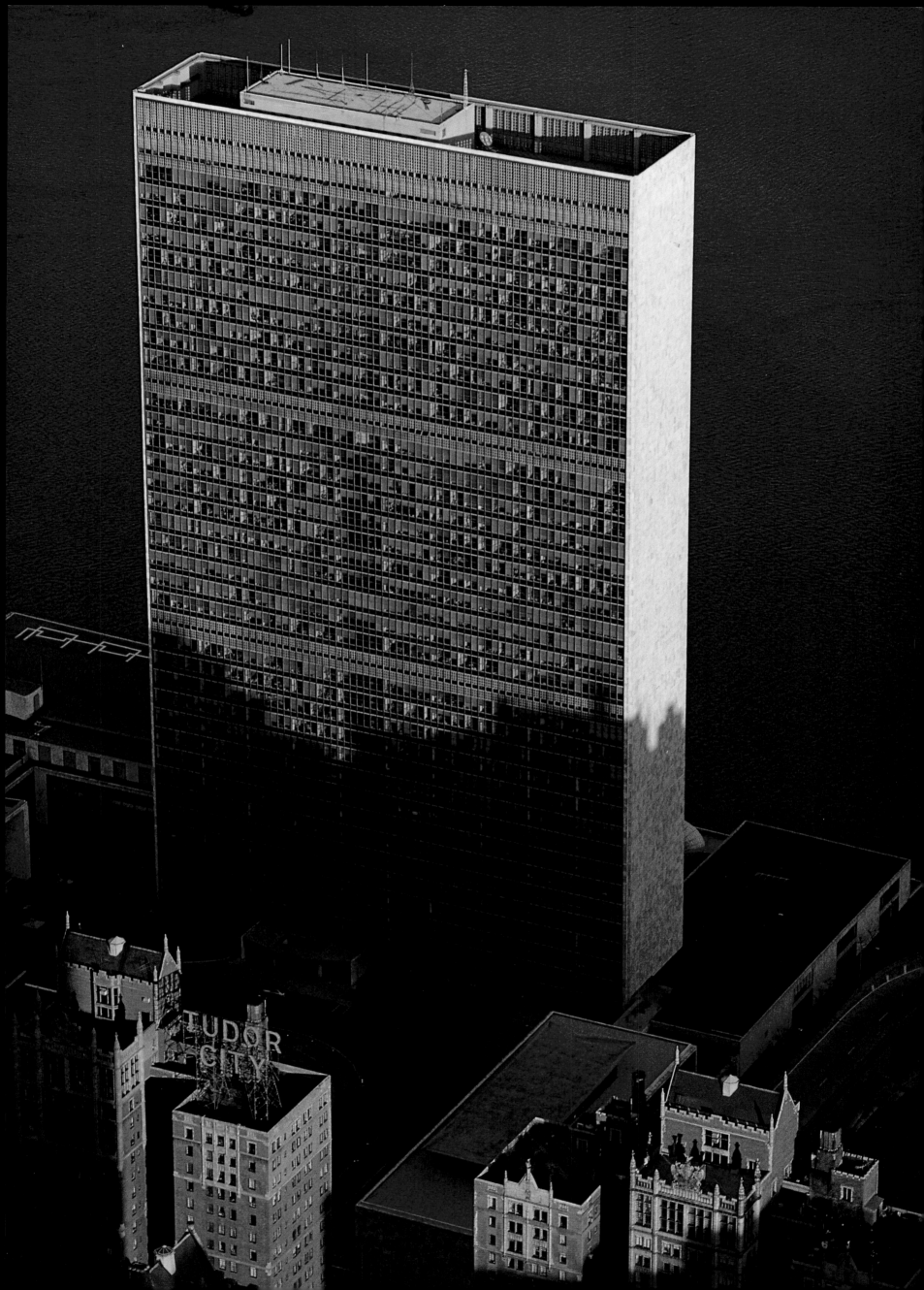

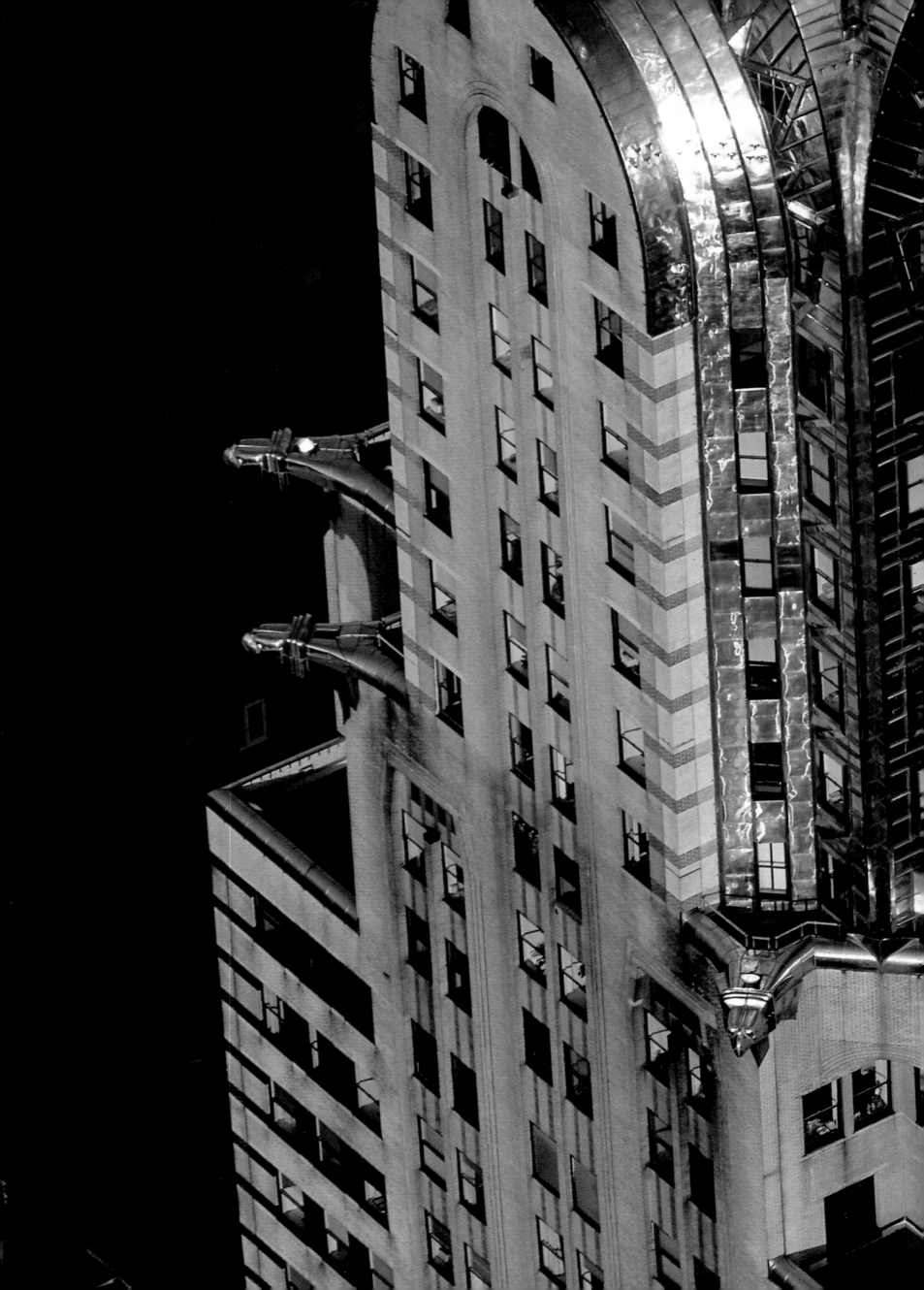

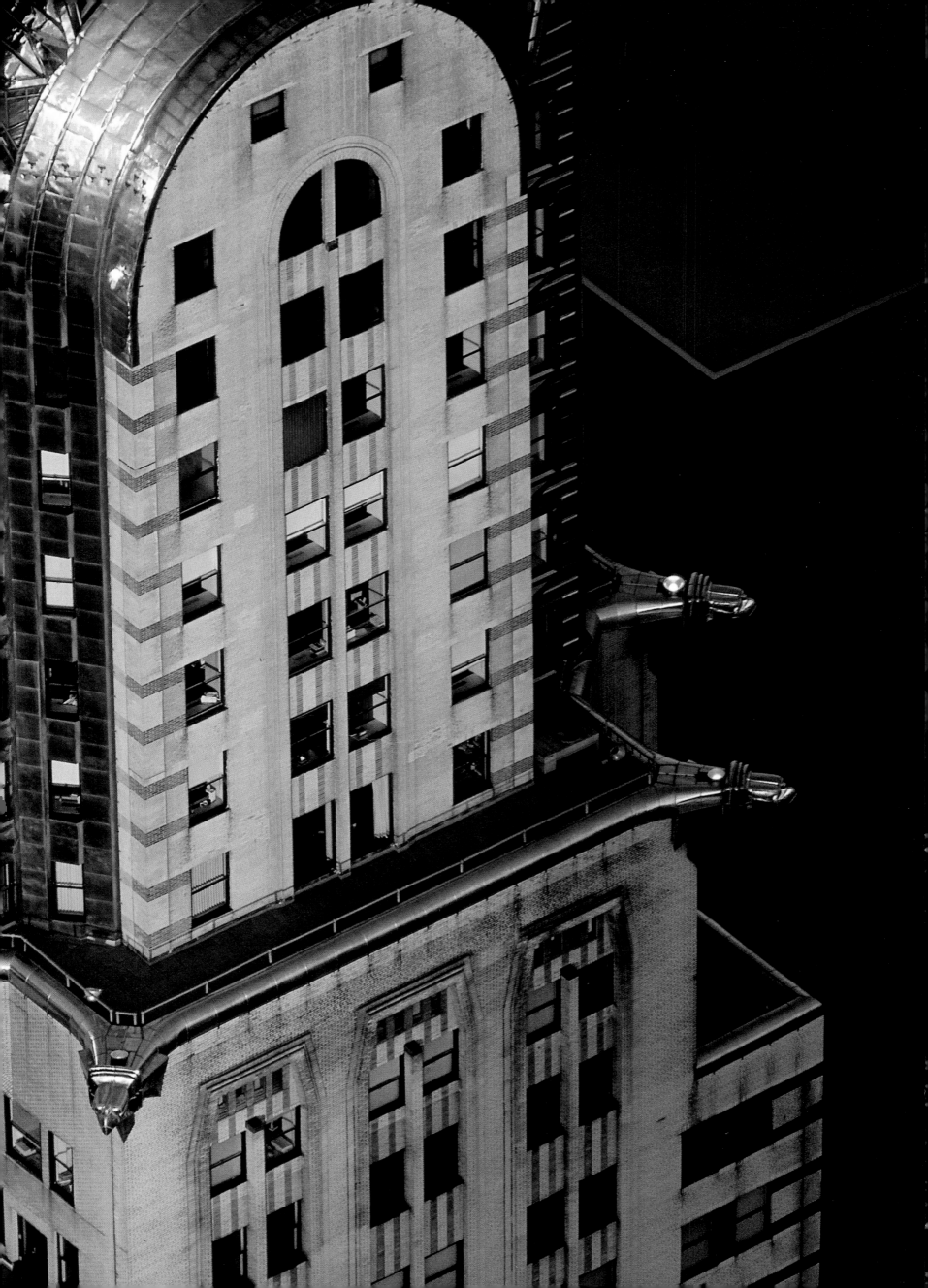

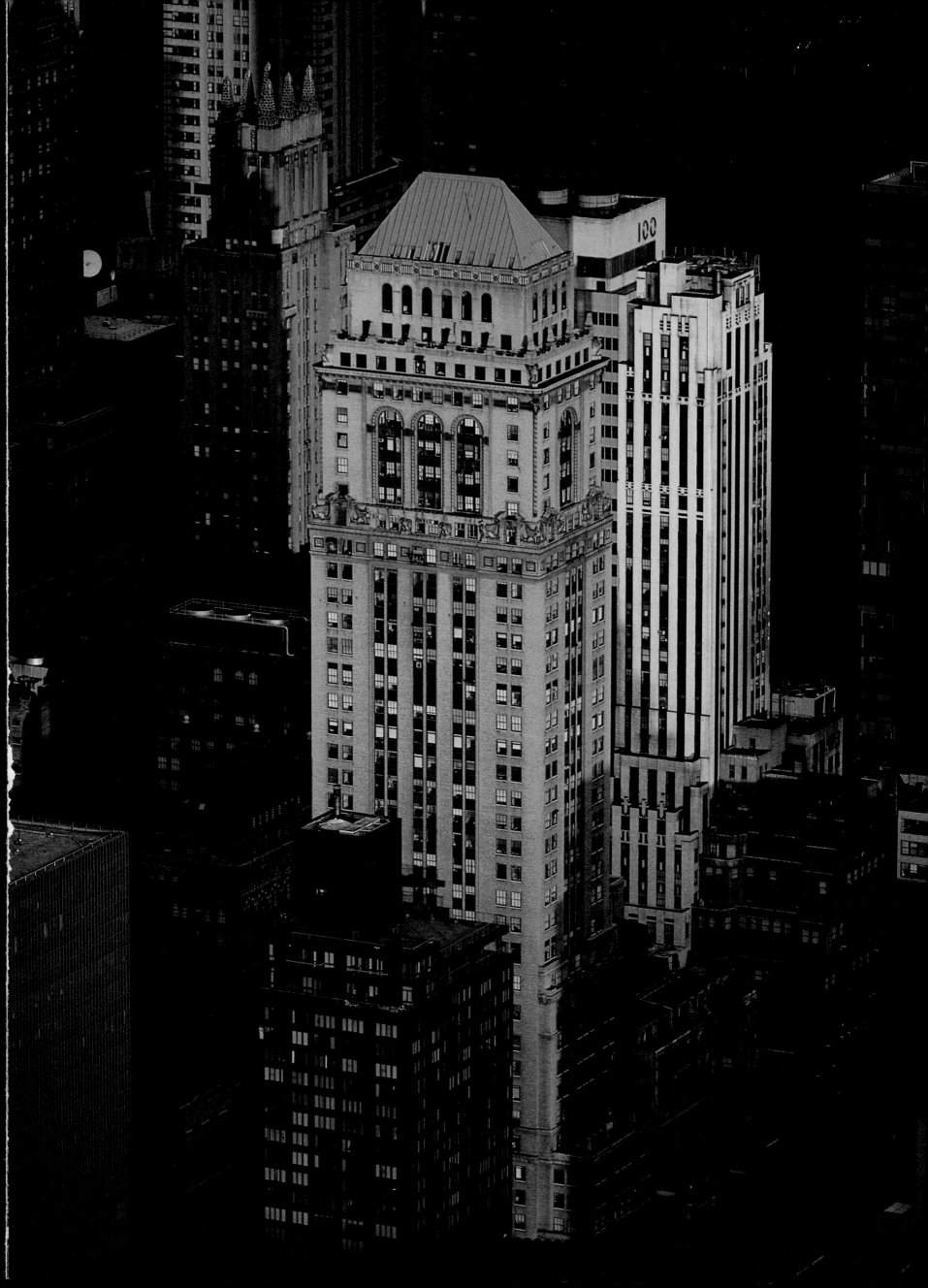

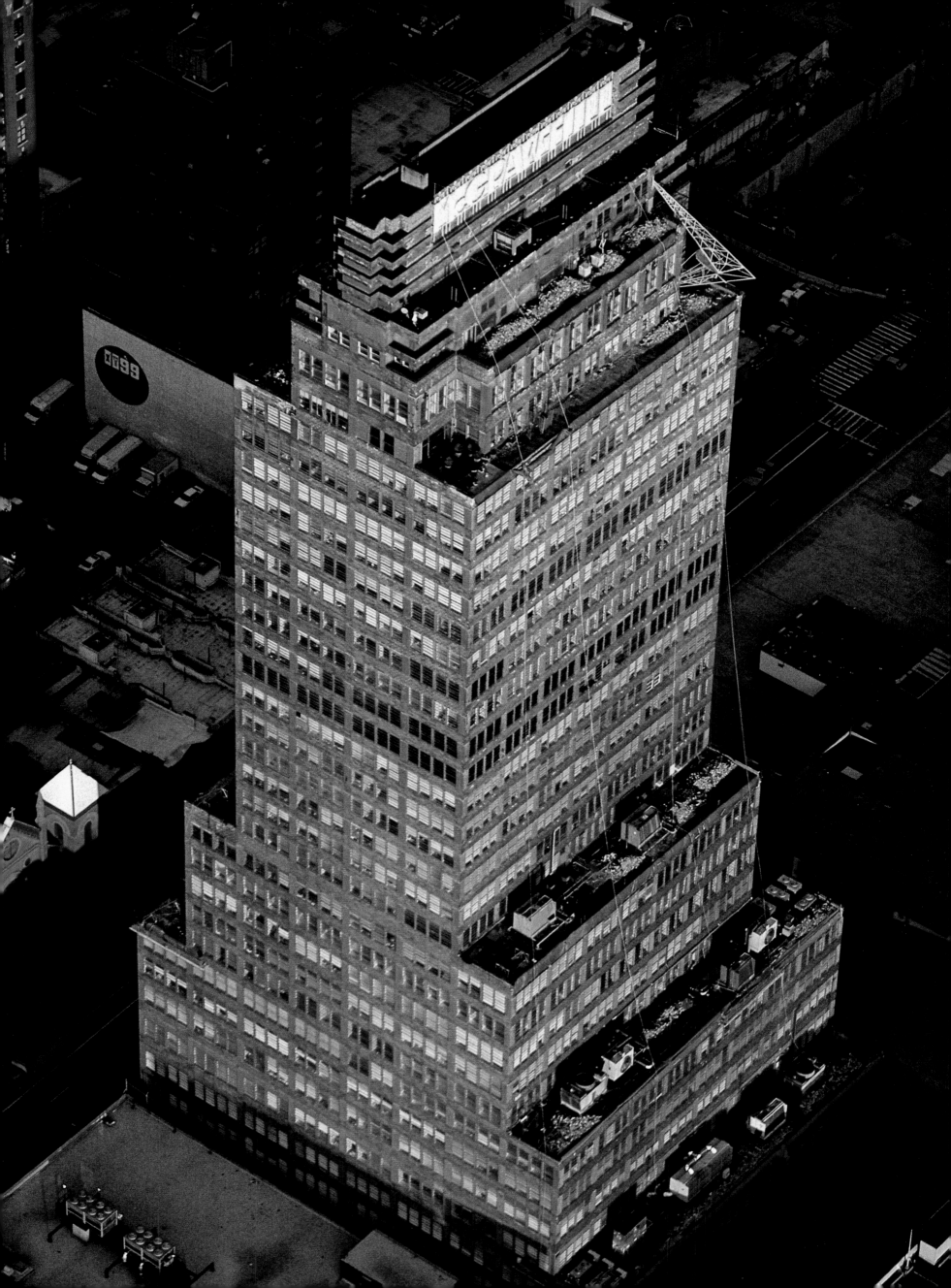

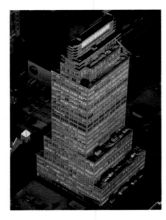

**McGraw-Hill Building,
330 West 42nd Street,
between Eighth and
Ninth Avenue
View looking
northeast**

With a roofline reminiscent of the superstructure of an aircraft carrier, the thirty-five-story McGraw-Hill Building has one of the city's most distinctive setback silhouettes. Its facade is little more than bands of sea-green terra cotta alternating with bands of windows. The only decoration, aside from the rooftop superstructure, is a very narrow and subtle tomato-red banding unifying the windows.

Here volume replaces mass, and purity of form supercedes decoration. In short, the 1931 building represented the tenets of the International Style as laid down by the masters of Modernism. But not even this spare building was spared criticism by Modernist purists, who felt that its crowning feature was "unnecessary" and "heavy." This, however, is the feature that most viewers appreciate most.

The piece of sculpture on the setback, titled *Boomerang*, was created by Owen Morrel for the site in 1980.

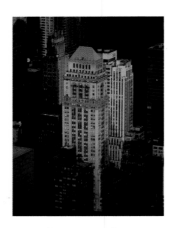

**10 East 40th Street,
between Fifth and
Madison Avenue
View looking
northeast**

Seldom do you find a forty-eight-story tower on a midblock site because developers are afraid that a neighbor will build a tower right alongside theirs and block the light. The developer Jesse Jones took a limited risk here. He had struck a deal with a neighboring Fifth Avenue store that needed to expand, so up went the building in 1928, with the Arnold Constable store occupying some of the lower floors.

The architects Ludlow & Peabody used griffins as a decorative motif on some of the setbacks, which might have been a prescient act. The mythological beasts made their nests out of gold, and this building is still a highly desirable nest for its office tenants—and a golden egg for its owners.

To the left is the Lefcourt Colonial Building (see pages 54–55).

To the left is the Lefcourt Colonial Building (see pages 54–55).

**Opposite: Bush Tower,
132 West 42nd Street,
between Sixth and Seventh Avenue
View looking northeast**

The architects Helmle & Corbett faced a predicament when they set out to design this building for Irving T. Bush—the shipping magnate who was then developing Bush Terminal, one of the city's largest industrial warehouses, on the Brooklyn waterfront. Bush wanted a tall building erected on a midblock site that was 200 feet deep but only fifty feet wide. The architects realized the distinct possibility that another developer might build a tower cheek by jowl to Bush Tower. Thus, the flanks of this thirty-two-story building, although decorated, are windowless for about three-quarters of the height of the building. In fact, a towering neighbor never appeared.

Bush Tower, planned just before the 1916 zoning law, was held up as the perfect example of a midblock building. One of its stylistic assets was that it was architecturally treated on all four sides, one of the requirements of the law.

When the developer asked architect Harvey Wiley Corbett how much revenue would be lost by having a tower like a cathedral, with setbacks and chamfered corners, Corbett told him that what he might lose in revenue he would gain in "beauty for all time." Obviously, Bush felt it was worth the price.

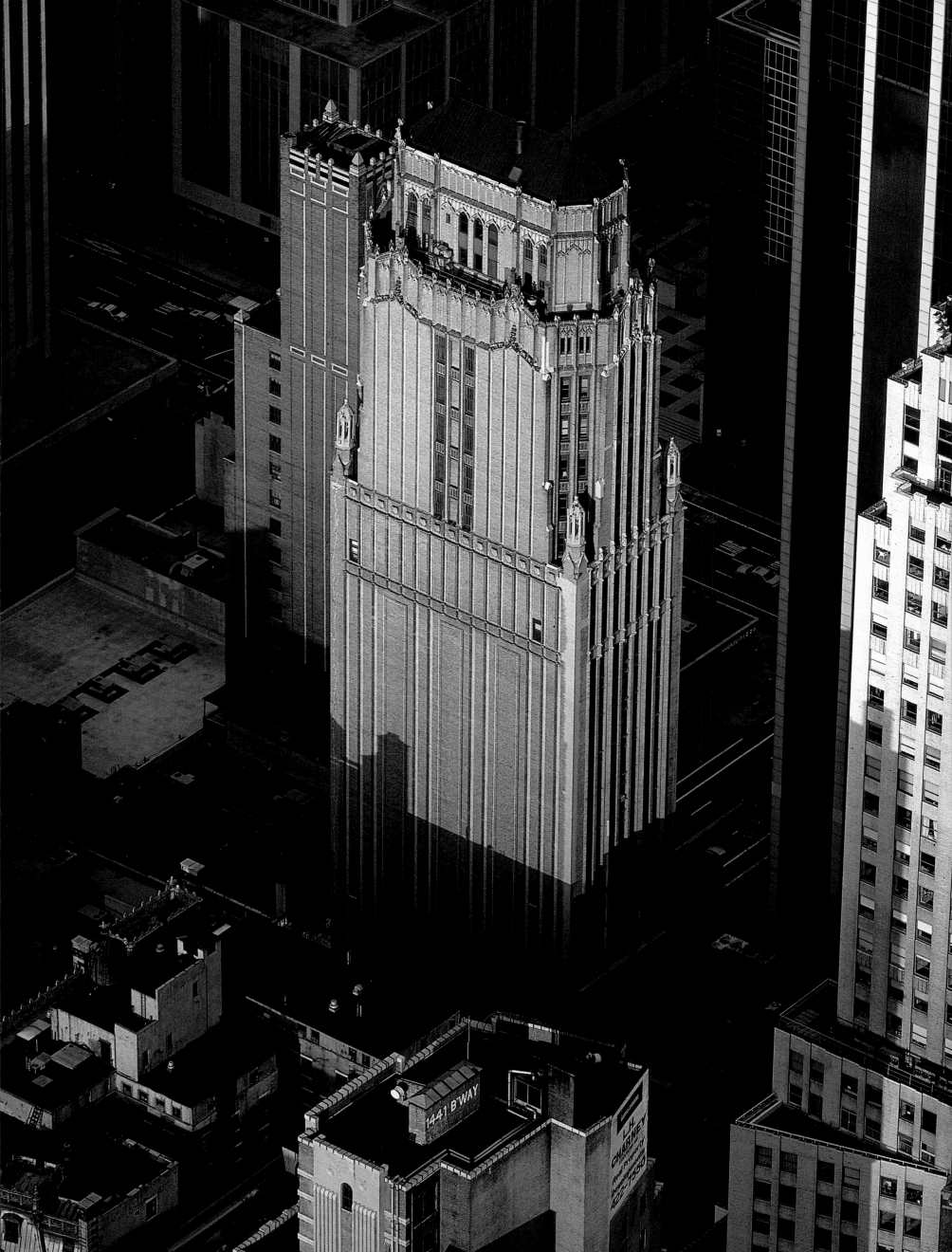

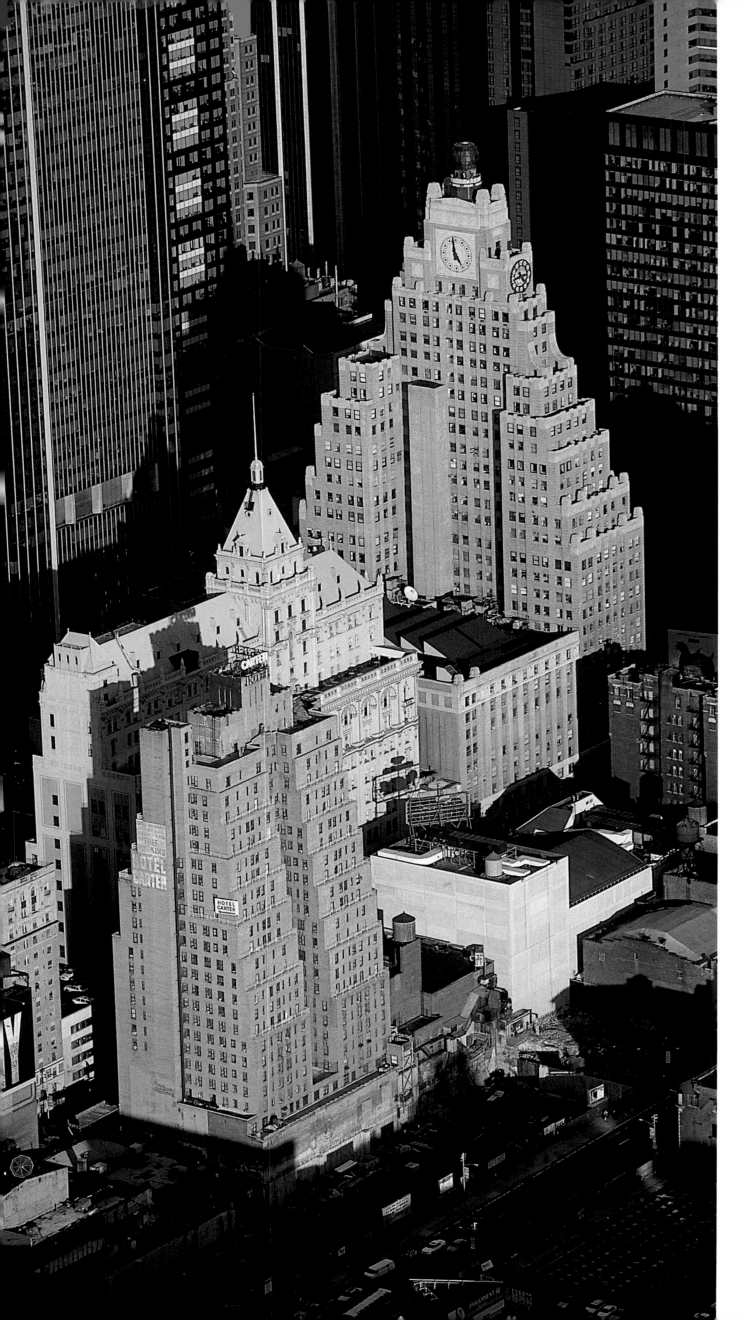

The Paramount Building is not to be confused with the building at Broadway and 50th Street that calls itself Paramount Plaza. That building was designed by Emery Roth & Sons and built by the Uris Brothers as a speculative venture in 1971. *The* Paramount Building was designed by masters of the theatrical, the Chicago-based firm Rapp & Rapp, and it was built by Paramount Pictures in 1926. It housed the Paramount Theater, where the likes of Frank Sinatra were mobbed by adoring fans, and where a movie like *Giant* did not seem so gigantic because it was dwarfed by the size of the auditorium, which was about ten stories high and had three balconies.

The building had a 450-foot-high observatory from which its publicists said you could see the entire city and the harbor. By the early 1930s, with competition from buildings such as the Empire State, RCA, and Chrysler, the observatory—to put it in theatrical terms—went "dark."

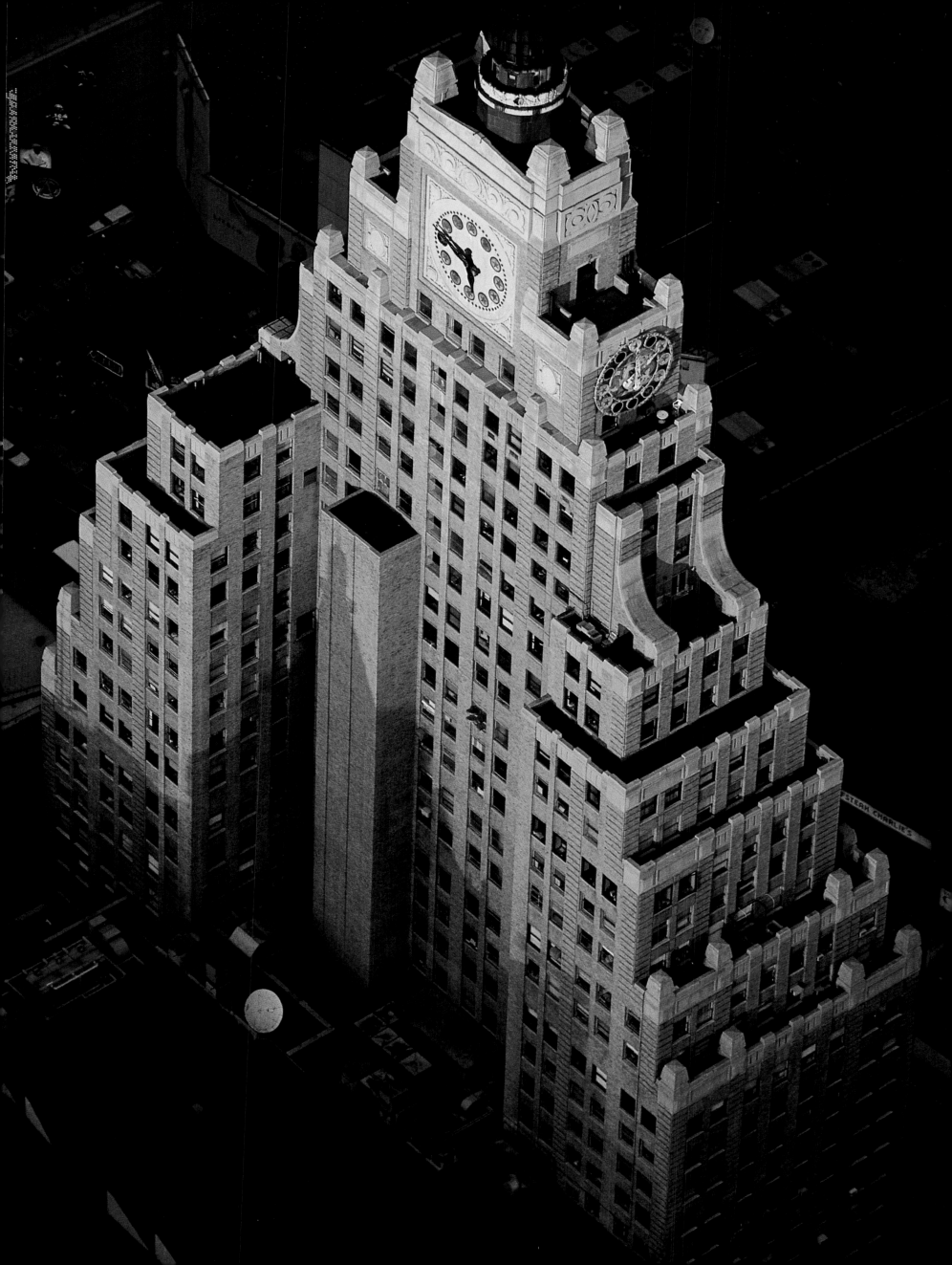

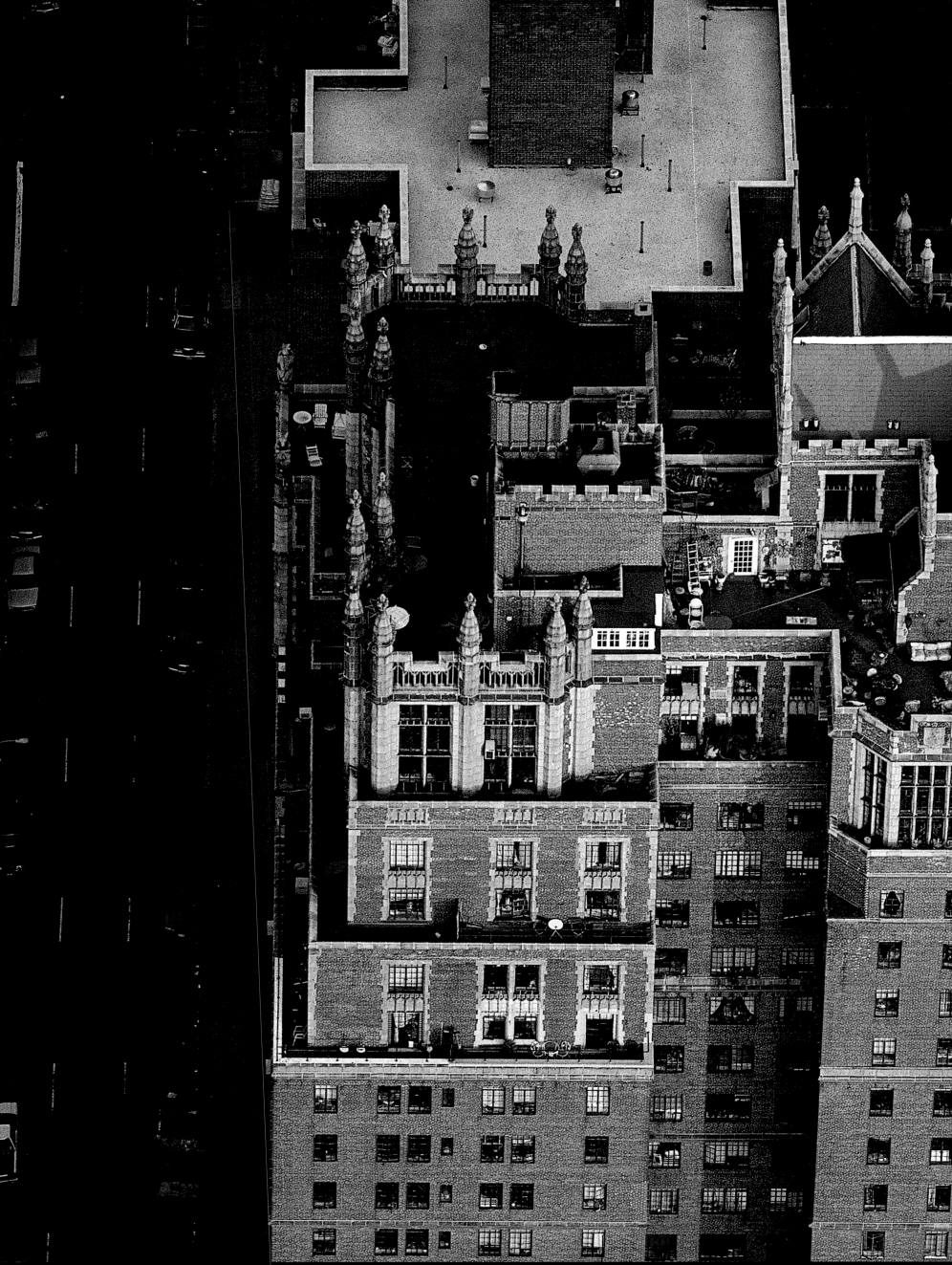

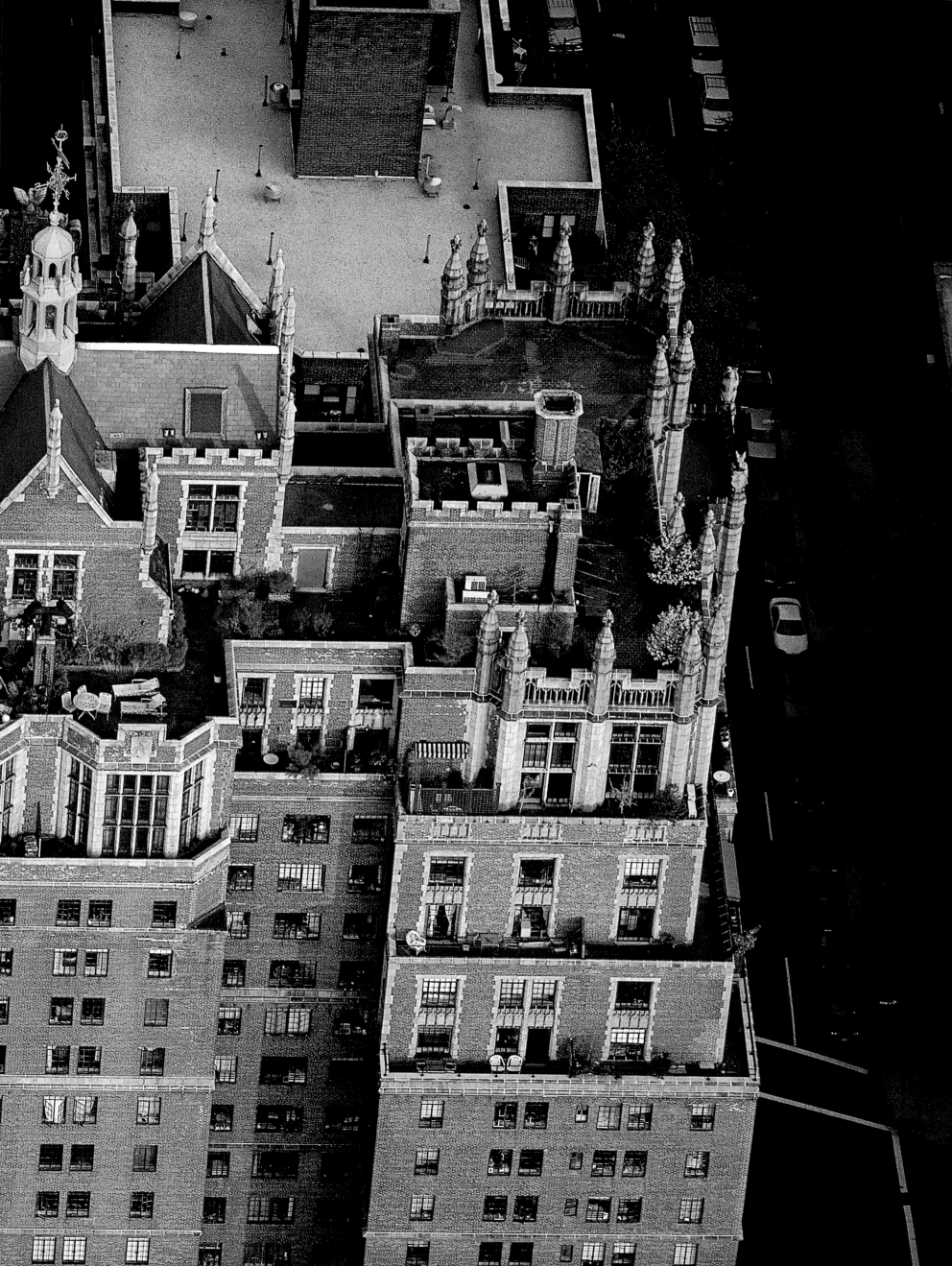

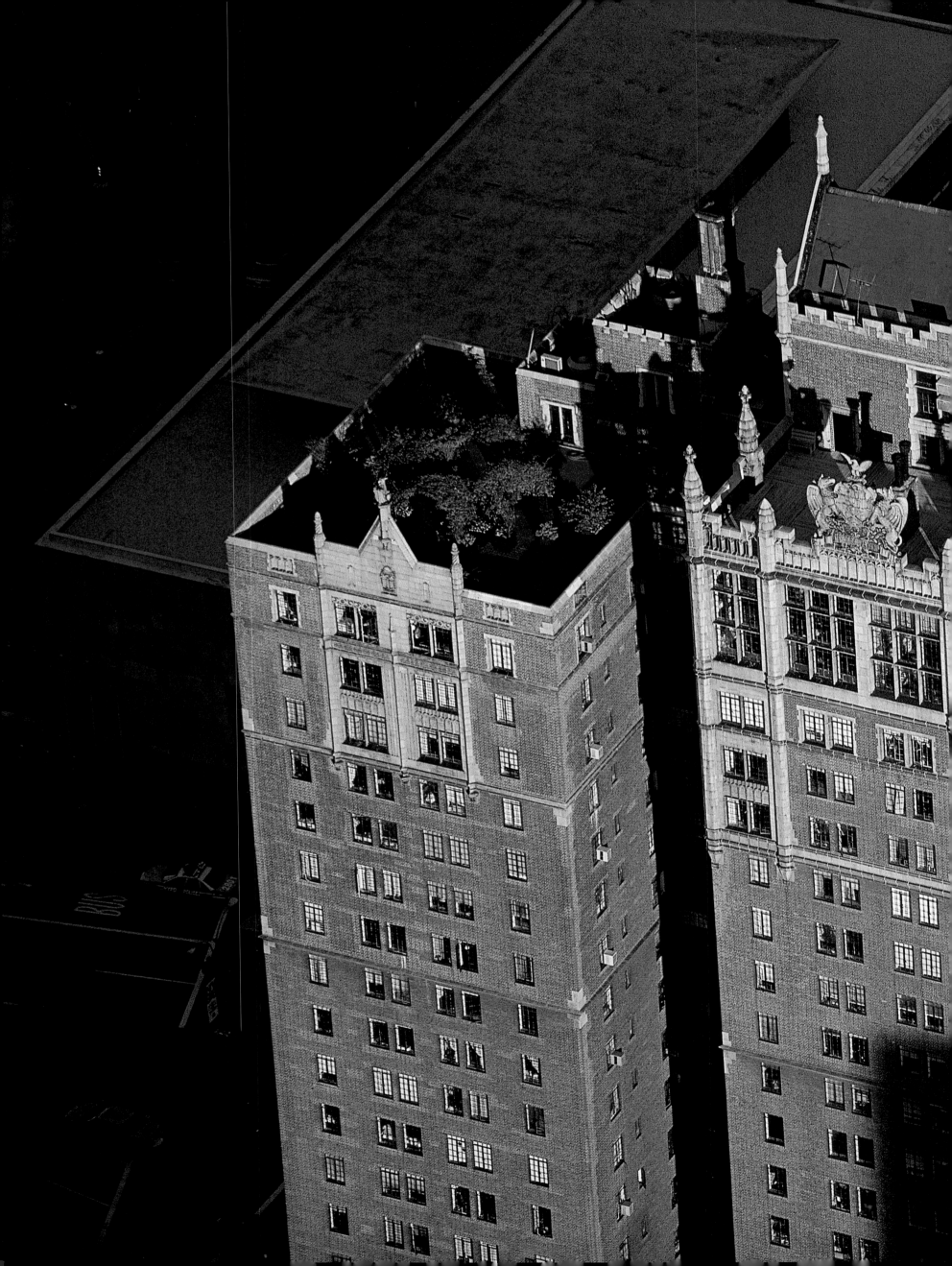

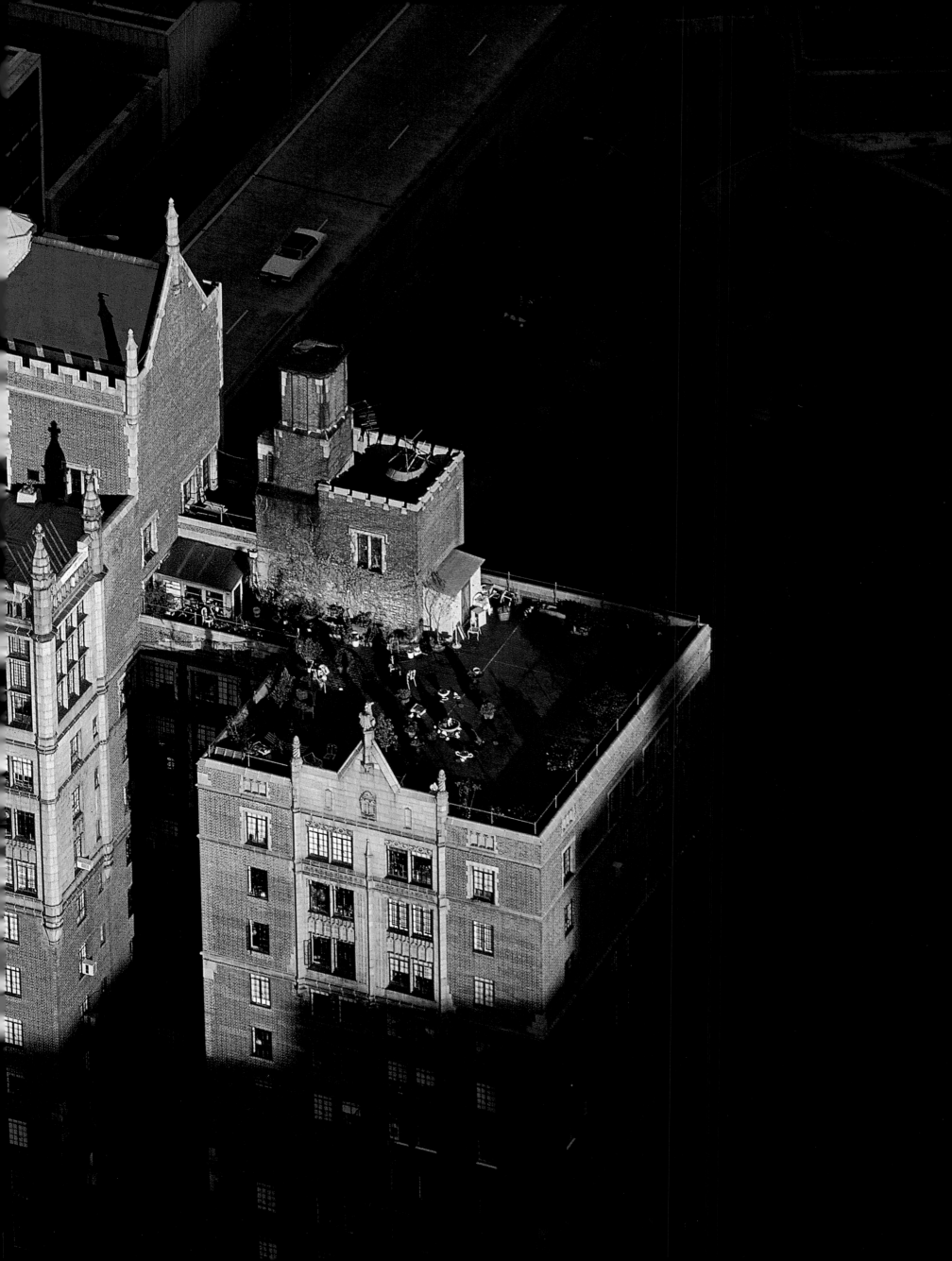

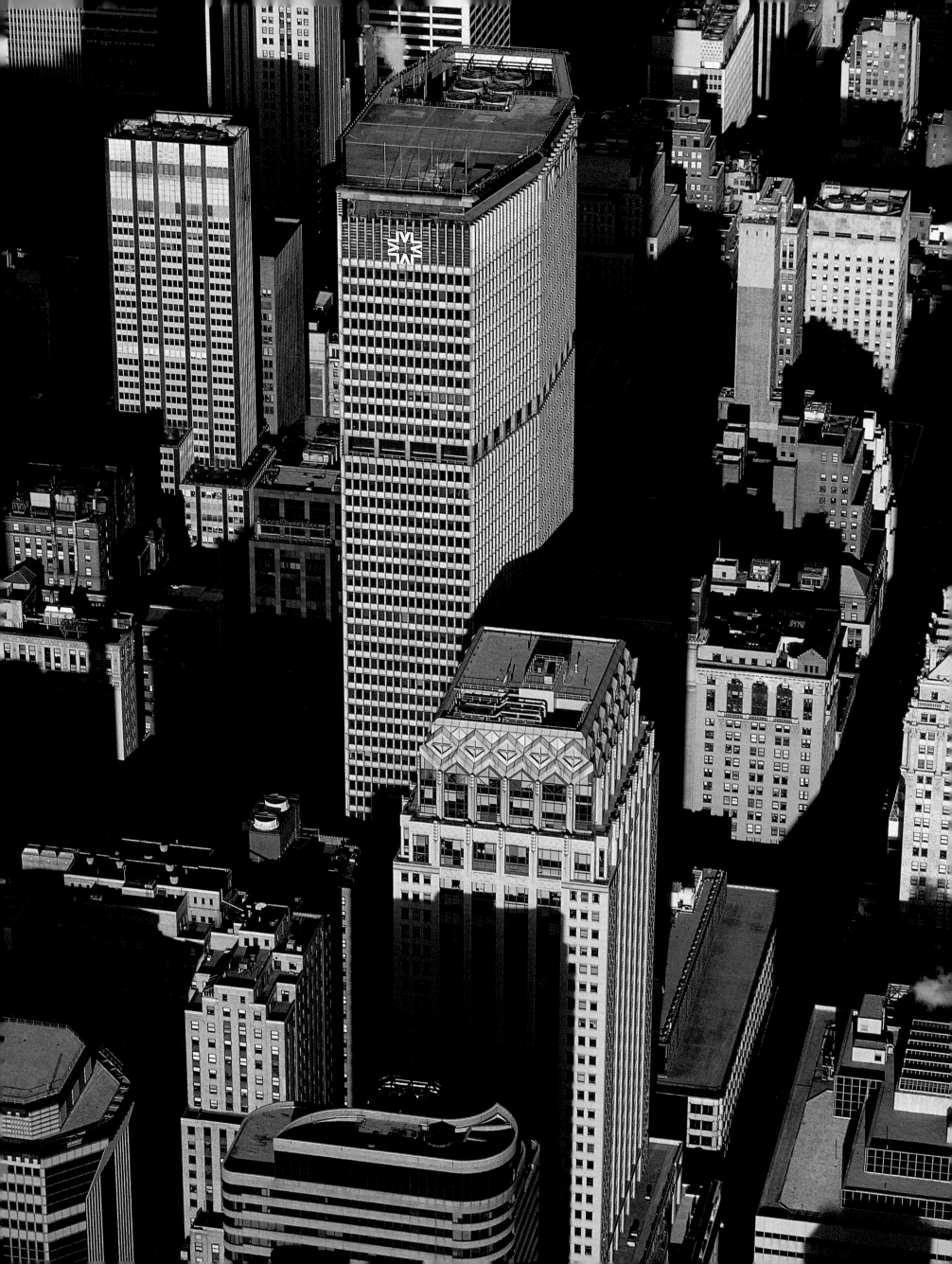

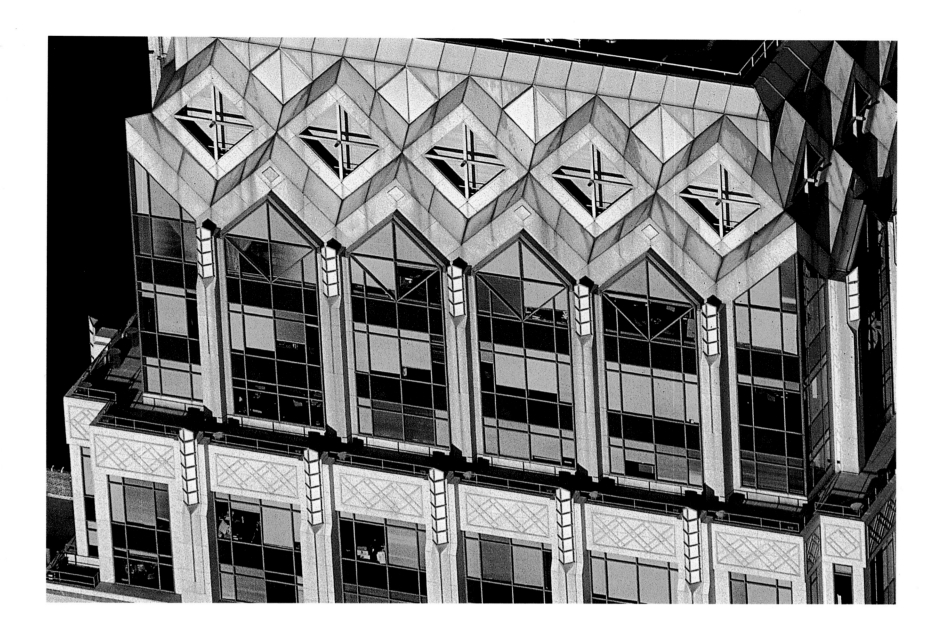

OPPOSITE AND ABOVE: METROPOLITAN LIFE BUILDING (FORMERLY PAN AM BUILDING), 200 PARK AVENUE, BETWEEN 44TH AND 45TH STREET; AND 450 LEXINGTON AVENUE, AT 45TH STREET

To those who remember a pre–Pan Am New York, this building is the monster that ate Park Avenue. It is the building whose form and bulk people still love to hate, the building that elicited cartoons such as the one set in an overbuilt future with picketers holding up placards saying "Save the Pan Am Building."

Pan Am housed its ticket office on the main floor, and the Clipper Club, a private luncheon club, was located on the fifty-ninth floor; the roof featured a heliport. The shadows cast by the helicopters regularly threw a chill into the hearts of those working below, and one day the seemingly inevitable happened—a helicopter crashed, and service was grounded.

The top of 450 Lexington Avenue, in the foreground on the opposite page, is seen above. In 1913 the New York Central Railroad built a six-story building whose steel frame was designed to support a twelve-story tower planned for a later date. That time came in 1992, and the style was not the "modernized Italian Renaissance" anticipated by the architects Warren & Wetmore, but a Postmodern design by the architects Skidmore, Owings & Merrill, and the tower grew to thirty-four stories.

PAGES 68-71: TUDOR TOWER, 41ST TO 42ND STREET, PART OF TUDOR CITY, 40TH TO 43RD STREET, BETWEEN FIRST AND SECOND AVENUE

With the coming of horse cars in the mid–nineteenth century, elevated railroads in the 1870s, and the subway by the early twentieth century, New York was no longer a walking city. Distances that people could comfortably commute between work and home doubled and tripled, and people started to live farther and farther away from their places of work.

A developer in the 1920s, Fred F. French, believed that people would be happy to live closer to their jobs if they had decent accommodations and could walk to work. French built his dream, gave it some English-style trim, and called it Tudor City. With about 1,200 apartments spread among three twenty-two-story and four ten-story apartment houses, the city's largest residential development of the 1920s opened and proved him right.

The design was convoluted, intentionally created so that tenants would look inward onto landscaped gardens. Few apartments had views east, out over the East River, and for good reason: on the east side of First Avenue, where the United Nations stands today, were coal yards and abattoirs.

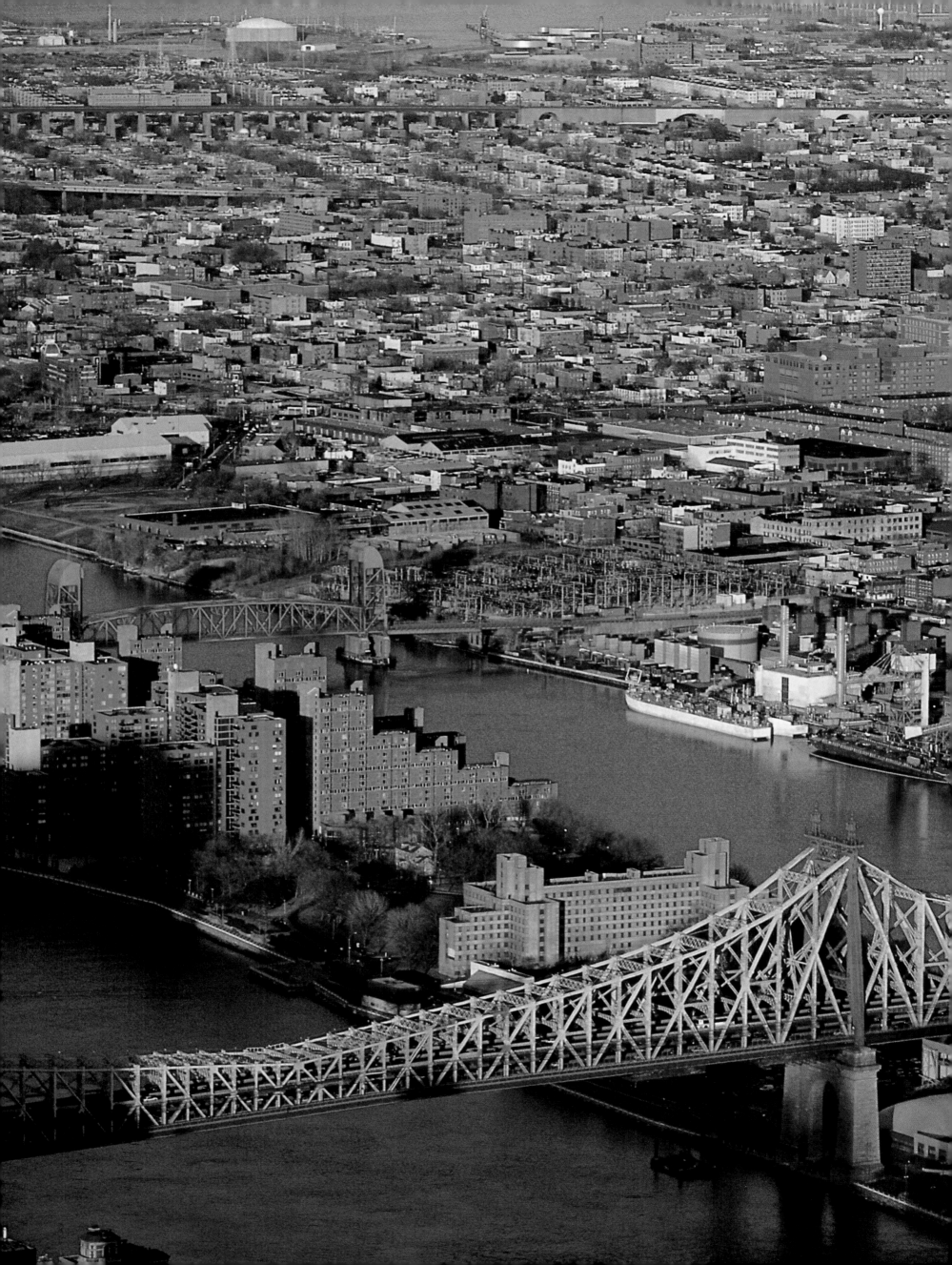

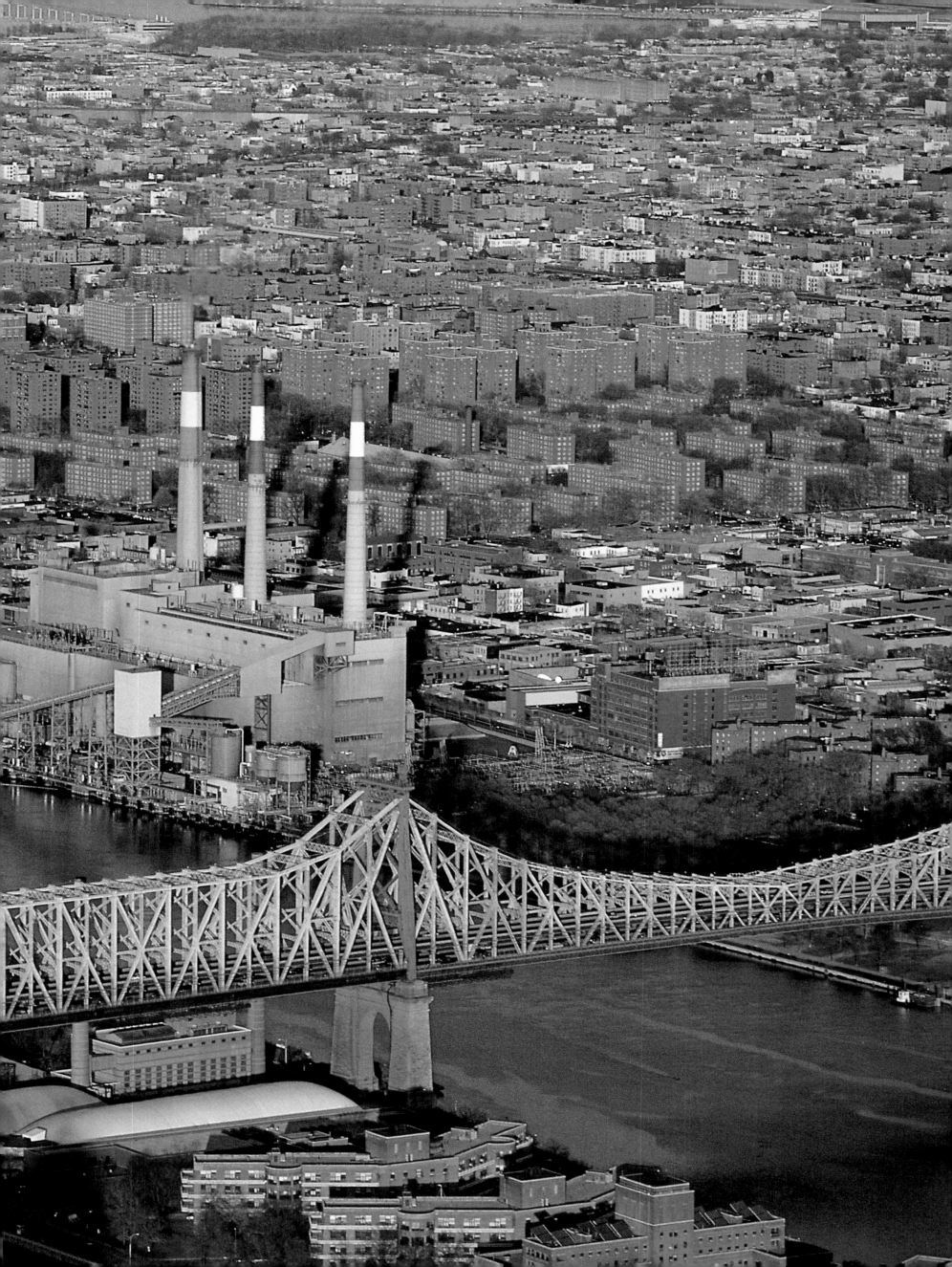

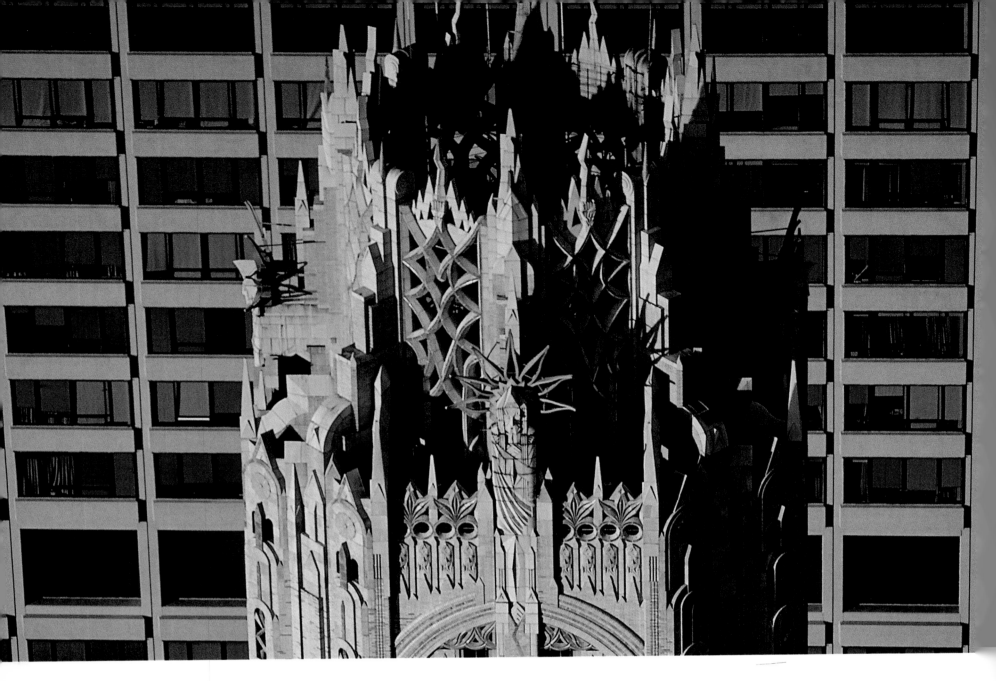

ABOVE AND OPPOSITE: **TOWER 570,
570 LEXINGTON AVENUE, AT 51ST STREET**

This idiosyncratic, highly stylized "Art Gotho" office building is adorned with symbols of electricity, and therein lies a confusing tale. For most of its existence, this building has been called the General Electric Building, which would explain the decorative motif. However, although General Electric occupied the building as recently as the 1980s, the primary tenant in 1930, and the tenant for whom the building was designed, was the Radio Corporation of America, and the building was originally called the RCA Building.

The symbolism was not designed to depict electricity in general, but radio waves in particular. However, in 1932 RCA moved into 30 Rockefeller Plaza, Rockefeller Center's flagship building, which was immediately called the RCA Building. GE now owns RCA, and in an act of corporate imperialism took over that building, which is still affectionately called the RCA

Building, and renamed it the GE Building. The building at 570 Lexington, however, which is still popularly called the GE Building, is now owned by Columbia University, whose real-estate marketers have dubbed it Tower 570, a name lacking in panache.

The building was designed by Cross & Cross, who, in an act of good neighborliness, gave it a facade of many-hued, salmon-colored bricks to match Saint Bartholomew's Church, its neighbor to the west on Park Avenue.

In the 1950s colored lights played within the grilles on the roofline, adding a magical quality to the night skyline. The tradition fell by the wayside, however, and today the building's roofline stands dark while all around it other buildings are lighting their rooflines, including, of course, the RCA—or, rather, the GE Building.

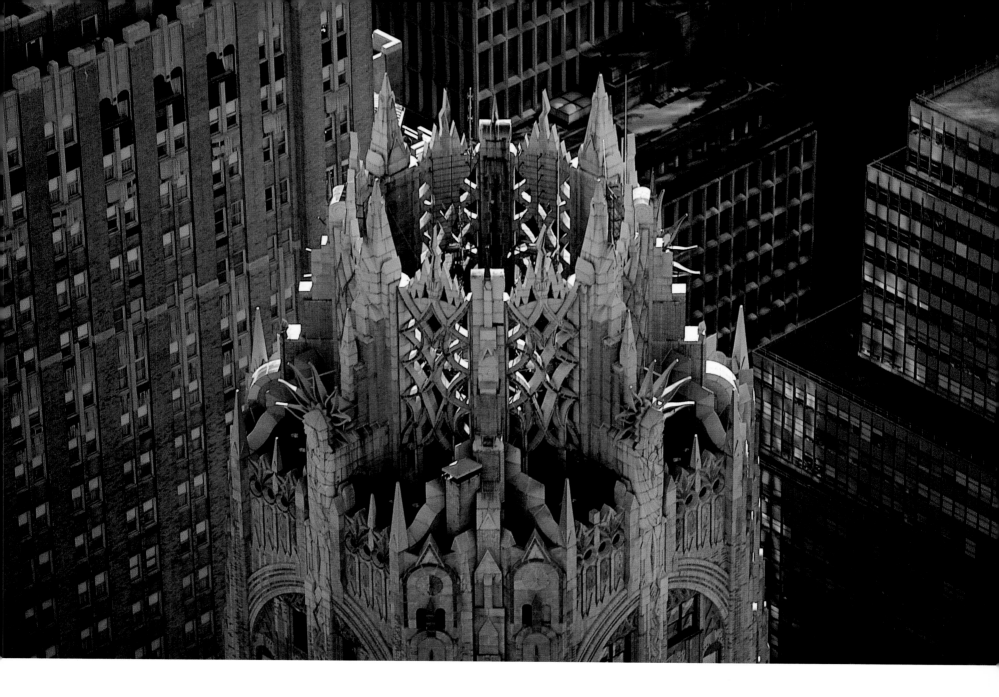

Previous spread: **Queensboro Bridge over Roosevelt Island**
View looking northeast

The Queensboro Bridge, which opened in 1909, straddles the East River and Roosevelt Island and links Queens and Manhattan. As a geocentric shorthand, Manhattanites frequently call it the 59th Street Bridge, as the singers Simon & Garfunkel did in their song title (subtitled "Feelin' Groovy").

Beginning in the mid–nineteenth century, Roosevelt Island, which was then called Blackwell's Island, was the social dumping ground for New York City. Buildings housed a workhouse, a penitentiary, and hospitals for "incurables" and the criminally insane. By the 1920s the face of the island had changed, and it was renamed Welfare Island, which it remained until 1973, when it was named in honor of Franklin D. Roosevelt. Now it is the site of a "new town," or, as the publicists called it, "Manhattan's Other Island." An aerial tram travels between Manhattan and Roosevelt Island, adding to the latter's almost ski-town ambience.

Overleaf: **Saint Patrick's Cathedral,**
Fifth Avenue, 50th to 51st Street
View looking northeast

Saint Patrick's Cathedral, which was consecrated in 1879, was the last of the great Gothic Revival churches in New York. Its architect, James Renwick II, who designed Grace Church in the same style in 1846, was acknowledged as an early master of his craft, and he showed his finely honed skills here.

The interior of Saint Patrick's features tall, slender columns and stained-glass windows that cast roseate hues on everything touched by their light, which combine with its sheer physicality to fill the cathedral with all the mystery and power of the great medieval houses of worship.

Although the spirit is genuine, not everything architectural is true. The buttresses, for instance, don't support much except themselves because the roof is plaster—they are there strictly for cosmetic reasons.

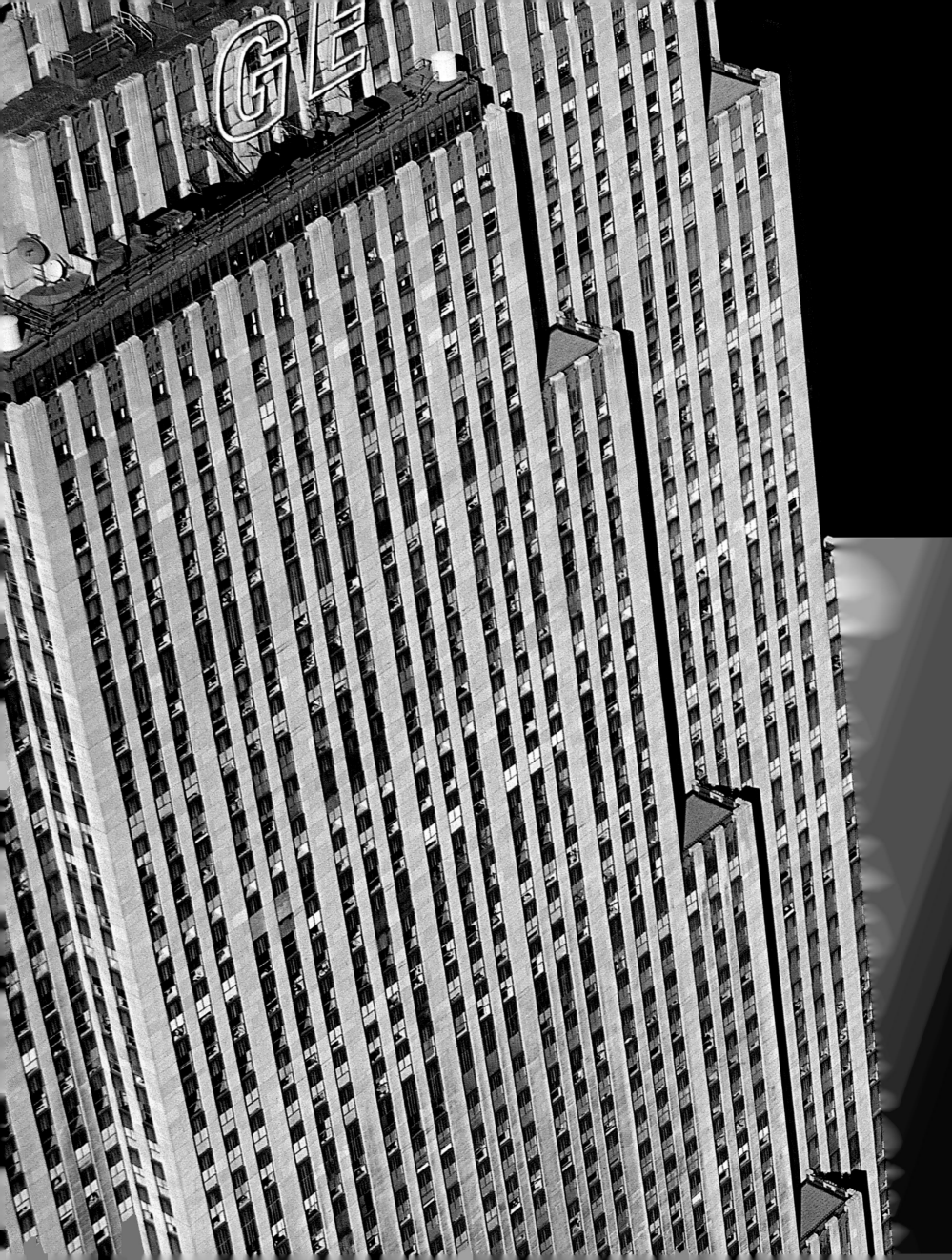

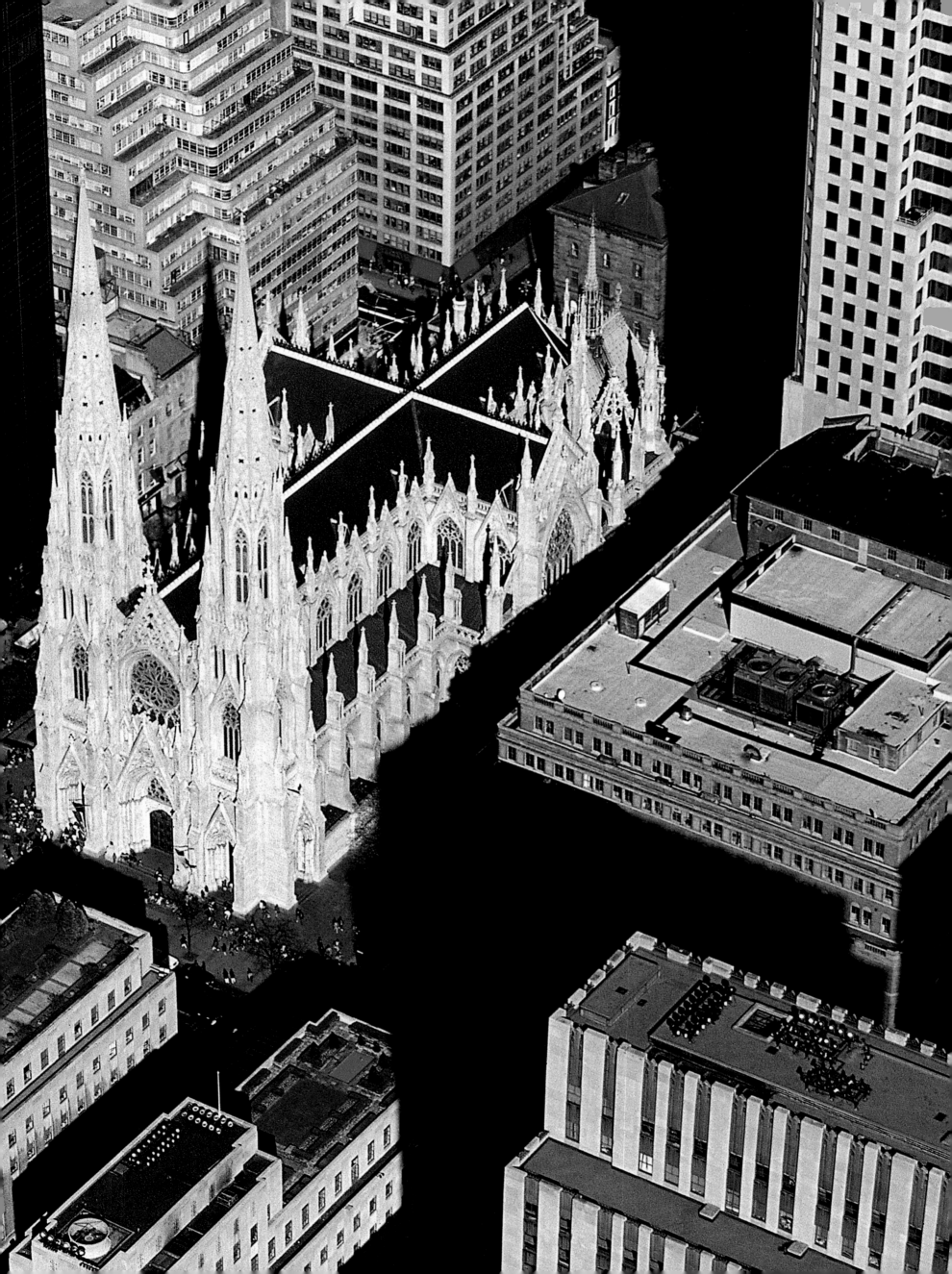

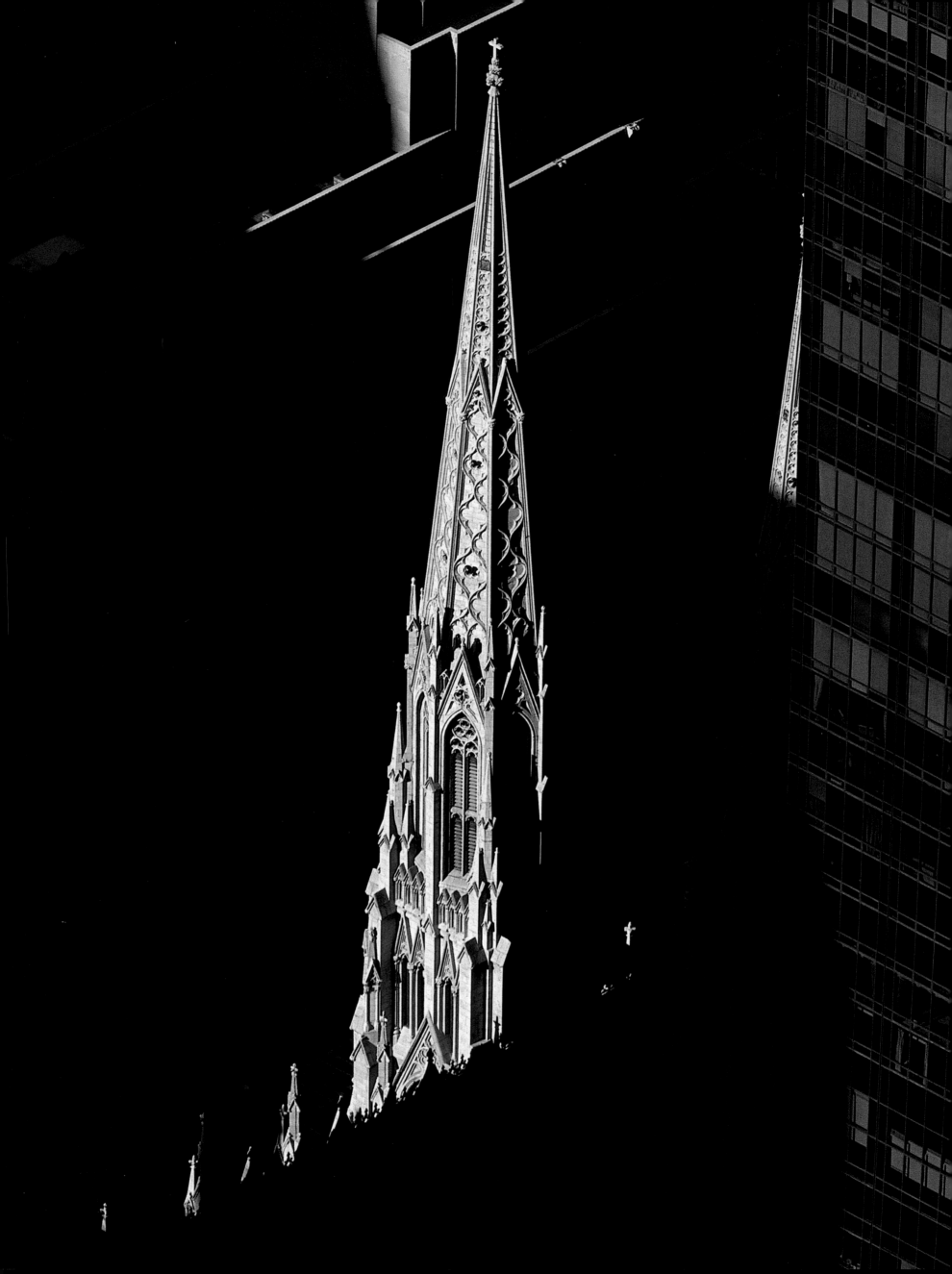

OPPOSITE: **SAINT PATRICK'S CATHEDRAL, FIFTH AVENUE, 50TH TO 51ST STREET VIEW LOOKING NORTHEAST**

In 1850, when the site for Saint Patrick's Cathedral was chosen as the seat of the Roman Catholic archdiocese, the built-up section of the city barely reached 42nd Street. By the time the cathedral opened, it was sitting in the middle of what was fast becoming New York's most exclusive residential district. Today, although dwarfed by mighty secular neighbors, the great spires still succeed in pointing heavenward.

OVERLEAF: **HELMSLEY BUILDING (FORMERLY NEW YORK CENTRAL BUILDING), 230 PARK AVENUE, 45TH TO 46TH STREET, IN CENTER VIEW LOOKING NORTHEAST**

The elegantly detailed and carefully scaled thirty-four-story building straddling Park Avenue was built by the New York Central Railroad as its headquarters in 1929. The railroad owned the property along Park Avenue from 42nd to 50th Street and planned an enormous development that included office buildings, hotels, and apartment houses. The individual buildings were planned with a unified cornice line above which towers would rise, based on the school of city planning inspired by Paris's École des Beaux-Arts. The architects Warren & Wetmore, who had designed the railroad terminal, designed what is today the Helmsley Building as the capstone of the development.

Although the building is built above the terminal's rail yards, it does not suffer vibrations created by the trains, thanks to an engineering solution that includes compressed cork. You can stand at the entrance with one foot inside the building and the other on the sidewalk, and although you'll feel the rumble of trains on the sidewalk, you won't feel it within the building.

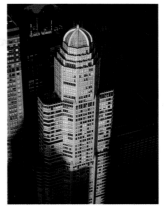

CITYSPIRE, 156 WEST 56TH STREET VIEW LOOKING NORTHEAST

Cityspire, a mixed-use building that rises seventy-four stories, sits between Sixth and Seventh Avenue on 56th Street. City planners traditionally placed large buildings at corner sites, with mid- or small-sized buildings at midblock sites, but the 1965 Landmark Preservation Law changed this preferred urban layout. The law stated that once a building is given a landmark designation it cannot be torn down, nor can the facade be altered. But this meant that property owners could not develop their sites to the maximum and would suffer economically. Hence, the notion was hatched that the air rights—the envelope of space—above a designated property could be transferred to a neighboring property, allowing the latter building to rise higher. By permitting the sale of air rights, the city gave landmark buildings a source of income, but in exchange had to accept the construction of enormous midblock buildings.

Cityspire was constructed after the transference of air rights from City Center, a performing arts space. The dome atop Cityspire was designed by the architects Murphy/Jahn as an homage to City Center's dome.

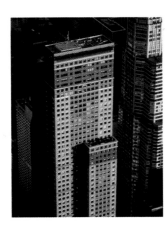

CARNEGIE HALL TOWER, 152 WEST 57TH STREET VIEW LOOKING SOUTHEAST

Carnegie Hall Tower, which opened in 1990, is another behemoth that resulted from the transference of air rights. The tower rises next to one of the city's greatest cultural and architectural landmarks, Carnegie Hall, a prize particularly savored because it was almost lost to the wrecking ball. The tower rises sixty stories from an irregular through-the-block site that measures only about sixty feet on 57th Street and an additional fifteen feet on 56th Street, between Sixth and Seventh Avenue, but its purchase of Carnegie Hall's air rights gave the Hall a more secure financial footing.

The architect Cesar Pelli extended the composition of Carnegie Hall and reinterpreted its system of ornamentation and massing in the tower, while at the same time recalling the shape of the Hall's studio additions. An open metal cornice and frieze, analogous to the attic story of the Hall but rescaled, top the structure, which is clad in colors chosen to complement—and compliment—what Andrew Carnegie modestly called "The Music Hall."

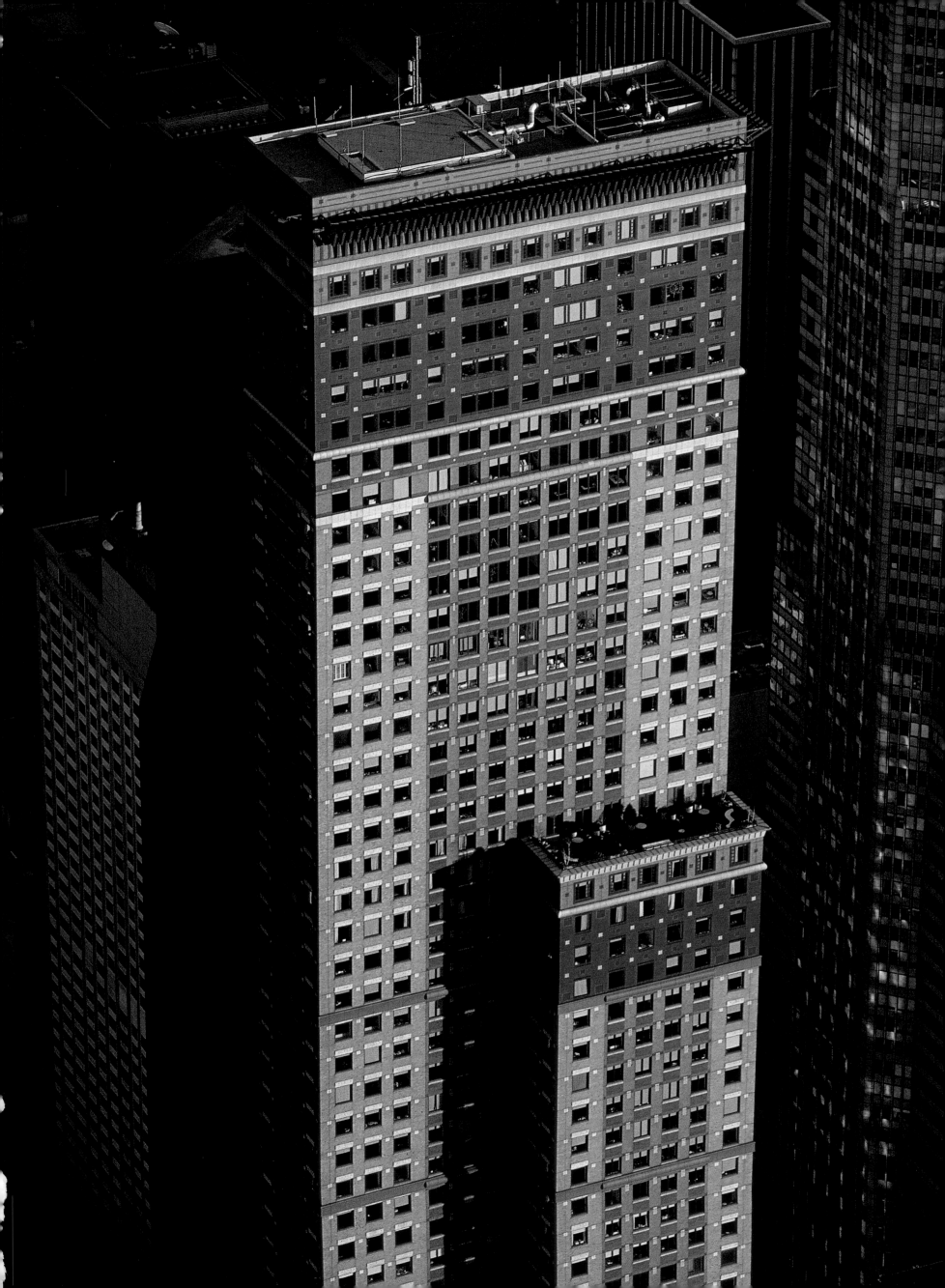

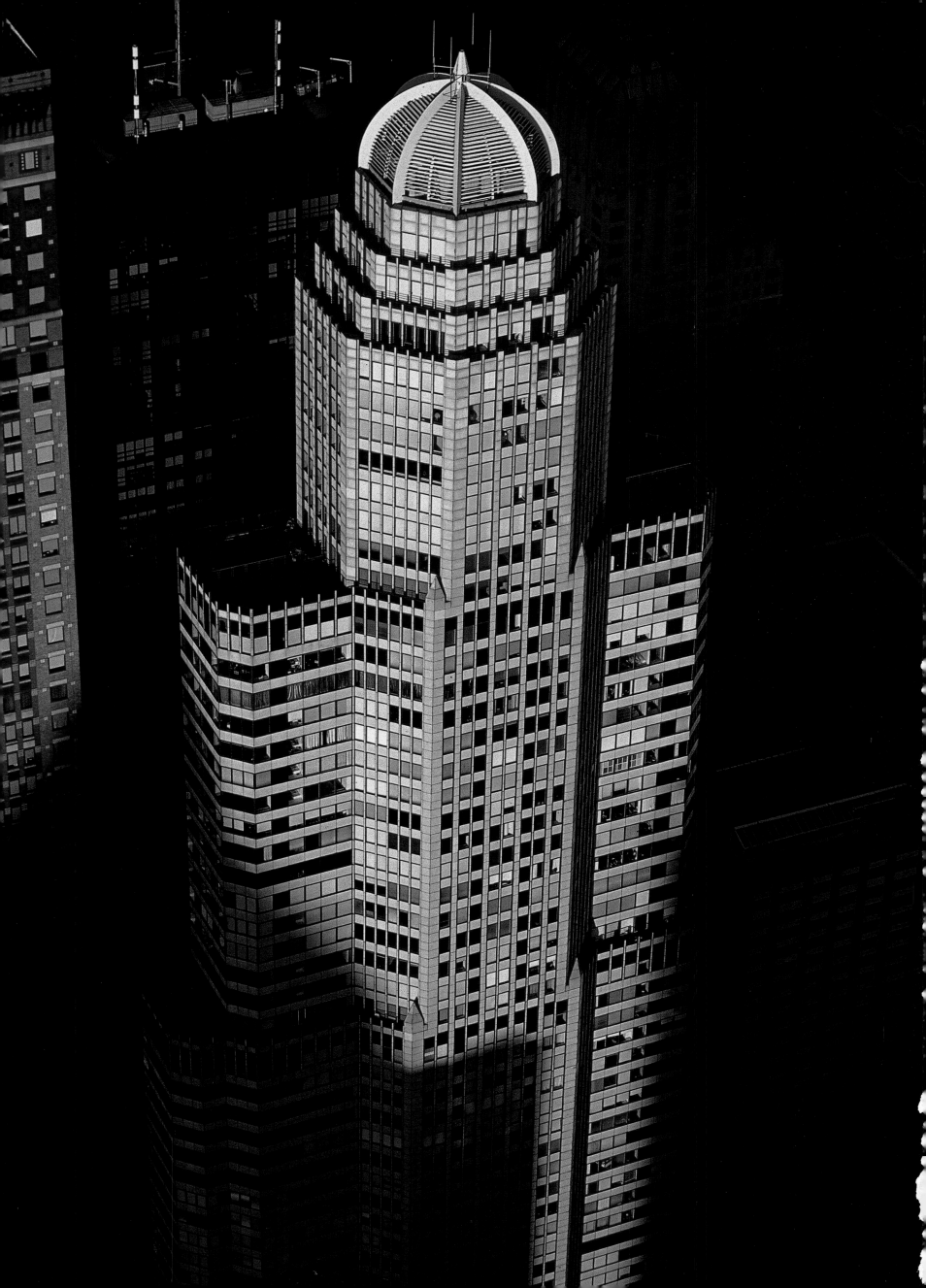

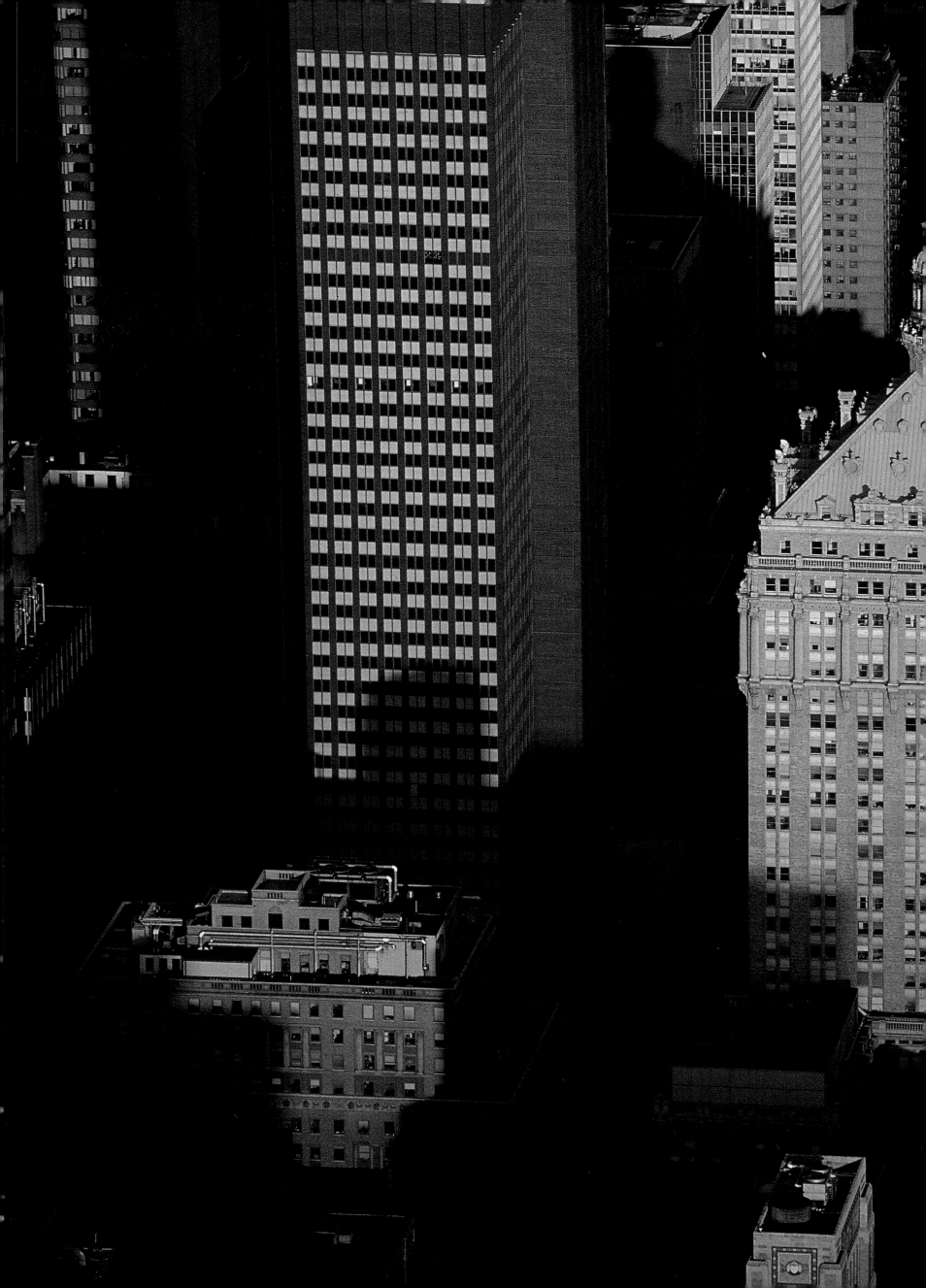

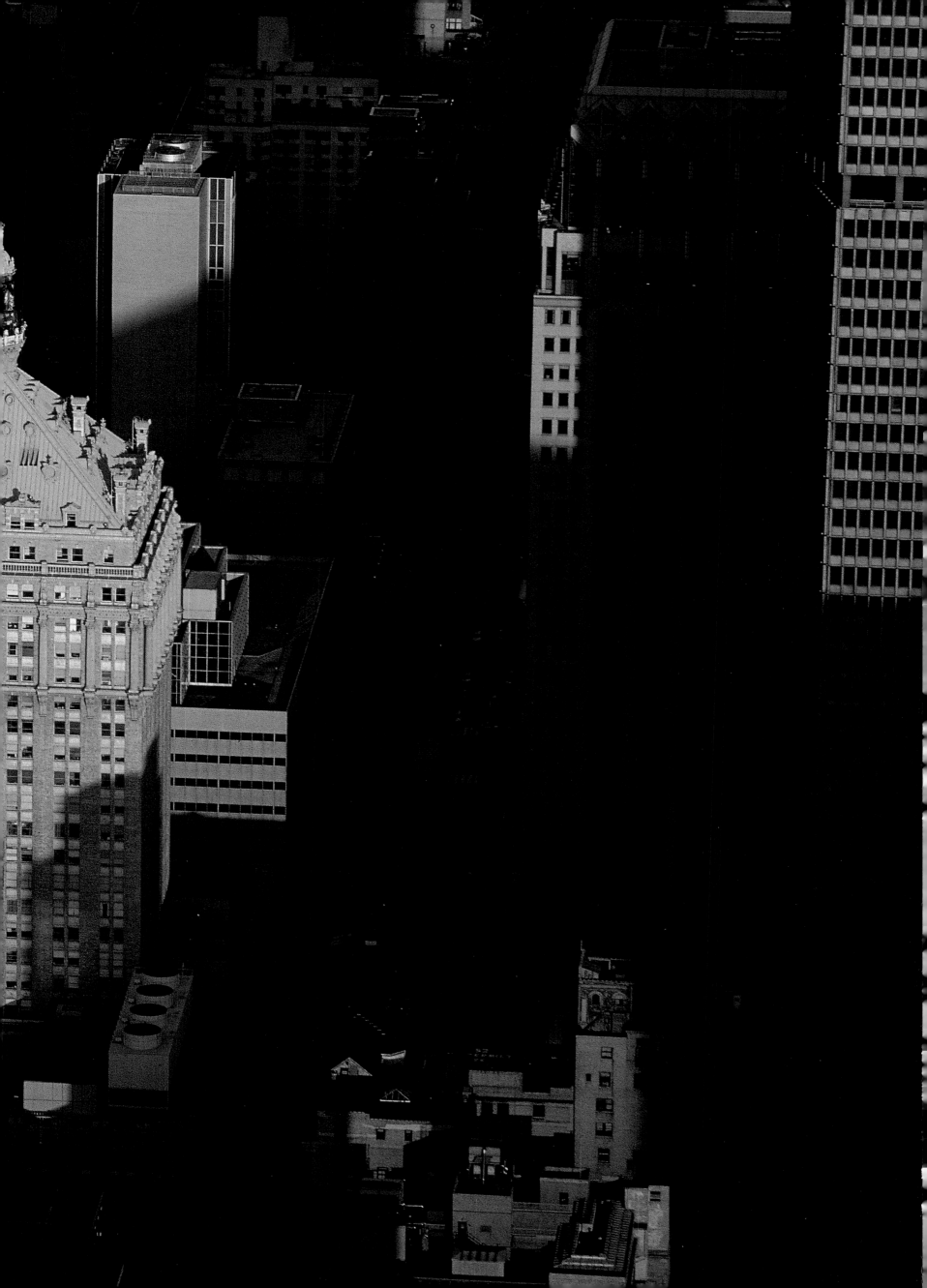

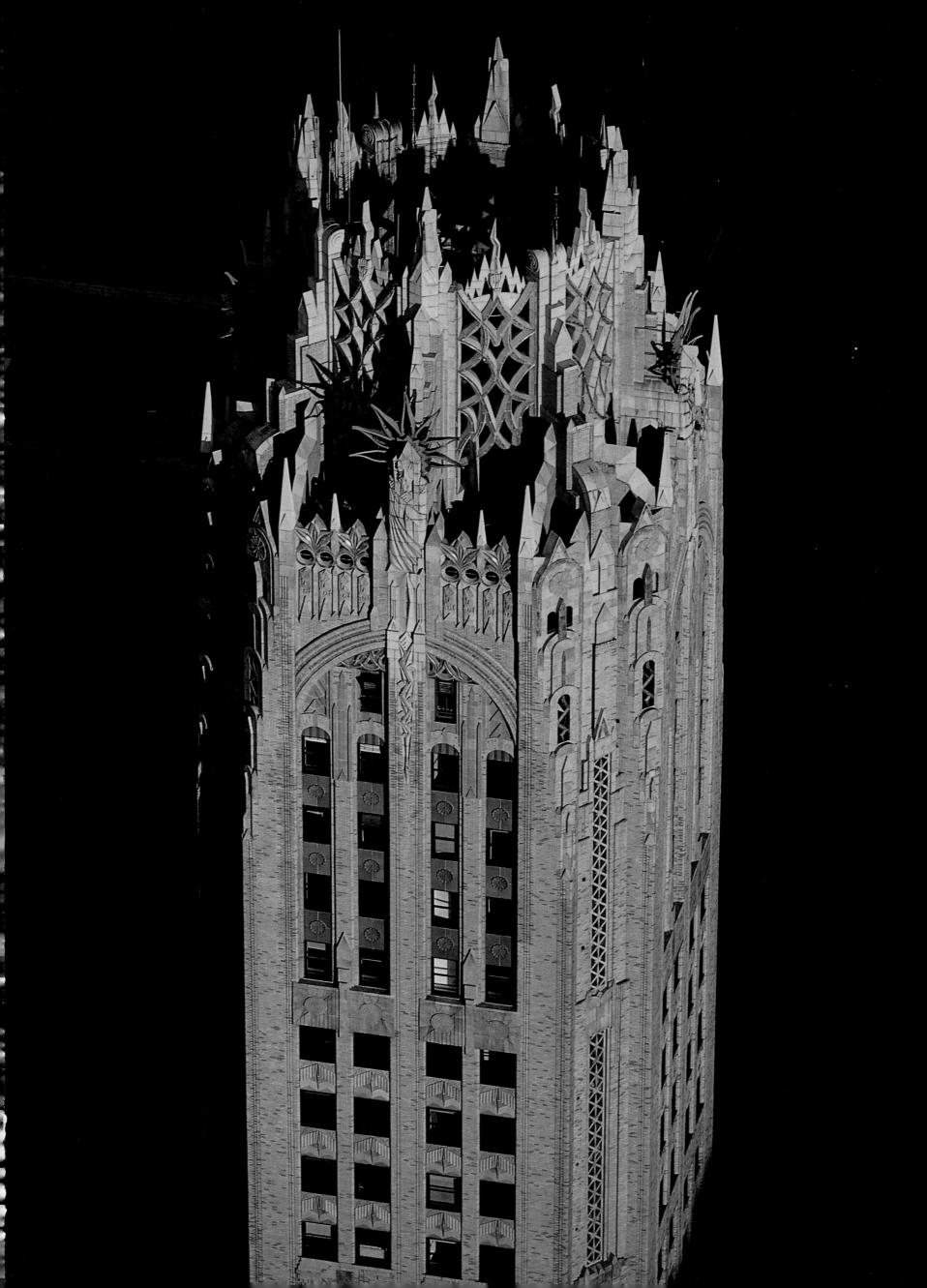

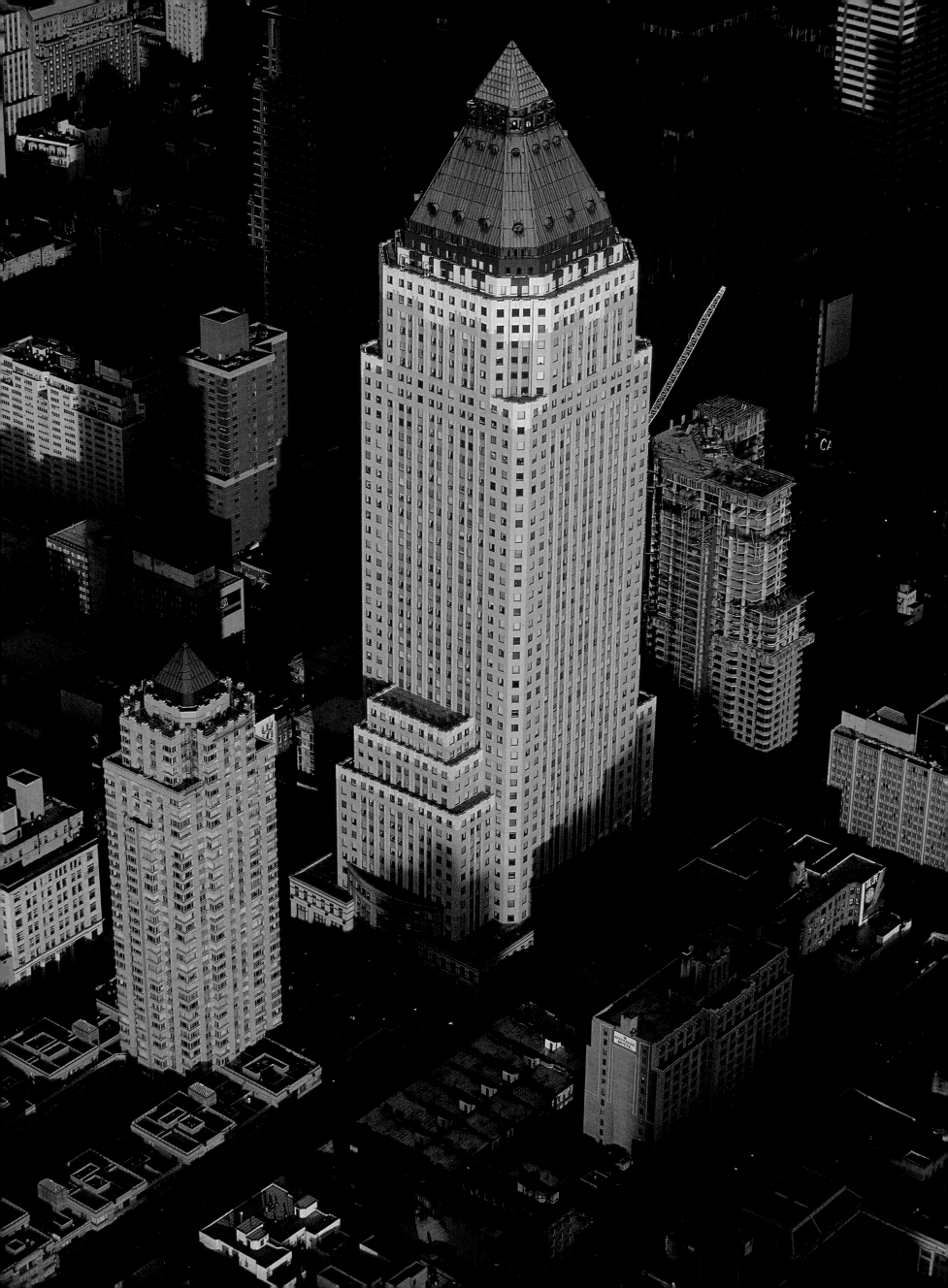

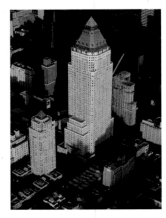

**WORLDWIDE PLAZA,
825 EIGHTH AVENUE,
49TH TO 50TH STREET
VIEW LOOKING
NORTHEAST**

The forty-nine-story tower at Worldwide Plaza is another atypical building for Skidmore, Owings & Merrill, who here dove into Postmodernism, creating a building that feels so right for the city that you have the sense that it was always here—in fact, it was built in only 1988.

The property was developed by William Zeckendorf, Jr., who felt that the risk in developing the site on the west side of Eighth Avenue was more than compensated by the planning commission's encouragement to develop the farther reaches of the West Side; the spine of the island in Midtown was overdeveloped, and the pressure had to be relieved. It's a gamble that seems to have paid off. The advertising agency Ogilvy & Mather occupies fourteen floors, and the law firm Cravath, Swaine & Moore occupies thirteen.

The site, which was home to the second Madison Square Garden from the mid-1920s until 1968, houses apartments in the low-lying cluster of buildings and in the tower that looks like a younger sibling of the office building.

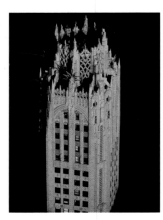

**TOWER 570,
570 LEXINGTON AVENUE,
AT 51ST STREET
VIEW LOOKING
NORTHEAST**

For caption, see page 76.

OPPOSITE: **CITIBANK,
44TH DRIVE AT JACKSON AVENUE,
LONG ISLAND CITY, QUEENS
VIEW LOOKING SOUTHEAST**

Citibank, one of the city's largest mortgage lenders, knows real-estate values. When more space was needed for back-office operations, the bank looked no farther than one subway stop away from its Manhattan headquarters on Lexington Avenue at 53rd Street and landed in Long Island City, Queens. The International Design Center (IDCNY) had already established itself in the neighborhood, and in the wake of these pioneers came new residential development on the river's edge.

The architects Skidmore, Owings & Merrill broke from the rigidity of the old Modernist school to create a multi-faceted building that is forty-eight stories high, making it the tallest building on Long Island.

The cemetery to the right is New Calvary; the elevated highway is the Long Island Expressway, frequently described as New York's longest parking lot.

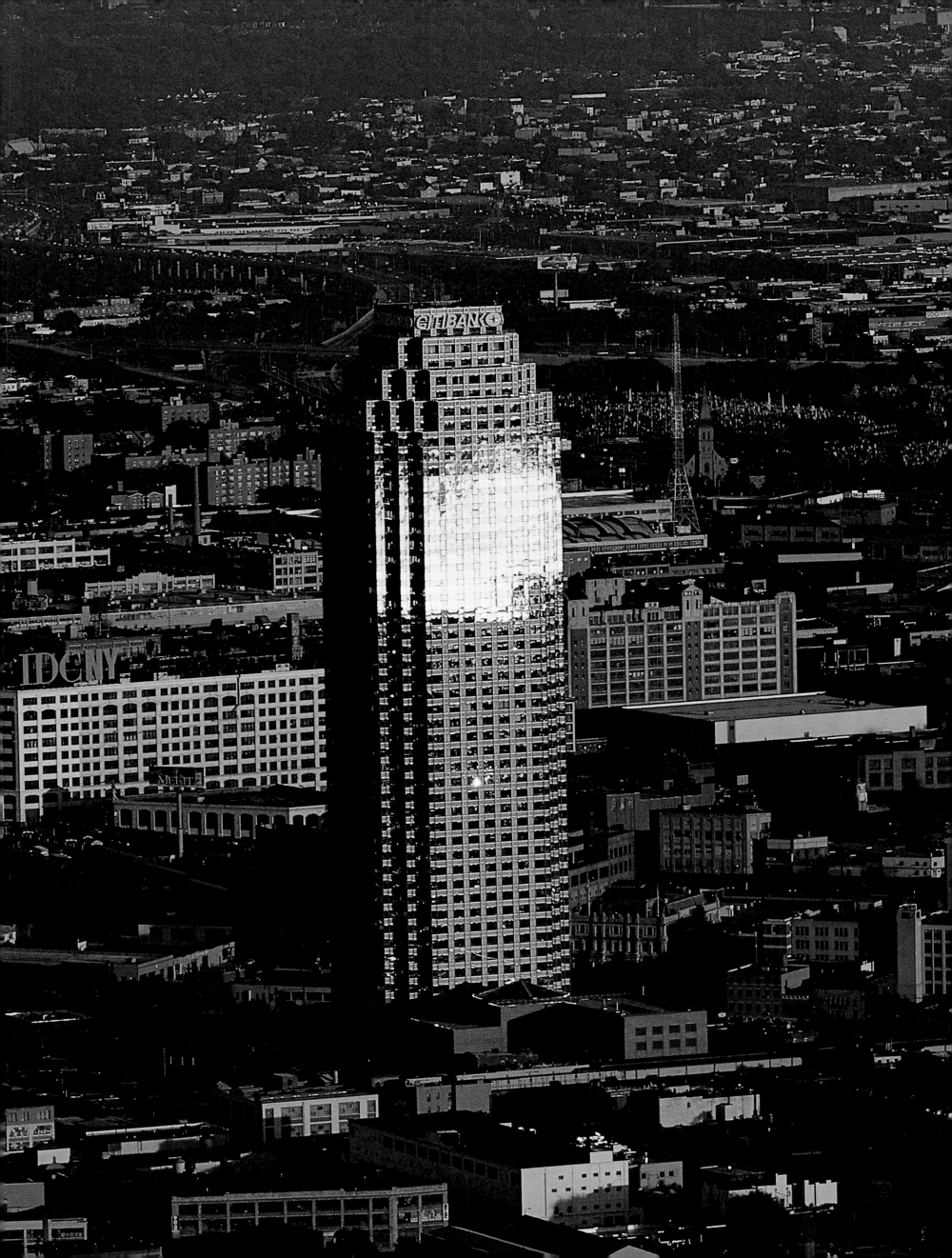

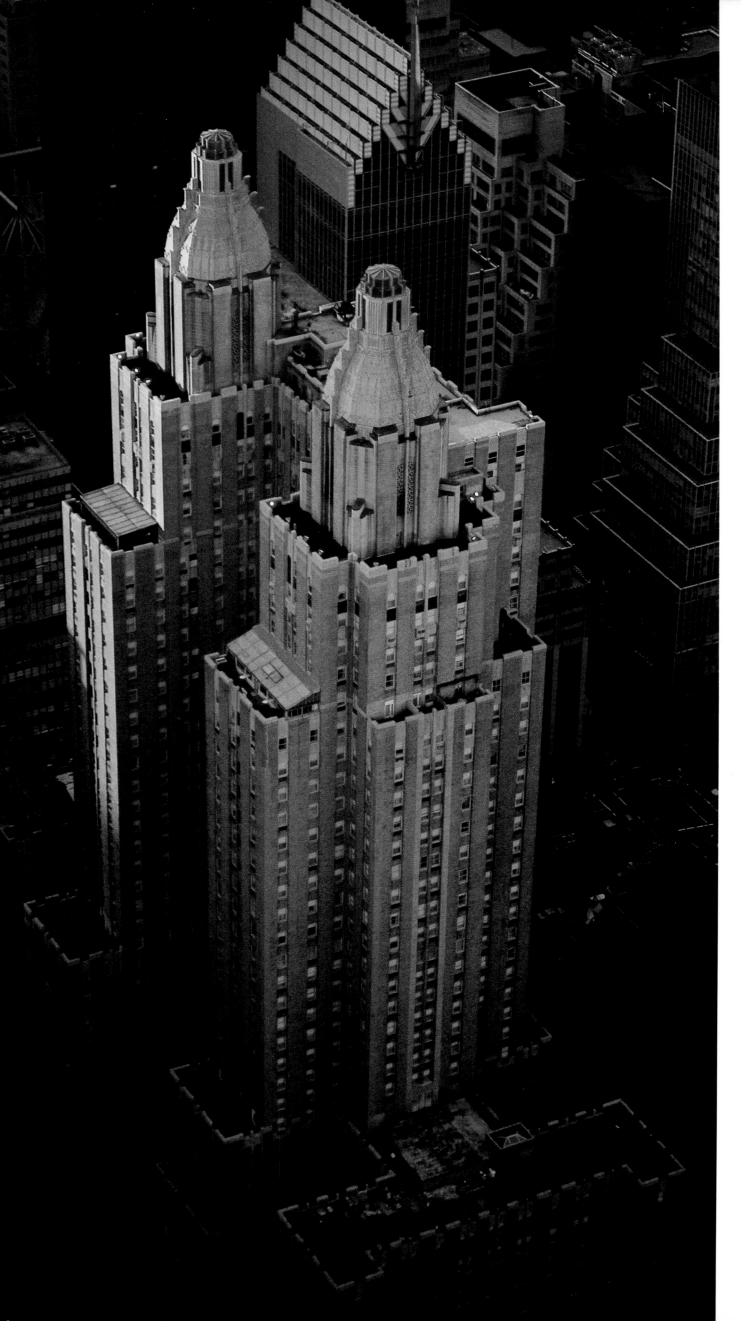

WALDORF-ASTORIA HOTEL, 301 PARK AVENUE, BETWEEN 50TH AND 51ST STREET VIEW LOOKING NORTHWEST

If one hotel synthesizes the essence of the luxury hotel in New York, it's the Waldorf-Astoria. Although not the city's most expensive hotel today, nor its most palatial, the Waldorf remains an icon.

Schultze & Weaver's design is still up-to-date and chic, which is to be expected from the masters of hotel design. The Waldorf's glory, with its 625-foot towers rising forty-seven stories and reaching for an Art Deco sky high above Park Avenue, eclipsed the majesty of its neighbors and set a new standard.

From its opening day in 1931, when Herbert Hoover addressed the nation on radio as part of the celebration, this has been the hotel of U.S. presidents. (The major exception was John F. Kennedy, who preferred the Carlyle.) Not all of the security details are public, but the windows in the presidential suite on the thirty-second floor are bulletproof, areas of the hotel can be sealed, elevators can be made to run nonstop or not at all, and the telecommunications system is, of course, state of the art.

Franklin D. Roosevelt made good use of one of the hotel's features. The hotel is built atop Grand Central's rail yards, and a railroad siding allowed Roosevelt to take a train directly to the platform, and then upstairs by elevator without having to set foot on actual stairs. The elevator door is visible in a side entrance on 50th Street.

The building with a ziggurat roofline is the Mutual of America Building, and it did not always look as it does now. When it was built in 1960, the building looked so much like its uptown neighbor that the joke was that one was the box the other came in. The building was "reconstructed" to designs by Swanke Hayden Connell and given the new look of the '90s.

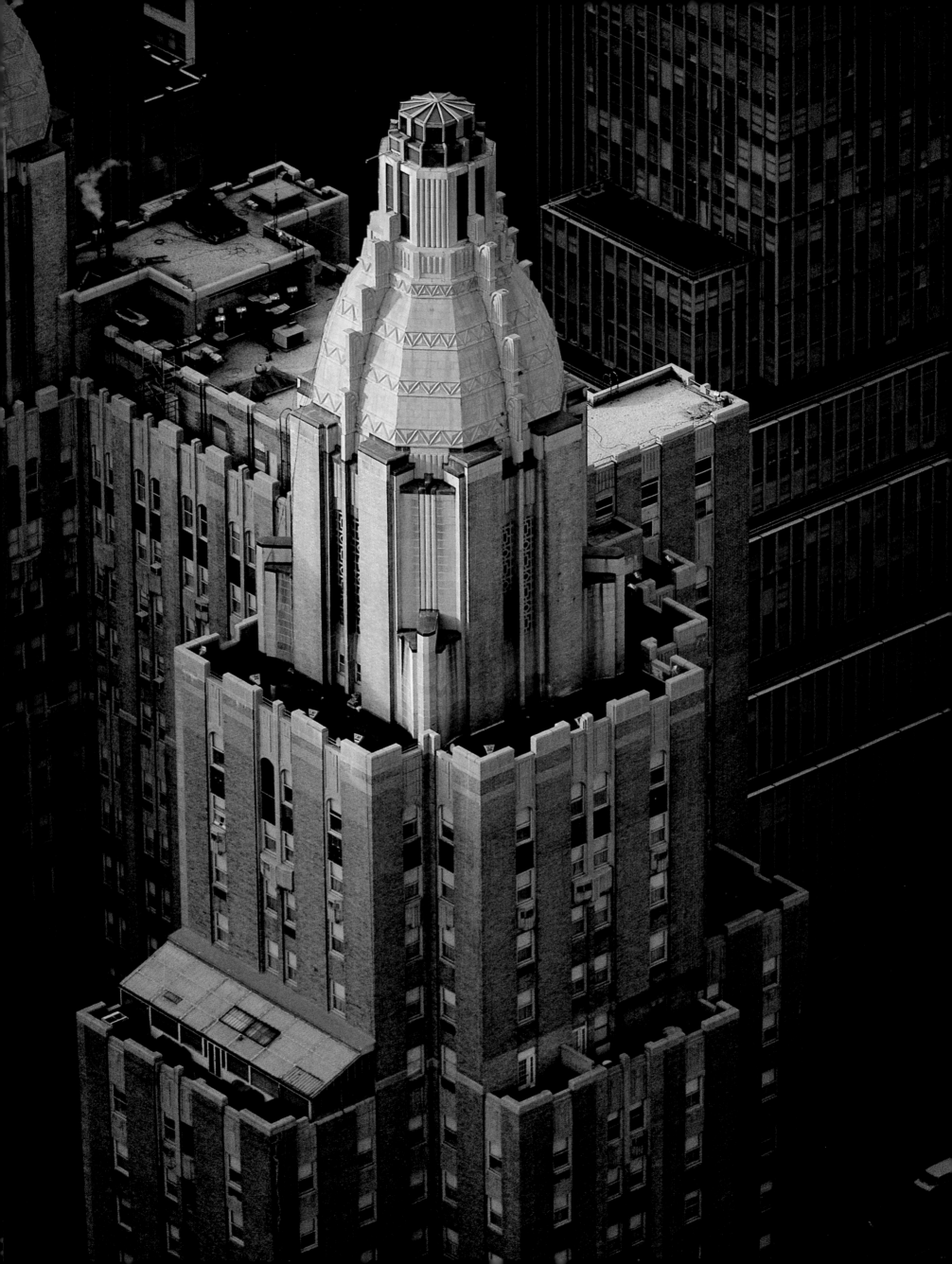

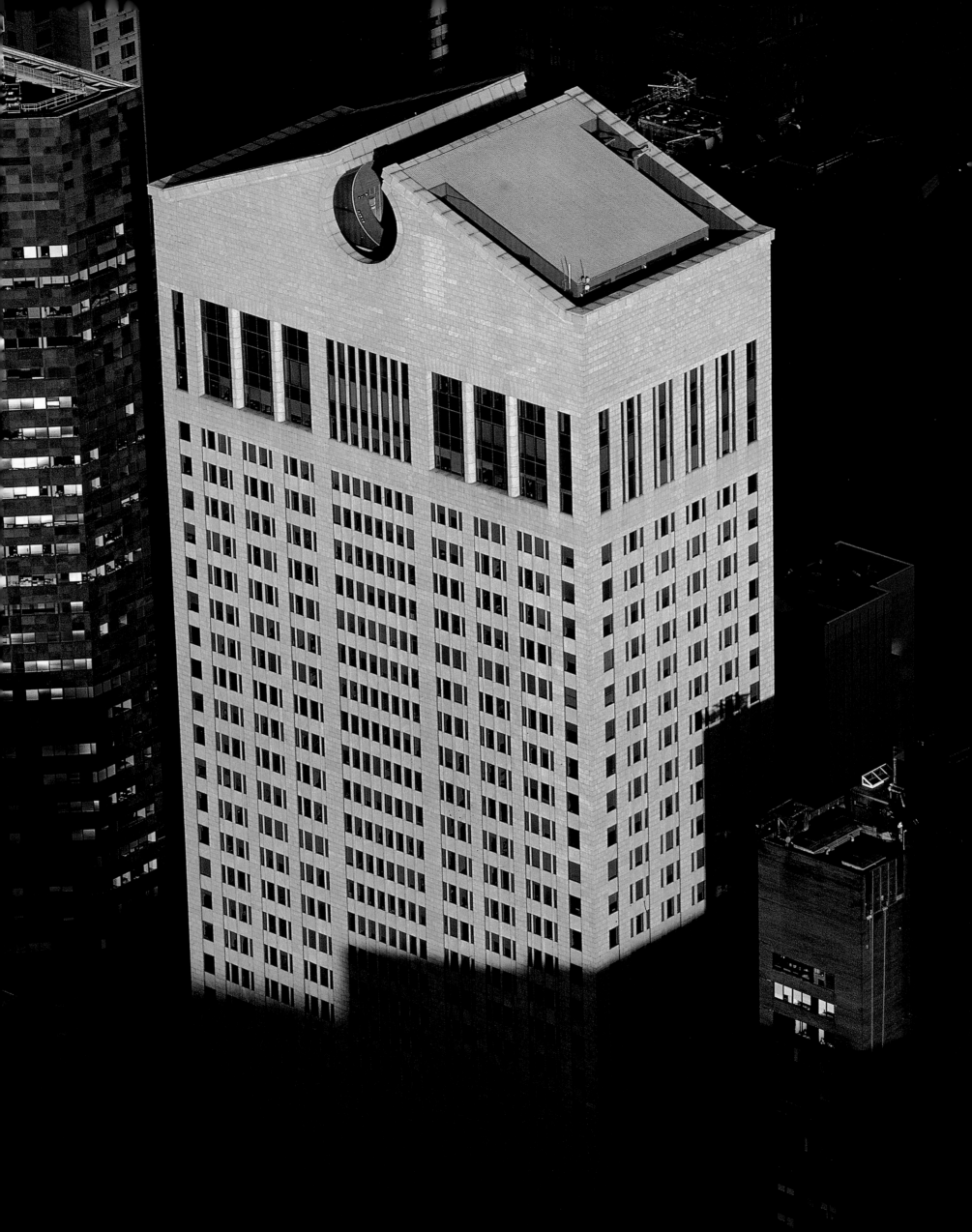

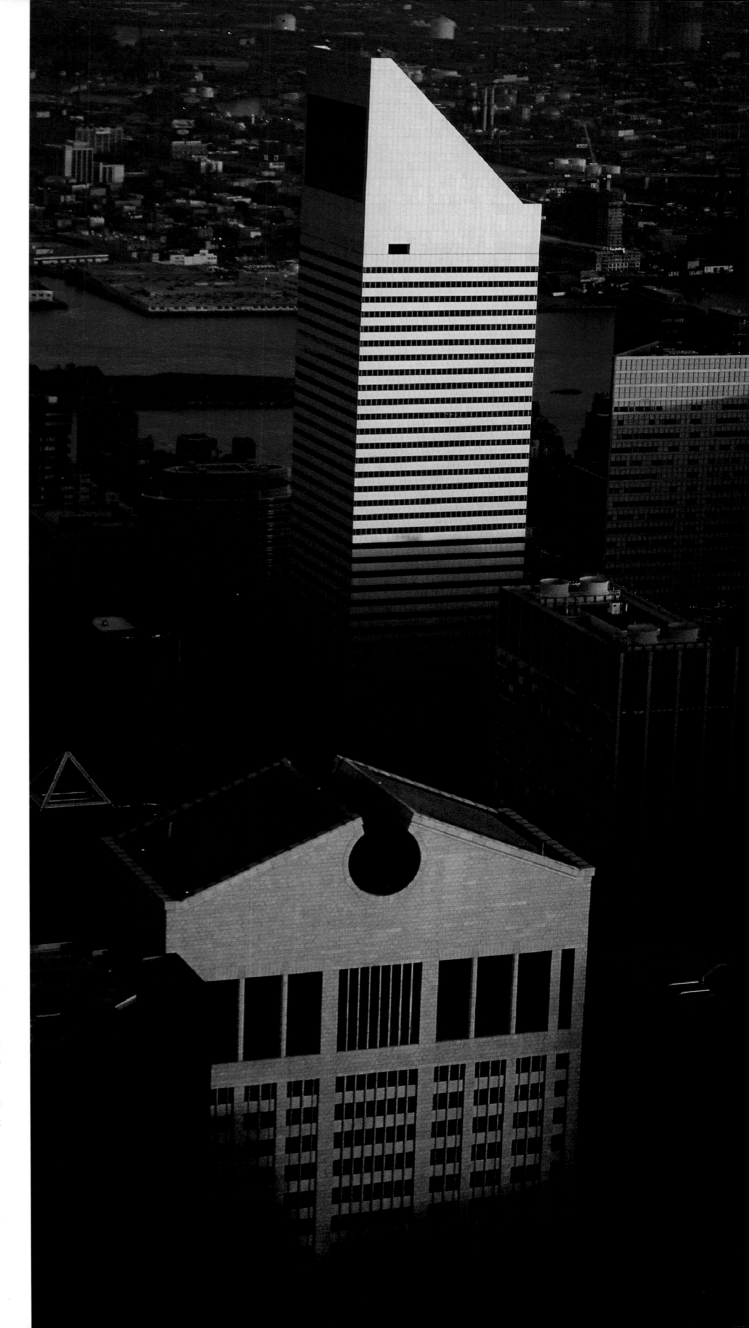

OPPOSITE: **SONY BUILDING (FORMERLY AT&T BUILDING), 550 MADISON AVENUE, BETWEEN 55TH AND 56TH STREET VIEW LOOKING NORTHEAST**

When the architect Philip Johnson unveiled his plans for the AT&T Building, barely contained sniggers were heard. A building in the form of a Chippendale highboy was different, no doubt about it, but the form that seemed so odd in 1984 quickly became assimilated into the hodgepodge that is the city's roofline.

With this Postmodern design Johnson broke with the tenets of Modernism, but the design is more classical and traditional than any convenient label. Similar to much classical design, the building is divided into three parts, with a beginning, middle, and end. It presents the introduction of the theme, the development, and then the recapitulation, a satisfying form that in architectural terms is translated into horizontal, vertical, and horizontal. He even divided the building into tripartite bandings horizontally and varied the windows to form minor variations.

The pink granite facing was a major break from the hegemony of the glass- and metal-clad buildings, and it was warmly greeted.

RIGHT: **CITICORP BUILDING IN CENTER; SONY BUILDING IN FOREGROUND VIEW LOOKING SOUTHEAST**

The Citicorp Building has a roofline as unusual as the Sony Building's. Citicorp's roofline was originally designed to house apartments, taking advantage of variances on the zoning law to become a mixed-used building. But the City's planning commission refused to grant the zoning variance.

Citicorp is every bit as interesting at the street level. The 915-foot building is entirely supported on four 127-foot-high super columns, or stilts, centered at the midpoints of the square tower. Where most buildings are at ground level, Citicorp is not.

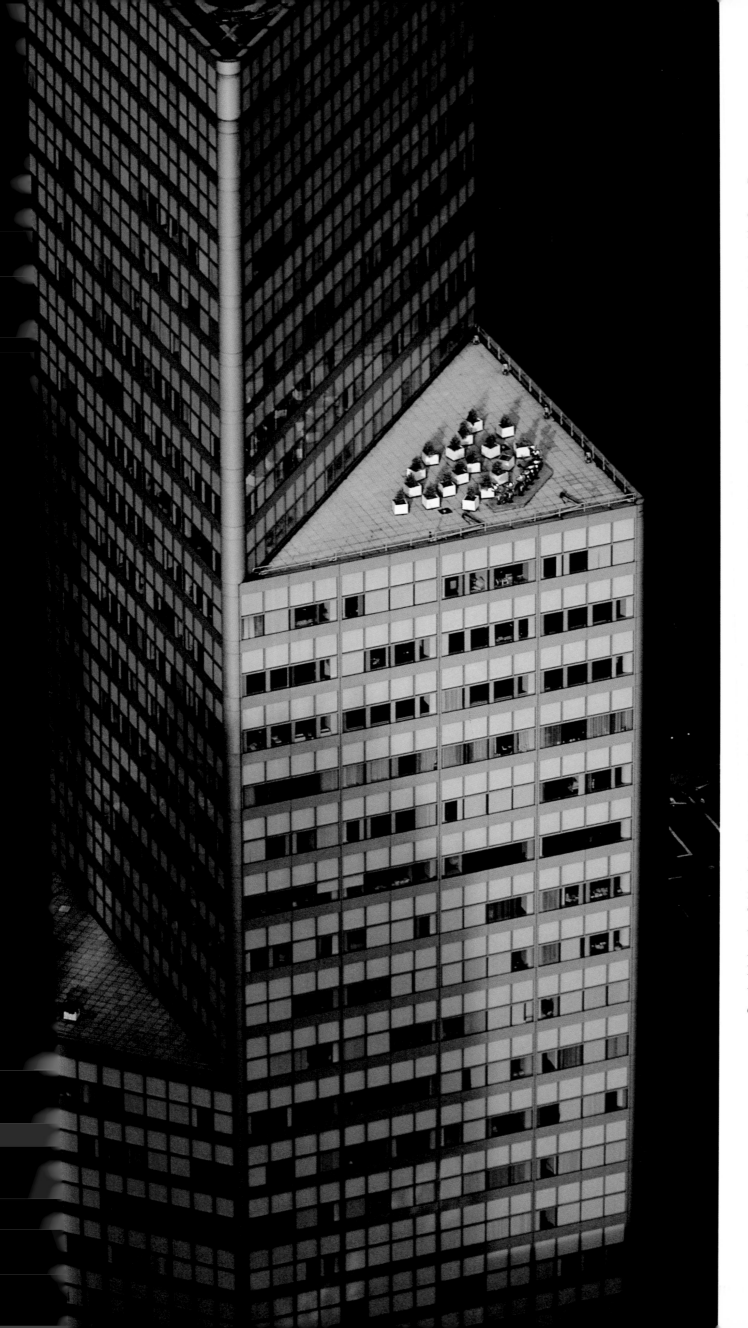

LEFT: **599 LEXINGTON AVENUE,
BETWEEN 52ND AND 53RD STREET
VIEW LOOKING NORTHWEST**

The architect Edward Larrabee Barnes often works with triangles. His plan for the IBM Building on Madison Avenue between 56th and 57th Street is triangular in plan. Adding to the basic plan, or rather, subtracting from it, Barnes cut a triangle out of the building at the street level on the corner of 57th Street, cantilevering the building above pedestrians.

This 1986 building is a series of triangles that are cut away from the building the higher it climbs, an intriguing variation on the right-angled setback. The subway entrance in front of 599 Lexington is a glass-enclosed kiosk whose pitched roof—triangular in shape—seemingly doffs its hat at Citicorp's roofline.

**OPPOSITE: MIDTOWN EAST
CITICORP BUILDING; 599 LEXINGTON
AVENUE; AND 53RD AT THIRD
VIEW LOOKING NORTHEAST**

Here is sacred geometry—the square, the triangle, and the circle—the elements that form the basis of all design. Circles, not usually found in New York buildings, exist in ovoid form in the "Lipstick Building," officially called 53rd at Third, the building with horizontal bands of brown facing alternating with horizontal bands of windows. Squares and rectangles, the basic building blocks, are everywhere. And in this photograph, triangles stand out. The green, glass-walled building featuring triangles is 599 Lexington Avenue. Next door to it is the Citicorp Building, with its unique roofline, which, depending on your view, is either triangular or trapezoidal.

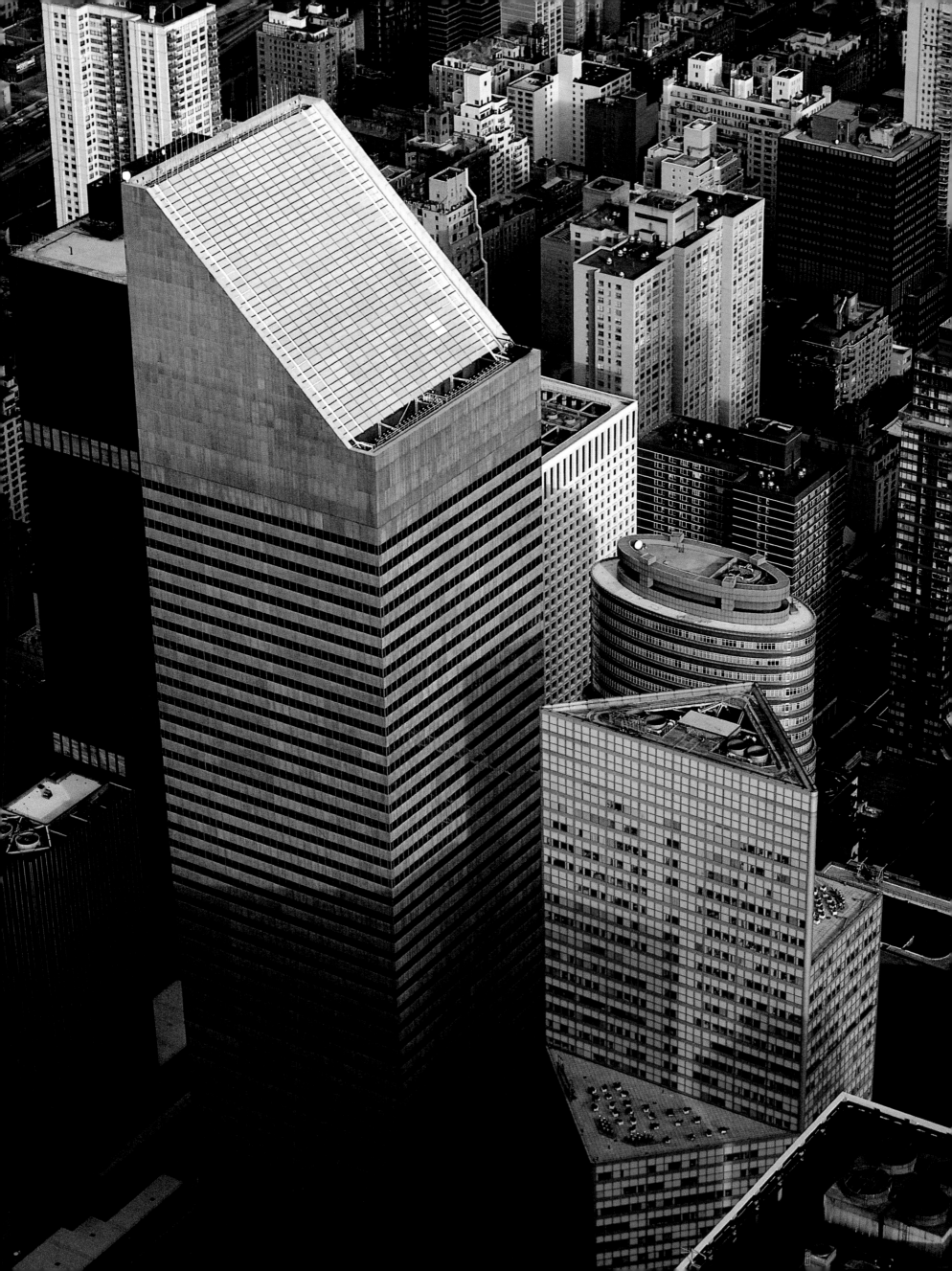

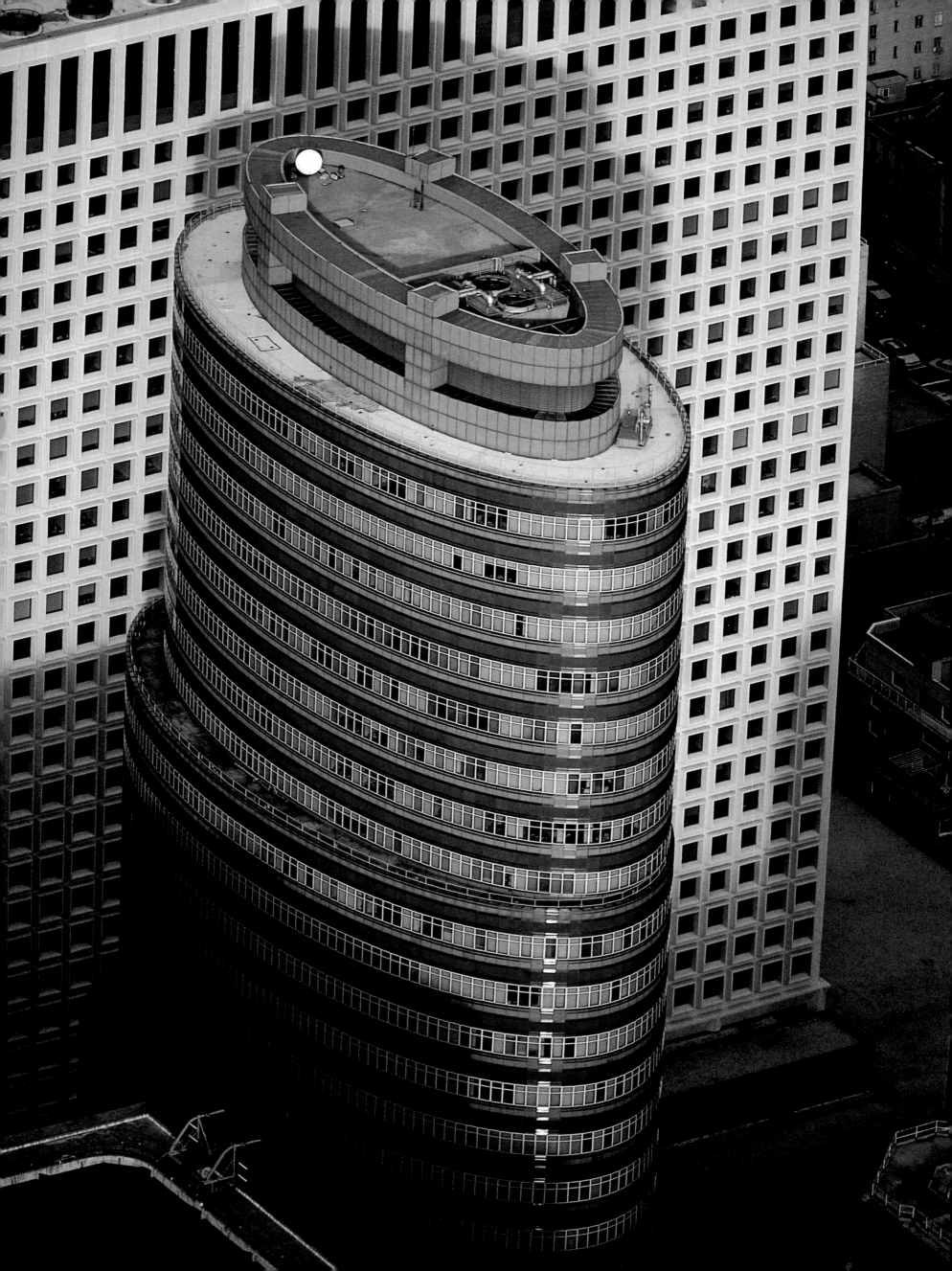

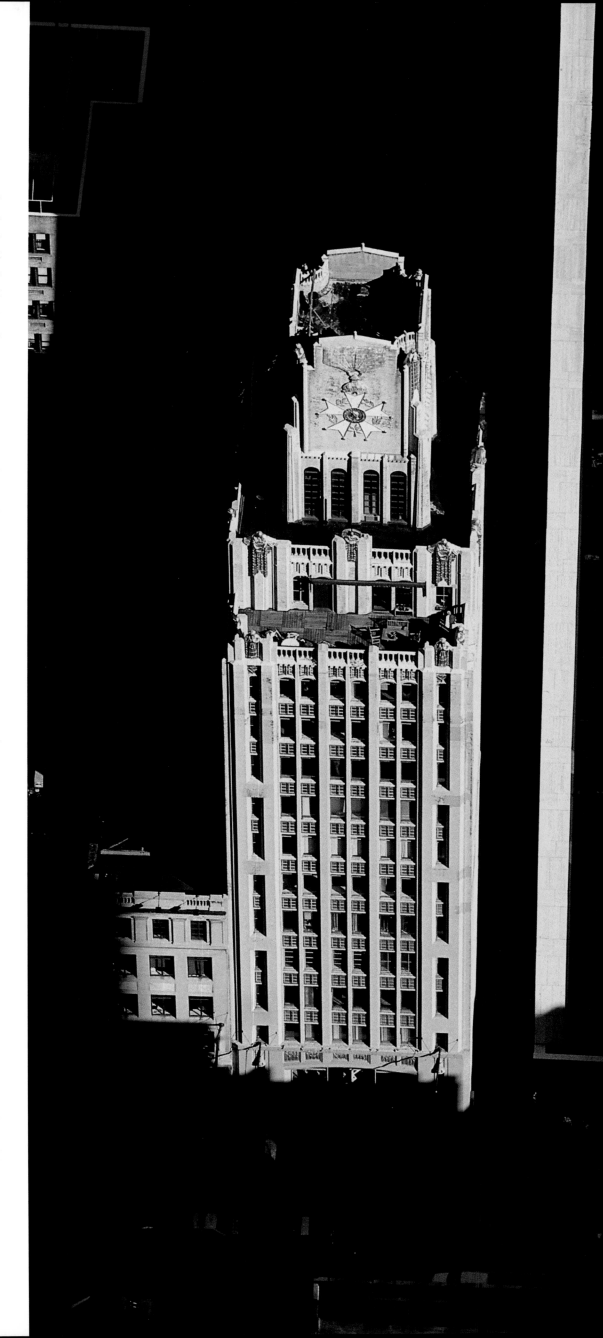

OPPOSITE: **53RD AT THIRD,
885 THIRD AVENUE**
VIEW LOOKING NORTHEAST

The street commissioners who designed Manhattan on the gridiron system of right-angled streets defended their plan on the basis that the most economically built houses were straight sided and right angled. That was 1811, before building elements were prefabricated. Even after modern technology had taken hold, however, the average building in New York was still straight sided and right angled, although rounded corners could just as easily be prefabricated.

The architects John Burgee and Philip Johnson decided that because a building with rounded corners was technologically feasible, and a break in the monotony of right-angled regularity was long overdue, they would design a building with a plan that consisted of a series of diminishing ellipses. The result in 1986 was immediately dubbed the "Lipstick Building."

RIGHT: **29 WEST 57TH STREET,
BETWEEN FIFTH AND SIXTH AVENUE**
VIEW LOOKING NORTH

Concentration of industry is one of the hallmarks of urban life, and 57th Street by the 1920s was already a concentration of culture. It boasted Carnegie Hall, the American Fine Arts Society and the Art Students League, and Louis Cahlif's School of Dancing. Steinway, "the piano of the immortals," soon moved to a site between Sixth and Seventh Avenue.

This 1924 building was the headquarters for the American Piano Company, which manufactured its own line of pianos and held a controlling interest in the companies Knabe, Chickering, and Mason & Hamlin. Relief medals representing the "Cross of the Legion of Honor" that Chickering won in Paris in 1867 were installed on the roofline. The medals served the double function of masking the housing for the elevators, while nettling Steinway down the block.

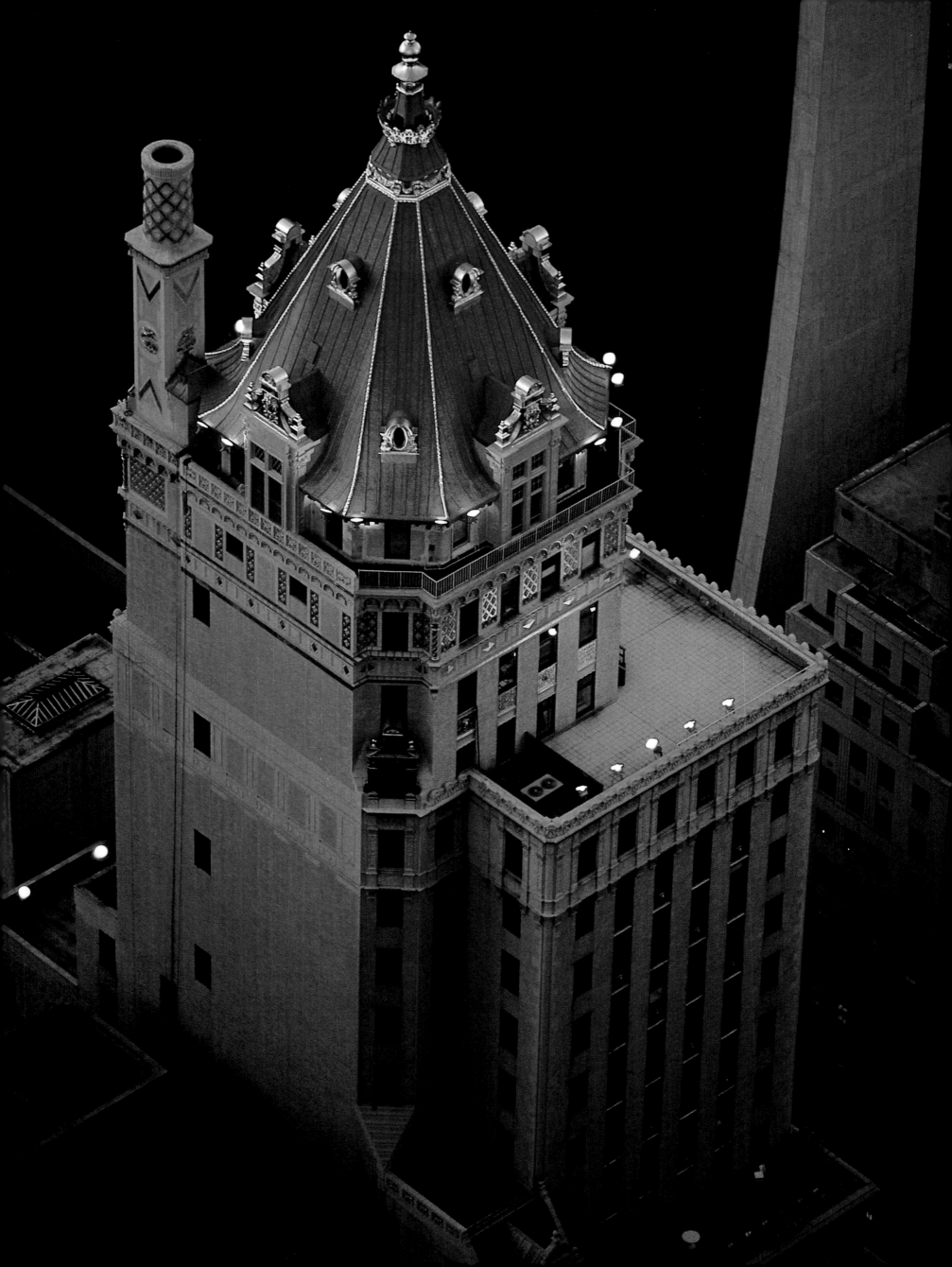

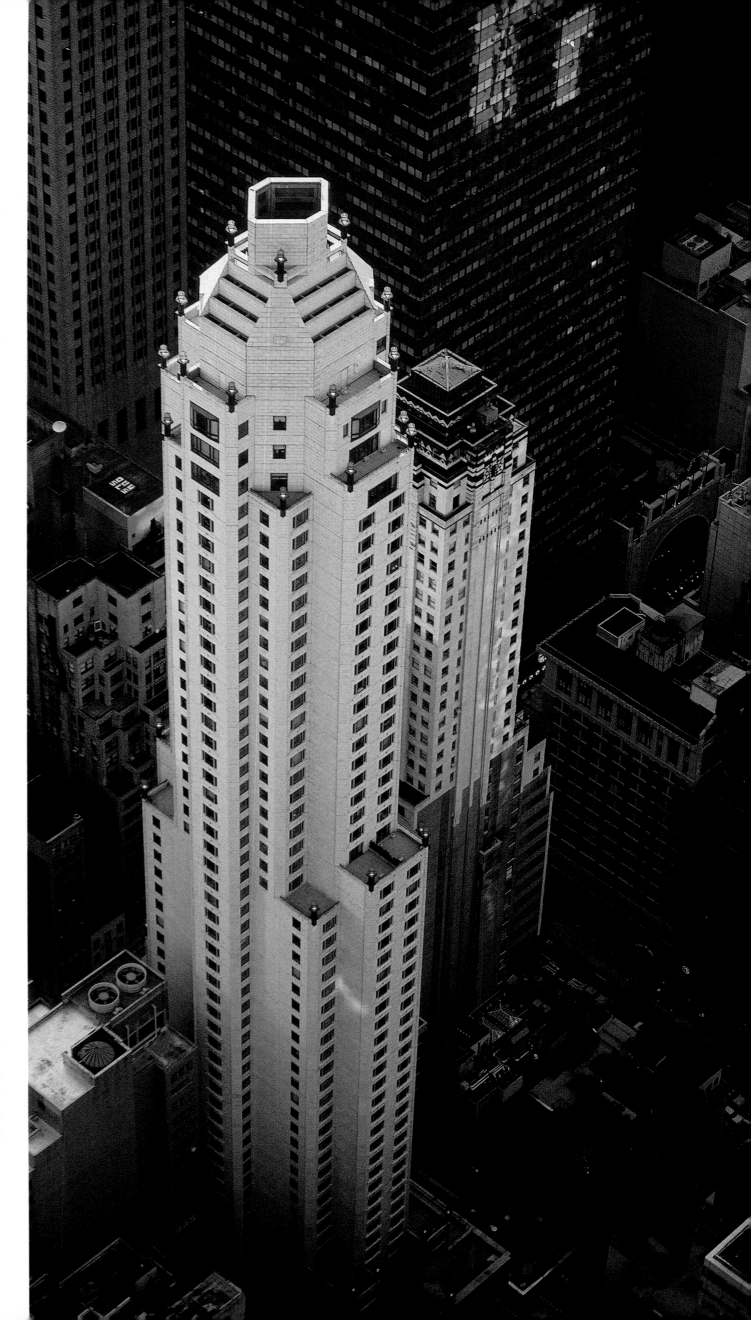

OPPOSITE: **CROWN BUILDING (FORMERLY HECKSCHER BUILDING), 730 FIFTH AVENUE, AT 57TH STREET VIEW LOOKING NORTHEAST**

Today's Crown Building was built by the real-estate developer and philanthropist August Heckscher, whose face is incorporated within the capitals of the pilasters that flank the entrance.

The 416-foot-high building, which opened in 1922, was the first tower erected under the influence of the zoning law of 1916. The designers, Warren & Wetmore, practiced contextualism long before the Postmodernists preached it. The roofline was clearly an homage to the "château" of Cornelius Vanderbilt II that stood across 57th Street at the time.

This building was owned by Ferdinand and Imelda Marcos until the collapse of his regime in the Philippines. It is perhaps no coincidence that the I. Miller Shoe Salon was on the ground floor.

RIGHT: **FOUR SEASONS HOTEL, 57 EAST 57TH STREET, BETWEEN MADISON AND PARK AVENUE VIEW LOOKING SOUTHWEST**

The Four Seasons Hotel is New York's newest grand hotel, a star in the constellation that includes the St. Regis, the Waldorf-Astoria, and the Plaza.

The Postmodern architect I. M. Pei created an Egyptoid–Art Deco look that is as sophisticated as the neighborhood. He specified French sandstone for the facade, which provides a soft, gentle quality. The setbacks and set-ins create not just an interesting facade but terraces as well. Finials with lights stand at the corners of the setbacks; at night, light cascades down the facade.

This is the most elegantly detailed hotel the city has seen since the Waldorf-Astoria. And for the price, it should be. It ranks as the most expensive hotel ever built in New York: with 360 rooms, the bill came to about $370 million, or a little more than $1 million per room.

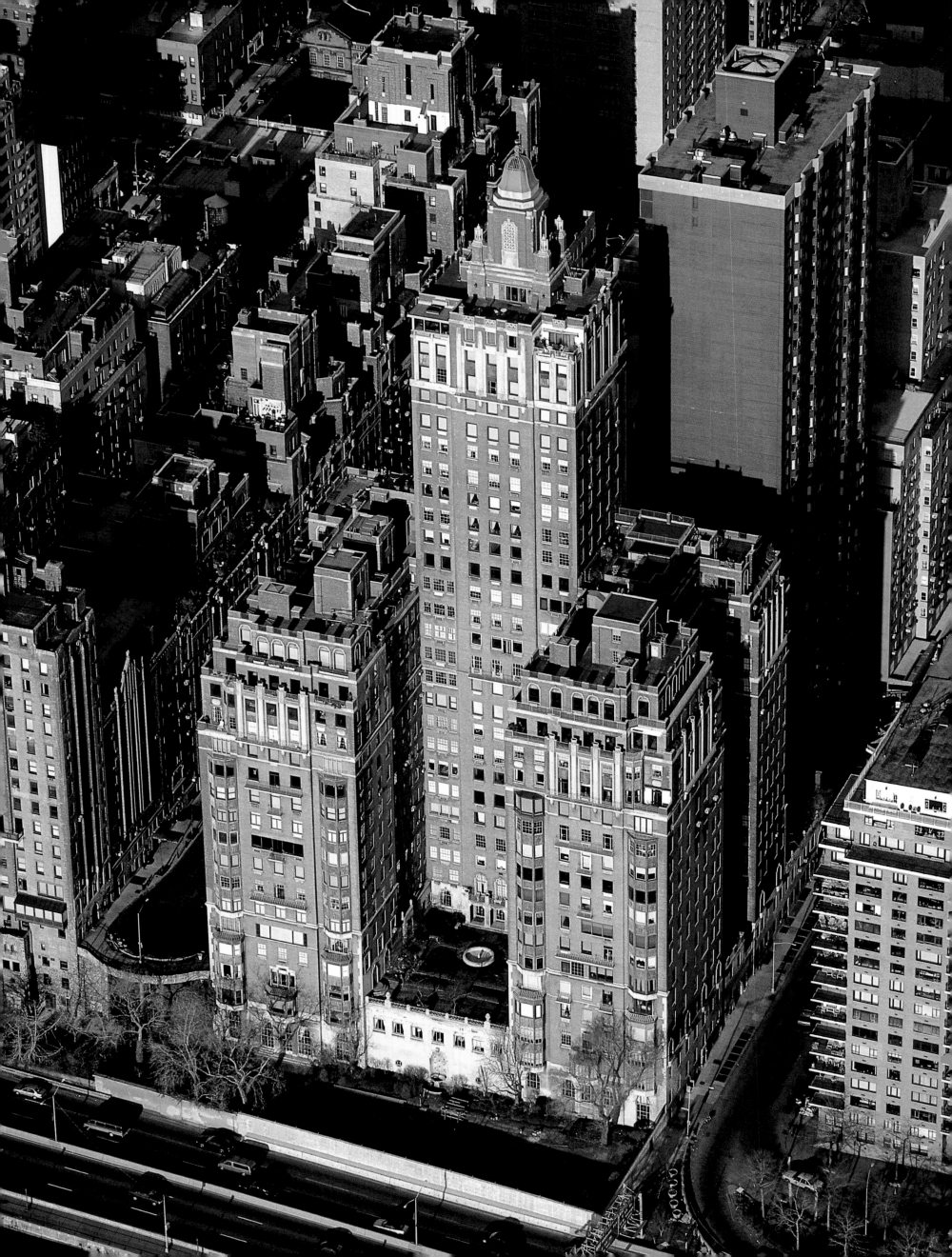

OPPOSITE: **RIVER HOUSE APARTMENTS,
435 EAST 52ND STREET,
OVERLOOKING THE EAST RIVER
VIEW LOOKING SOUTHWEST**

"Bedroom" isn't a word you read in the plans for this 1930 apartment house. The word is "chamber," and the average duplex came with six of them, the largest over nineteen by twenty-two feet. A full bathroom was attached to each of the chambers, and the master suite had a boudoir and a dressing room. Downstairs, the suite included a nineteen-by-thirty-eight-foot drawing room, and an eighteen-by-twenty-seven-foot dining room. There were five maid's rooms and a servants' hall that, not including bathrooms and closets, occupied about 550 square feet. That would qualify as a large one-bedroom apartment in the average apartment house today.

The FDR Drive, the highway along the East River in the bottom of the photograph, had not been built on landfill when River House was erected, and the building sat directly on the the riverbank. There, as at a Venetian *palazzo*, the yachts of the tenants and members of River Club tied up.

RIGHT: **TRUMP PARC APARTMENTS,
106 CENTRAL PARK SOUTH,
AT SIXTH AVENUE
VIEW LOOKING NORTHEAST**

Today's Trump Parc, a condominium apartment building since 1986, when Donald Trump converted it and changed its name, was originally built as the Barbizon Plaza Hotel in 1930. Designed as a residential hotel by Murgatroyd & Ogden, its name was meant to recall the Barbizon school of painting. Its goal was to attract artists, whether engaged in the "art of business, or the business of art."

In the days when New York telephone exchanges provided a clue to neighborhoods, the telephone number for the Barbizon Plaza was CIrcle 7-7000. The "CIrcle" refers to Columbus Circle, which is just down the block.

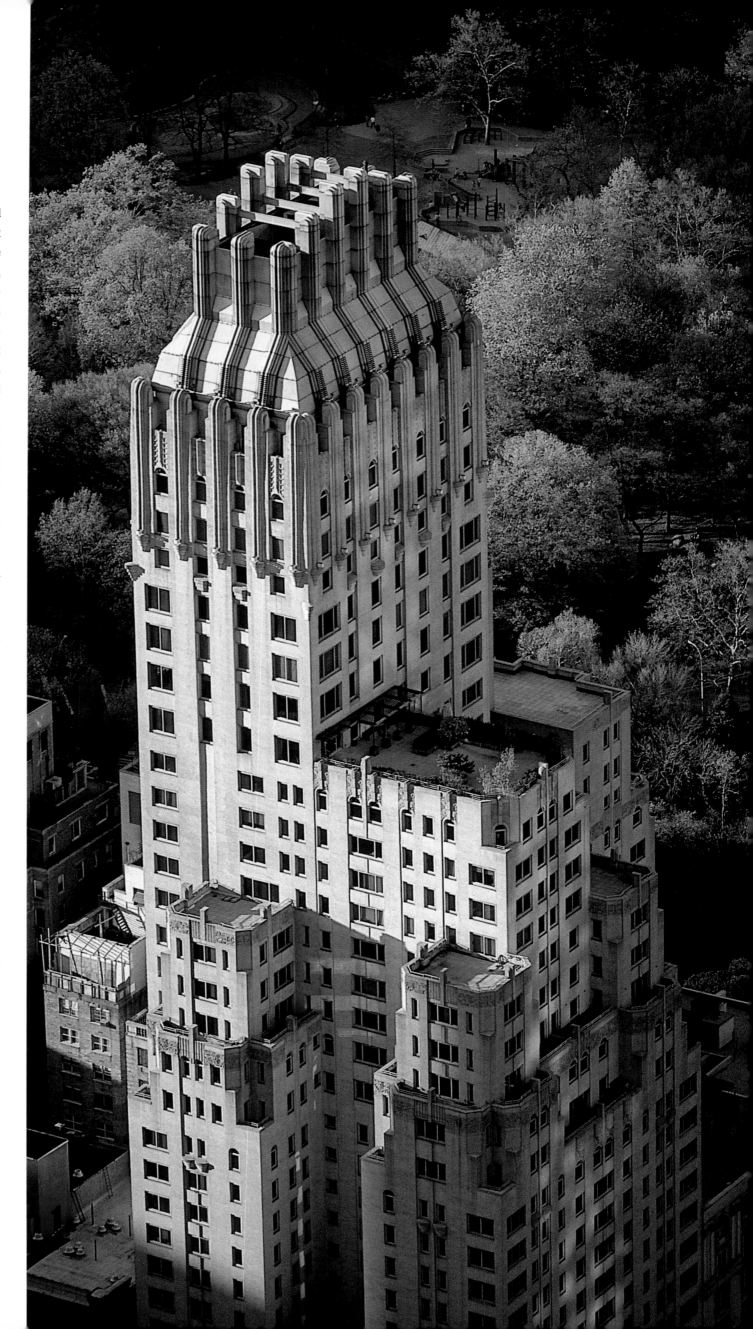

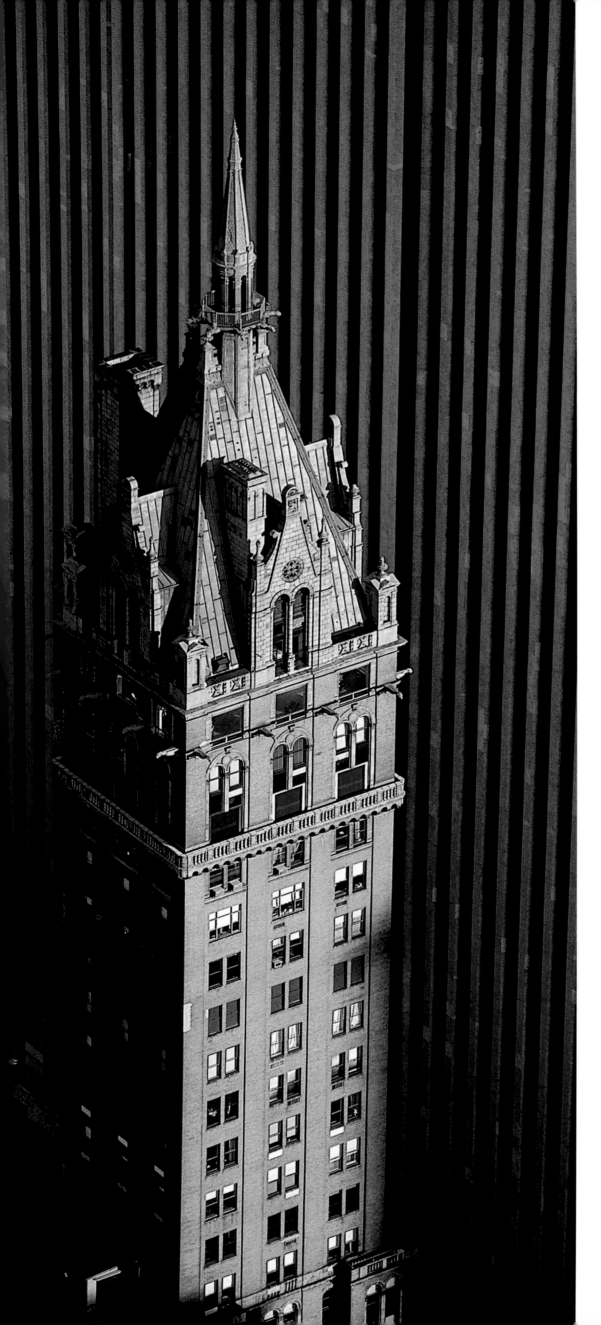

At thirty-eight stories and 570 feet, the Sherry-Netherland was the tallest hotel in the world when it was built in 1927. The name of the hotel was created by merging the name of the very successful but outdated hotel that had stood on the site since 1892 with that of Louis Sherry, a confectioner and restaurateur.

The motif for the design of the roofline was an updated version of a Loire Valley château. The architects Schultze & Weaver would later turn away from this kind of architectural eclecticism; one wag quipped that "the flèche was willing but the spirit was not."

If all you saw of the Pierre were the copper-clad mansard roof and bull's-eye windows, with French doors leading onto a private terrace, you would swear that you were looking at a manor house somewhere south of Paris. But that terrace is a palace in the sky forty-four stories up, and all the French neoclassicism cannot mask the reality of twentieth-century urban life. Down two stories you will see air-conditioning units artfully installed.

The hotel was named for Charles Pierre, another great New York restaurateur whose aspirations were realized with the help of wealthy backers. Pierre died only months before the hotel opened.

The highly touted kitchens were visited by the great chef Escoffier in 1930, who decided to sample a sauce that had been prepared without benefit of brandy or wine. He stuck his finger in the pot, licked his finger, and—sotto voce—said to the translator: "*merde.*" Out of consideration for the kitchen staff and for the reputation of the hotel itself, no translation was made.

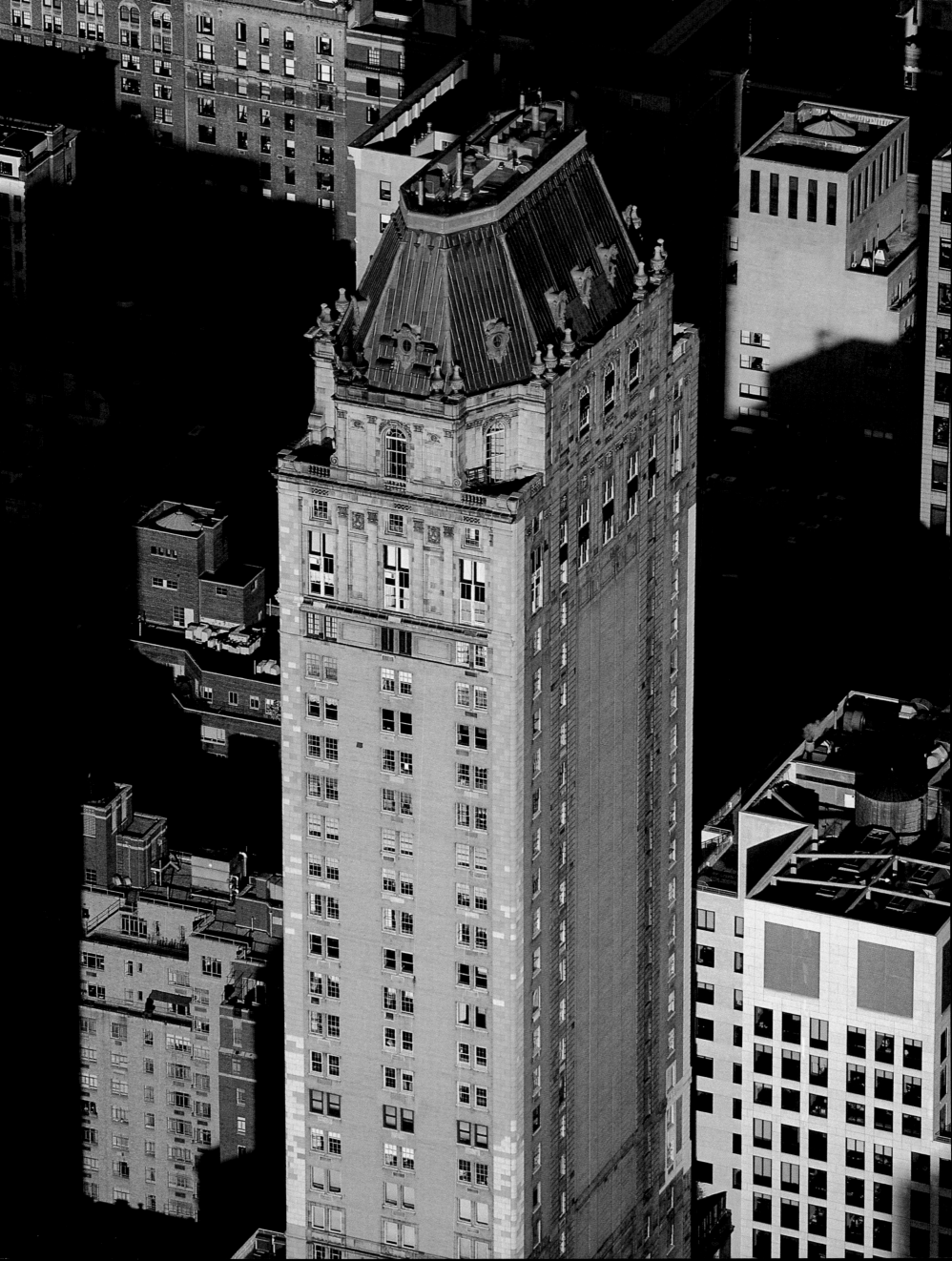

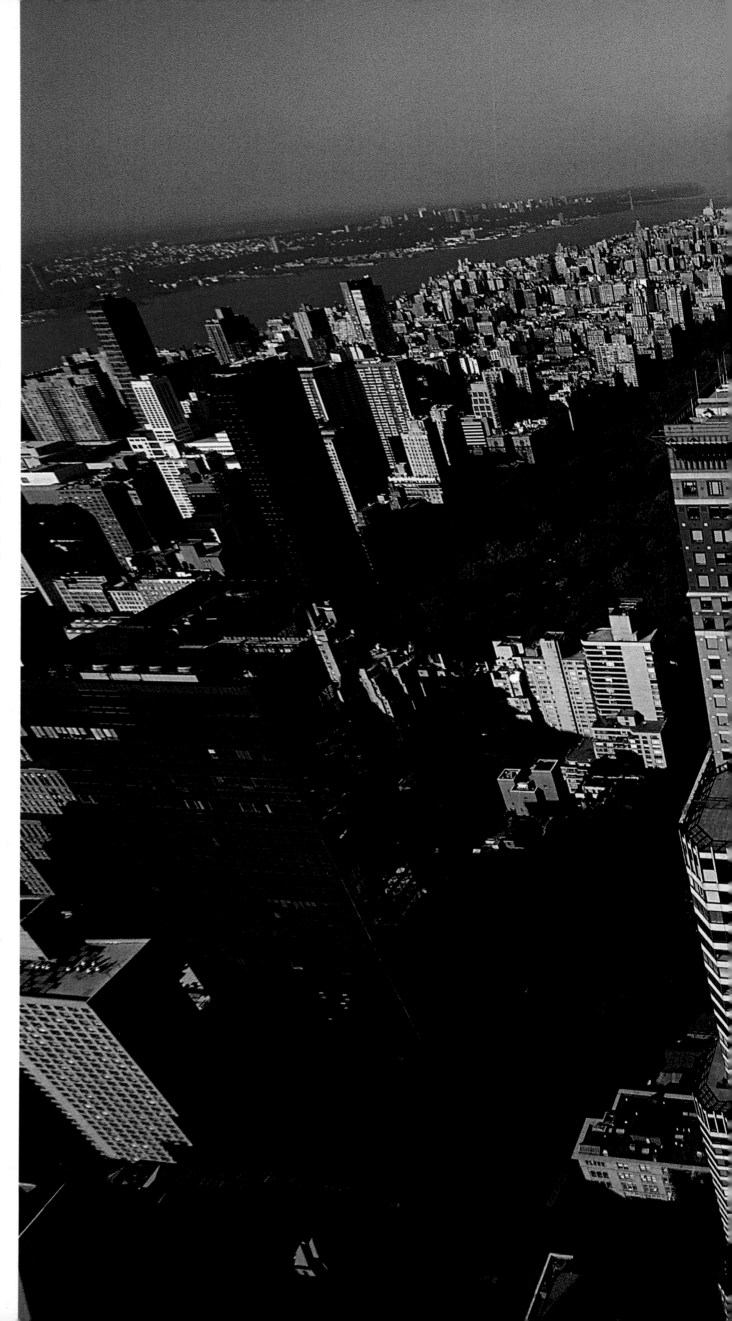

CENTRAL PARK,
WITH CITYSPIRE IN FOREGROUND
VIEW LOOKING NORTH

Central Park, with the Upper West Side to the left and the Upper East to the right, and Harlem and the northern sections of the city beyond, dominates this view. The park extends from 59th Street to 110th Street, and spans the area between Fifth Avenue and Central Park West. It is about two-and-a-half miles long, about a half mile wide, and it adds up to the city's very own backyard, the place where children and adults go to play, to work out, or just to take life easy.

Planned by Frederick Law Olmsted and Calvert Vaux in 1858, it was America's first major urban park in a Romantic setting. Every inch of the park was planned. Streams were diverted, rocks were blasted, hills and valleys were sculpted, trees were planted to frame vistas, and ten million cartloads of earth and stone were transported, all to give us this great playground.

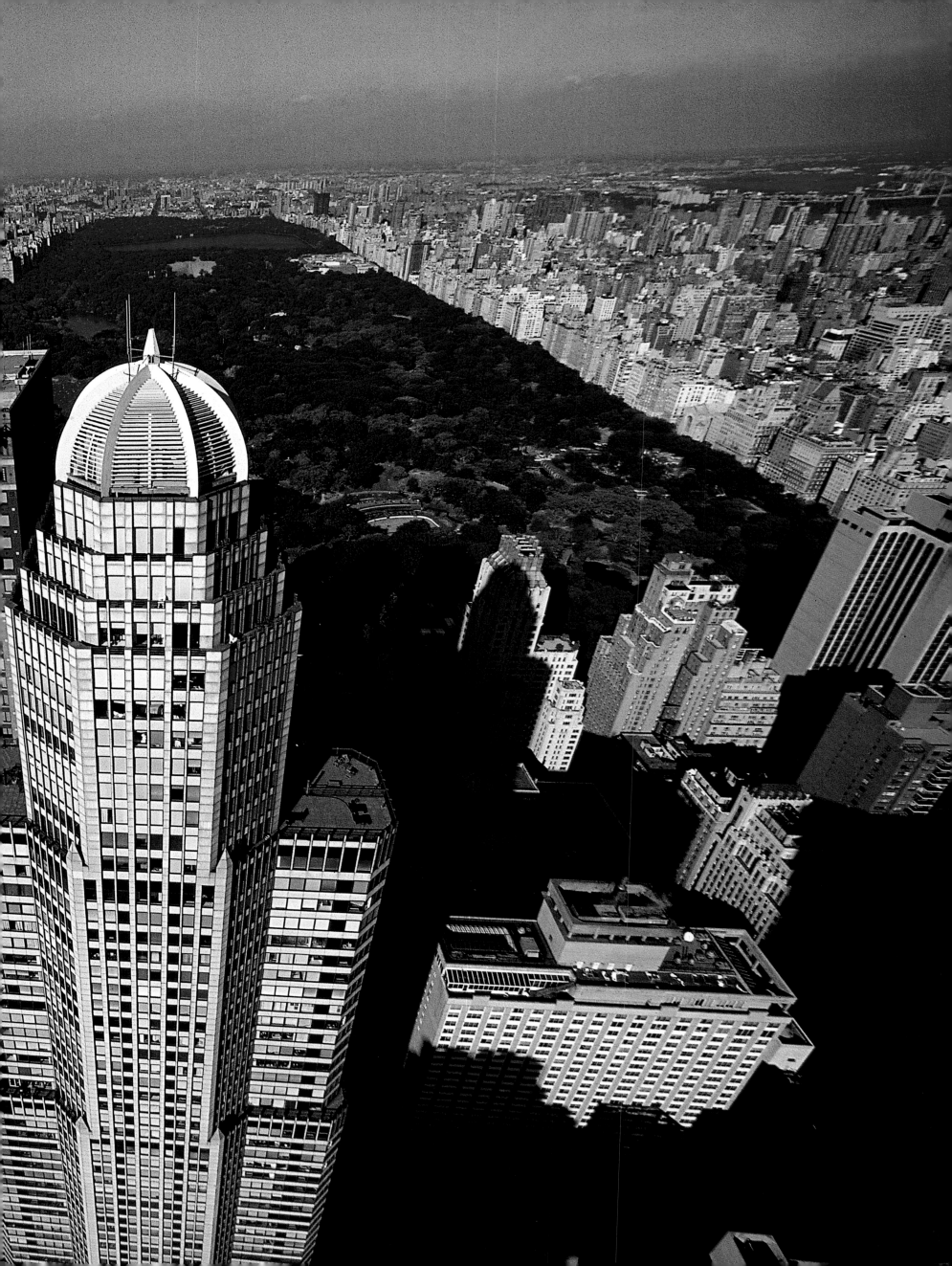

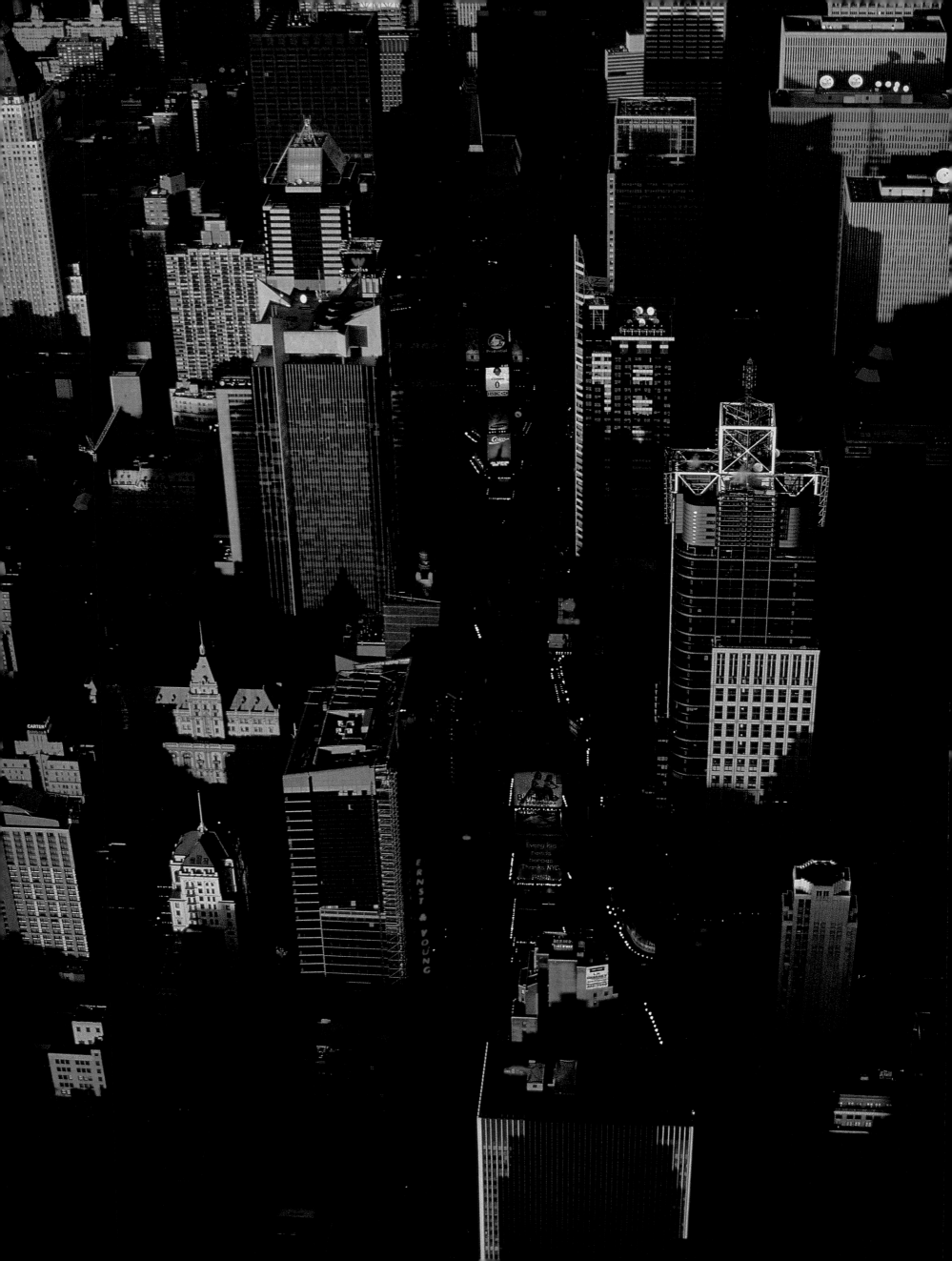

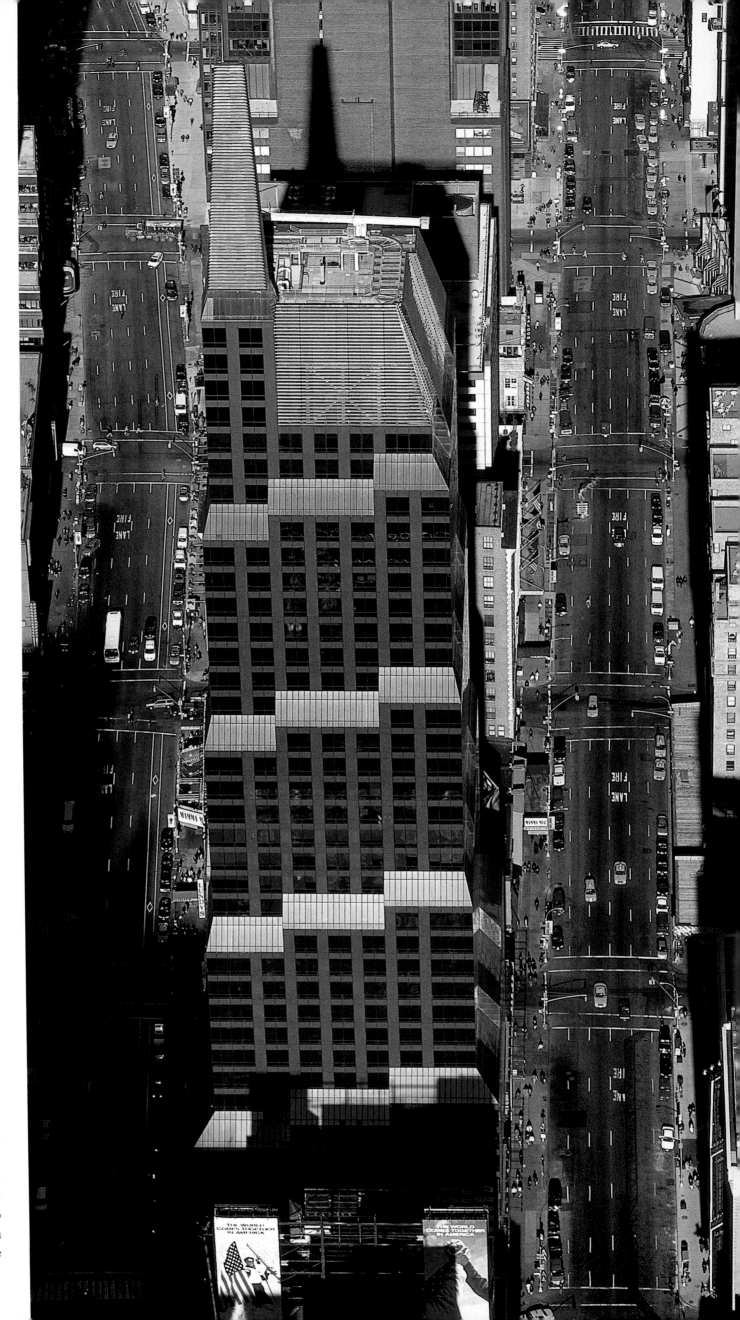

OPPOSITE: TIMES SQUARE, CROSSING OF SEVENTH AVENUE AND BROADWAY, AT 45TH STREET VIEW LOOKING NORTH

Times Square is often called "The Crossroads of the World" because everyone is said to cross it at some time in their life, or "The Great White Way" because of its blazing electric signage.

The peep shows, dance halls, and adult movie houses of yesteryear have been replaced with office towers housing law firms, Disney corporate offices, and even Madame Tussaud's wax museum. This is the new Times Square, a sanitized version.

If for certain romantics the place has lost its soul, its streets nonetheless remain animated, as thousands of visitors converge there nightly seeking entertainment. On average, each evening sees nearly 30,000 people flocking to the Broadway and movie theaters.

The attractions are, to be sure, sometimes artificial. ABC News, recently installed on Broadway and 44th Street, attracts gawkers to its glass-walled studios. And with the arrival of MTV, young music fans can hope to catch a glimpse of their favorite pop star in the heart of Times Square.

RIGHT: MORGAN STANLEY BUILDING, 750 SEVENTH AVENUE, AT 49TH STREET AND BROADWAY VIEW LOOKING NORTH

This 34-story office building by Kevin Roche, John Dinkeloo & Associates was built in 1990. It is one of the most dramatic buildings erected in Times Square in recent years.

It is both classical—balance and harmony are created by its wide windows—and modern although it breaks with several tenets of modernism. The south wall, seen here, is far from being uniform in its series of setbacks that give it a life of its own. Most interesting are its setbacks and roofline slope that break with the modernist rule of rooflines being at 90º angles to the wall. This is not the architects' first building designed with sloping roofs but this one reflects new stylistic innovations. It is multifaceted, as if a diamond or prism. The architects also weren't satisfied until they created a pyramid-like structure rising from the roof, almost a postmodernist finial.

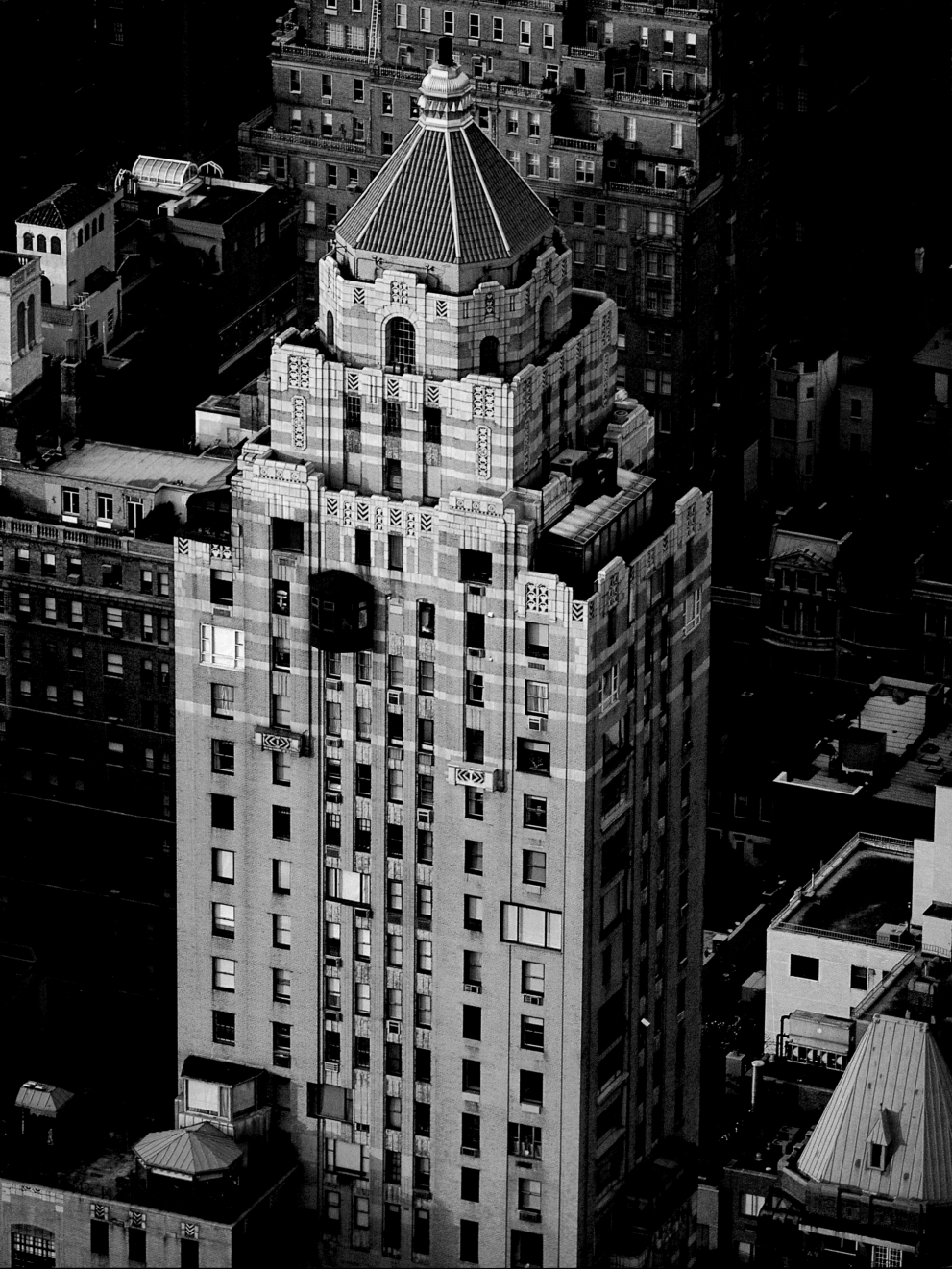

OPPOSITE: **CARLYLE HOTEL, 35 EAST 76TH STREET, AT MADISON AVENUE** **VIEW LOOKING SOUTHEAST**

The subtle horizontal banding in the brickwork and the geometric forms used in the spandrels and parapets add up to a classic example of New York architecture in the late 1920s, just the sort of style that Donald Trump was seeking in Trump Palace.

The Carlyle is a true palace at times, a temporary home to royalty and visiting heads of state. It was the favorite New York hotel of John F. Kennedy, and King Carlos of Spain stays here today.

OVERLEAF: **WEST 74TH AND 75TH STREET, BETWEEN CENTRAL PARK WEST AND COLUMBUS AVENUE** **VIEW LOOKING NORTHEAST**

The Upper West Side was spared the monotony of brownstone row houses stamped out of the same mold when it was developed in the late nineteenth and early twentieth centuries, and the row houses on the Central Park blocks were especially varied.

These row houses were developed as private homes. They were usually staffed by live-in servants who occupied the top floor (the houses were not elevator equipped, so the servants had to climb the greatest number of stairs). The family quarters included the parlor floor, which was reached by the front stoop, with bedrooms and sewing rooms and libraries on the second and third floors. A family dining room usually occupied the front room in the half-basement, with the kitchen in the rear.

The parlor floors were ordinarily used for entertaining and formal functions, with the front parlor filled with overstuffed horsehair furniture, and the back parlor used as the formal dining room (it was usually linked to the kitchen below by a dumbwaiter).

The vast majority of these houses have been metamorphosed into apartments over the years, but some private homes still remain on these side streets.

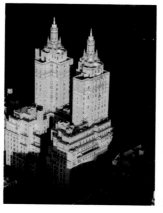

SAN REMO APARTMENTS, 145 CENTRAL PARK WEST, BETWEEN 74TH AND 75TH STREET **VIEW LOOKING SOUTHEAST**

The late 1920s witnessed the rise of four great twin-towered apartment houses on Central Park West, a phenomenon that gave the avenue the most distinctive residential skyline in the city.

The apartment houses all rise from solid U-shaped bases that provide open-ended courtyards, and all have their main entrances on the avenue, with ancillary side-street entrances leading to lobbies that serve both wings.

Two of the apartment houses—the Century and the Majestic—have rooflines that are sleek, and the emphasis is placed on the massing. The Eldorado and the San Remo, on the other hand, are both crowned by architectural doodads. The San Remo, with a pair of choragic monuments arising from a surround of urns, supported by volutes flanked by Mediterranean-style tiled roofs, and topped by finials, is clearly the neoclassical champion.

This is the work of Emery Roth, who was at the height of his prodigious powers when he created this building.

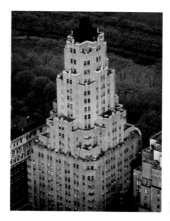

MASTER APARTMENTS, 310 RIVERSIDE DRIVE, AT 103RD STREET **VIEW LOOKING SOUTHWEST**

This 1929 building began life as the Master Institute of United Arts. It was the brainchild of the artist Nicholas Roerich, who wanted to promote interculturism in the arts, and the building was specifically designed to combine a residential hotel with a base for his artistic operations—classes, theater, and a museum displaying his own work and the work of others.

The massing and detailing of the building are suggestive of both One Fifth Avenue and the New Yorker Hotel, and for good reason—the Master Institute was designed by Helmle, Corbett & Harrison, who created One Fifth, and Sugarman & Berger, who created the New Yorker (see pages 34 and 42–43).

The height of the twenty-eight-story building and its silhouette make it a beacon on the Upper West Side.

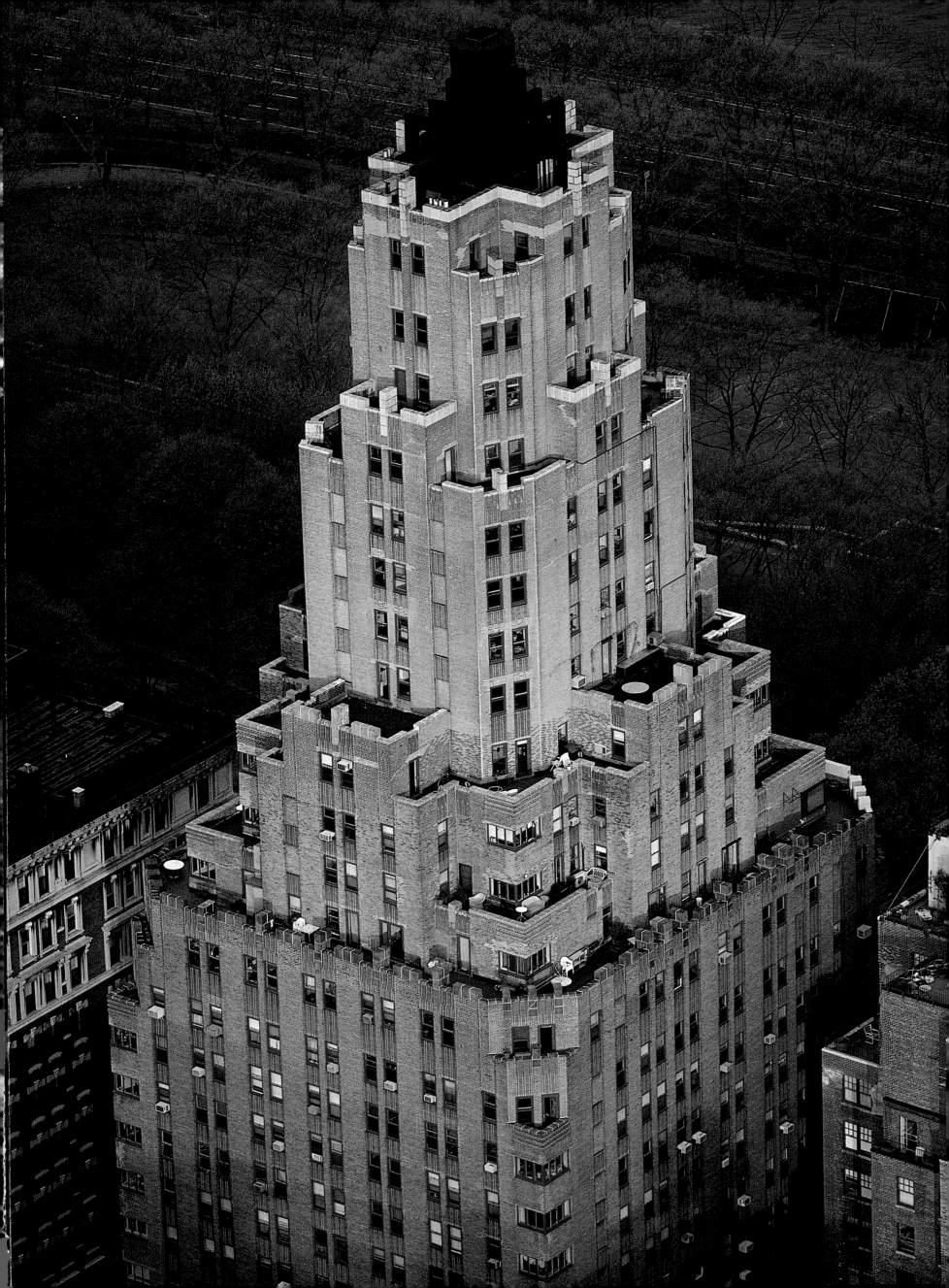

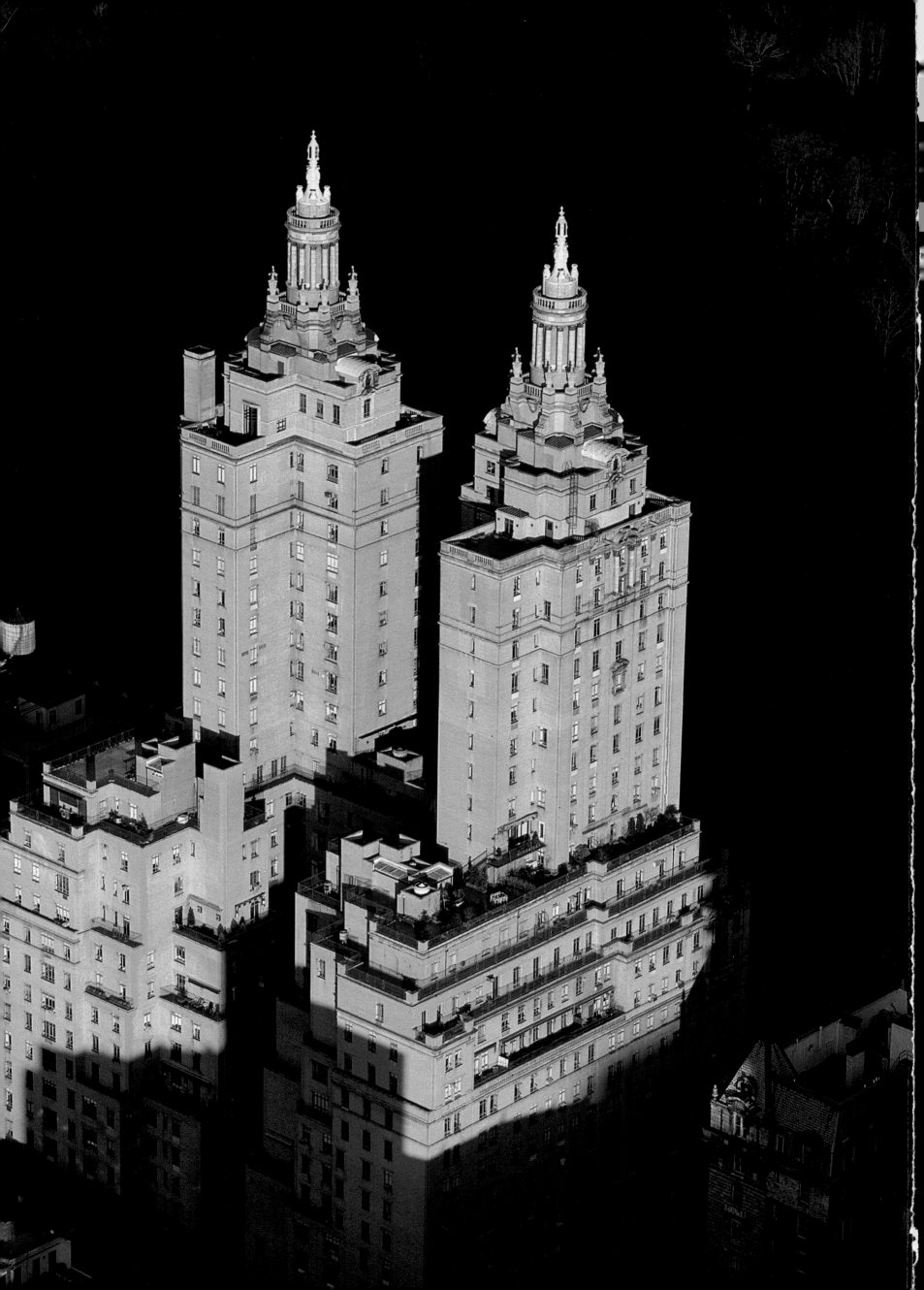

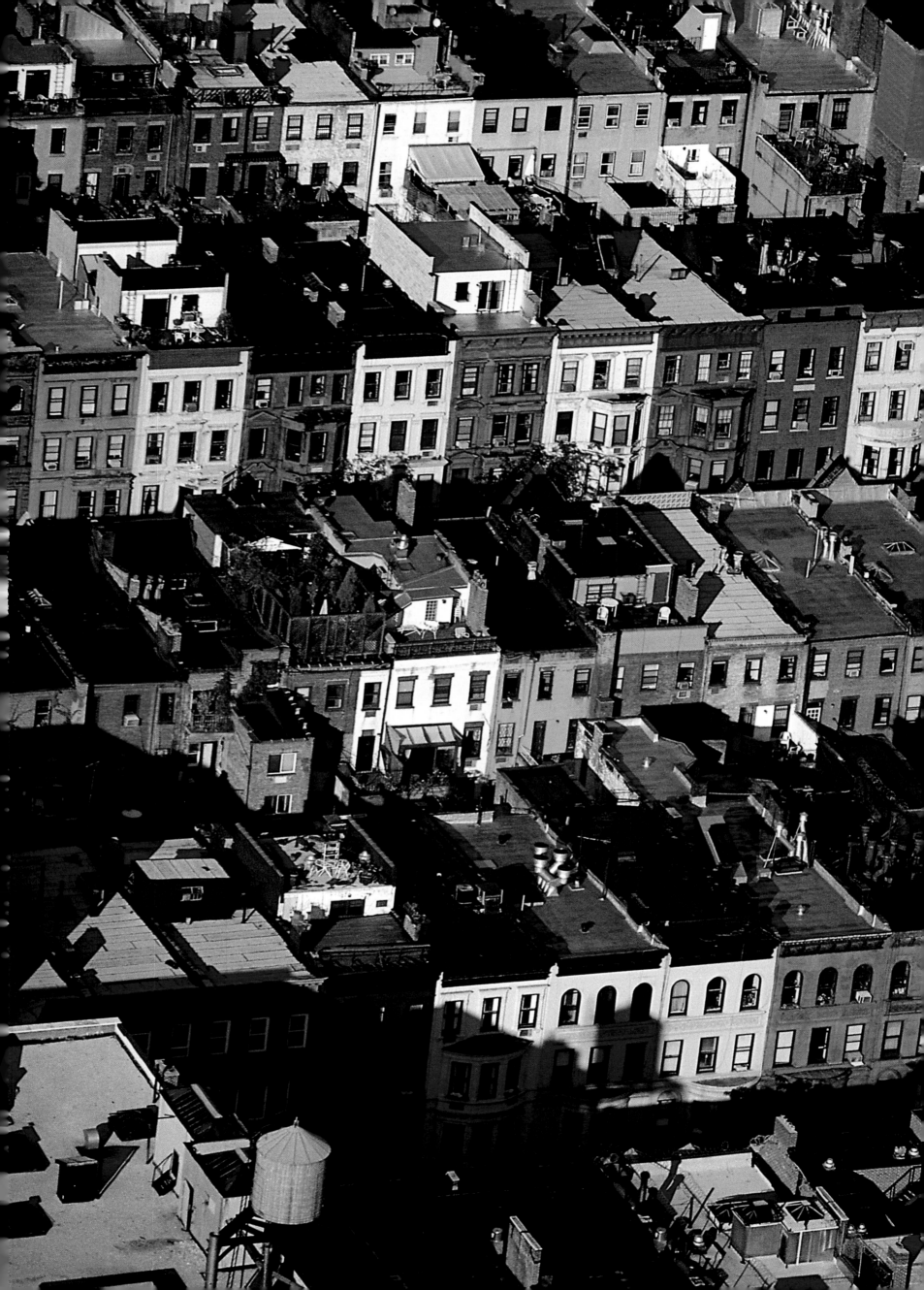

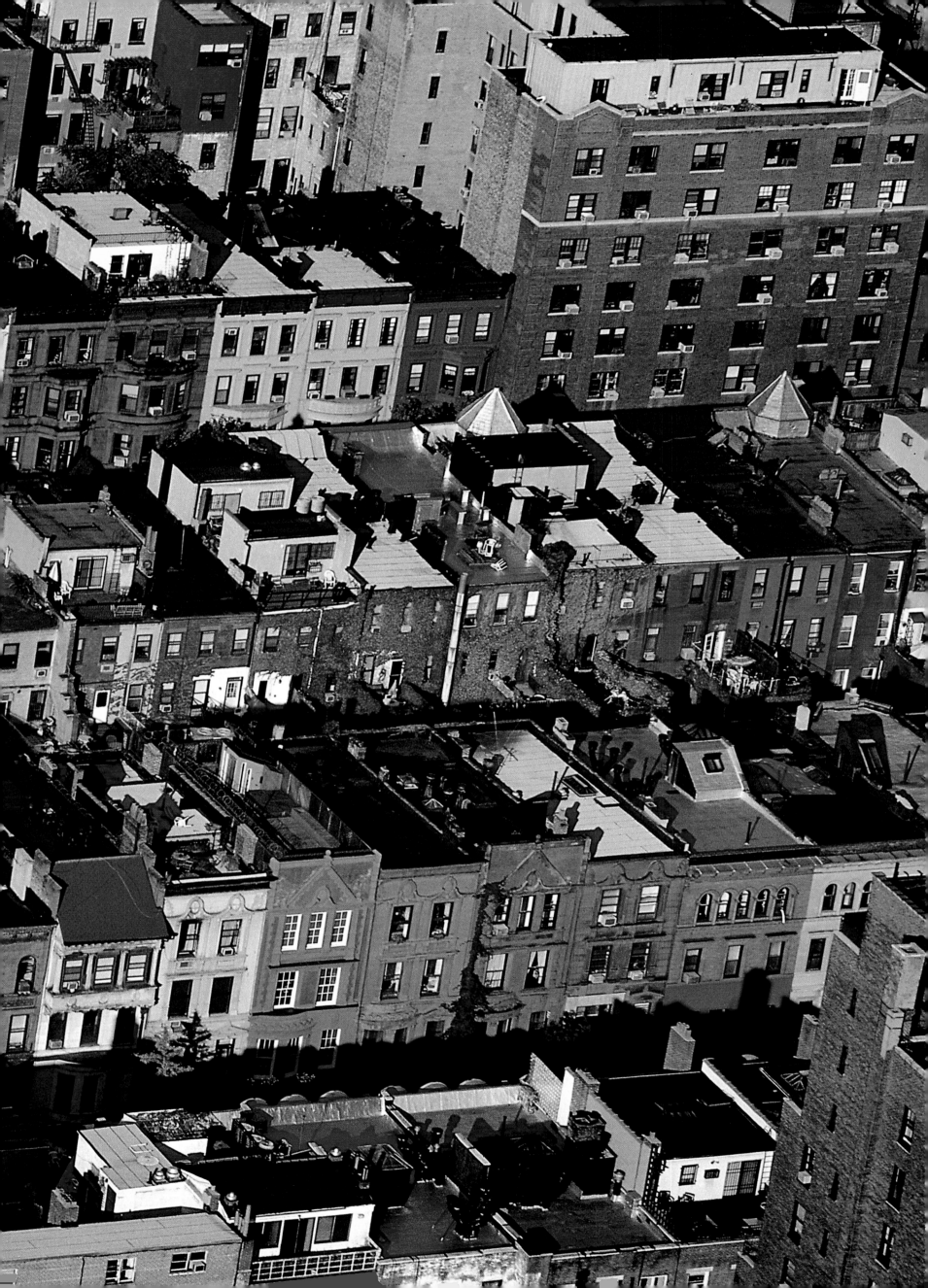

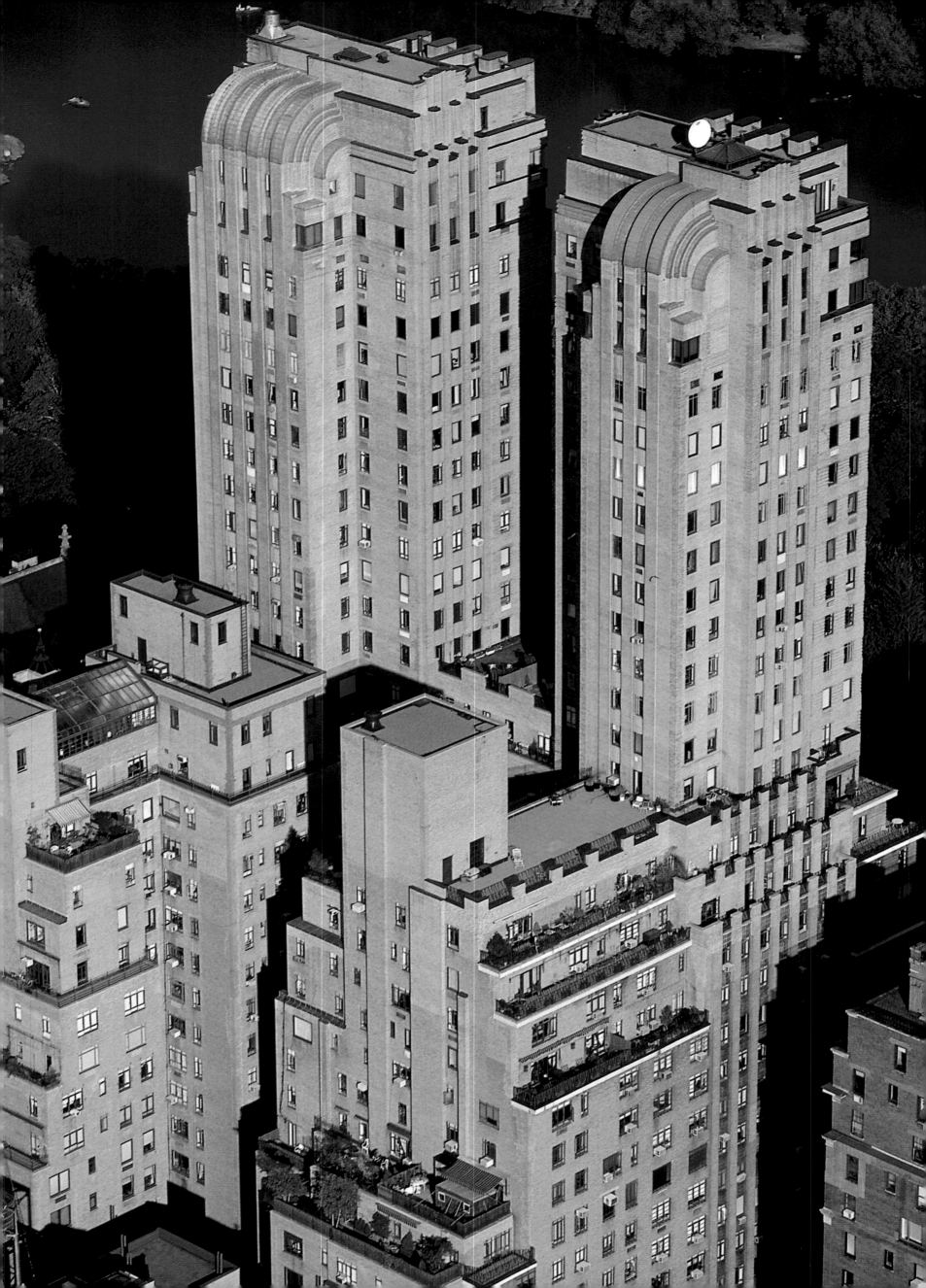

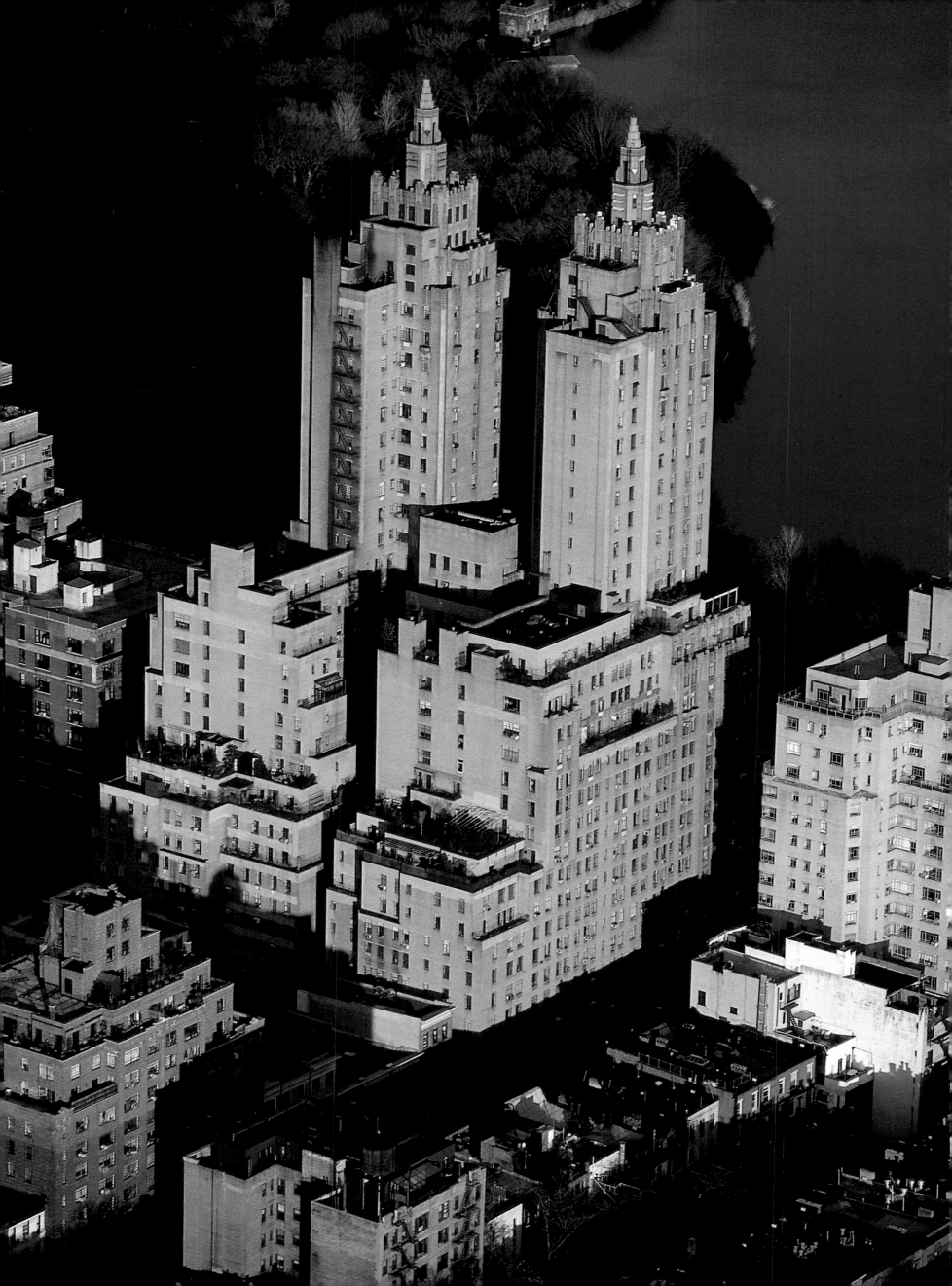

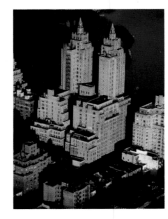

ELDORADO APARTMENTS, 300 CENTRAL PARK WEST, BETWEEN 90TH AND 91ST STREET VIEW LOOKING NORTHWEST

The Eldorado—literally, the City of Gold—was the home of the family of Marjorie Morningstar, the title character in Herman Wouk's classic tale of upward (and downward) mobility.

Marjorie's father told her that he and her mother used to come down from The Bronx and go rowing in Central Park before she was born. He pointed to the big houses on Fifth Avenue and said that they would live there someday. "Listen," he said, "we came pretty close, after all—Central Park West."

This stretch of Central Park West, and, to a lesser extent, West End Avenue and Riverside Drive, was by midcentury a place where, if you had it, you could flaunt it. Apartments on a palatial scale, apartments that have aptly been called mansions in the sky, are the norm.

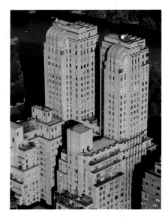

MAJESTIC APARTMENTS, 115 CENTRAL PARK WEST, BETWEEN 71ST AND 72ND STREET VIEW LOOKING NORTHEAST

When the Majestic Hotel opened in the early 1890s, it was described as the largest, most magnificent hotel in the world; by the 1920s, the hotel had run its course. It was snapped up by the developer Irwin Chanin, who saw his opportunities and took them. He wanted to build an apartment house for his era as grand as the Majestic Hotel had been for its own.

Chanin's original plan was to have apartments that ranged in size from eleven to twenty-four rooms, but it was a plan made in the boom of the '20s. The Crash of 1929 forced him to change his plans. When the thirty-story apartment house opened in 1931, the largest apartments had "only" fourteen rooms, such as an eight-by-nineteen-foot solarium, a wood-burning fireplace in its eighteen-by-thirty drawing room, a fourteen-by-twenty-eight dining room, and a servants' wing. Not bad for living in reduced circumstances.

OPPOSITE: **55 CENTRAL PARK WEST, AT 66TH STREET VIEW LOOKING WEST**

"Flamboyant" is the architectural term for the fifteenth-century Gothic style characterized by ornate tracery suggesting flames. This 1929 apartment house doesn't have tracery, but its brickwork is designed in a flamelike motif, with its hues diminishing in intensity the higher they climb.

The architects, Schwartz & Gross, had spent most of their careers to this point designing buildings in the style of the Renaissance, but here they changed course and freely adapted the Art Deco as their own. At 55 Central Park West the architects took the ziggurat as their theme, incorporating three-dimensional ziggurats as buttresses and finials, even repeating the theme in the awning.

The building looms large in popular culture. It played a prominent role in the movie *Ghostbusters*, as an apartment building haunted by ghosts.

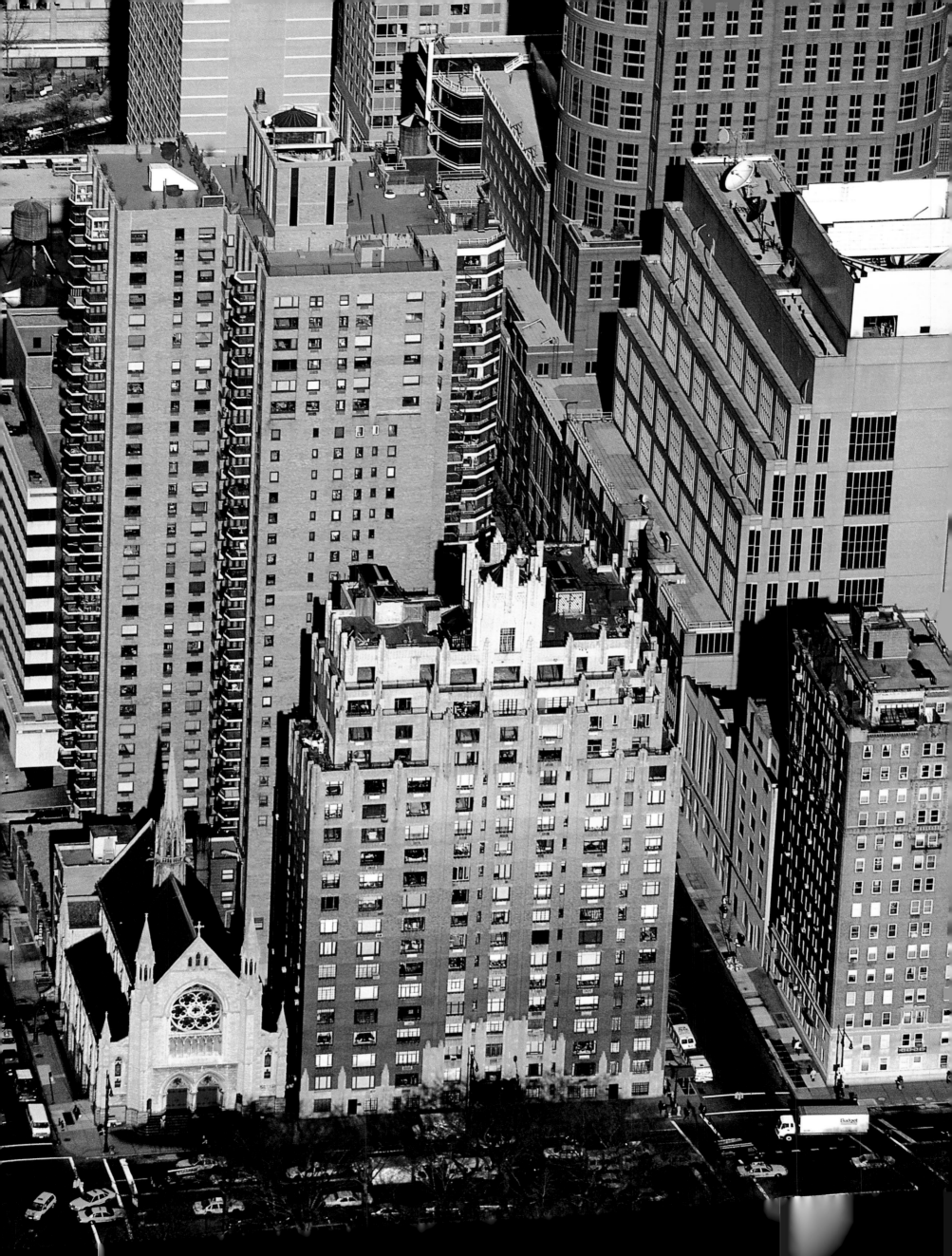

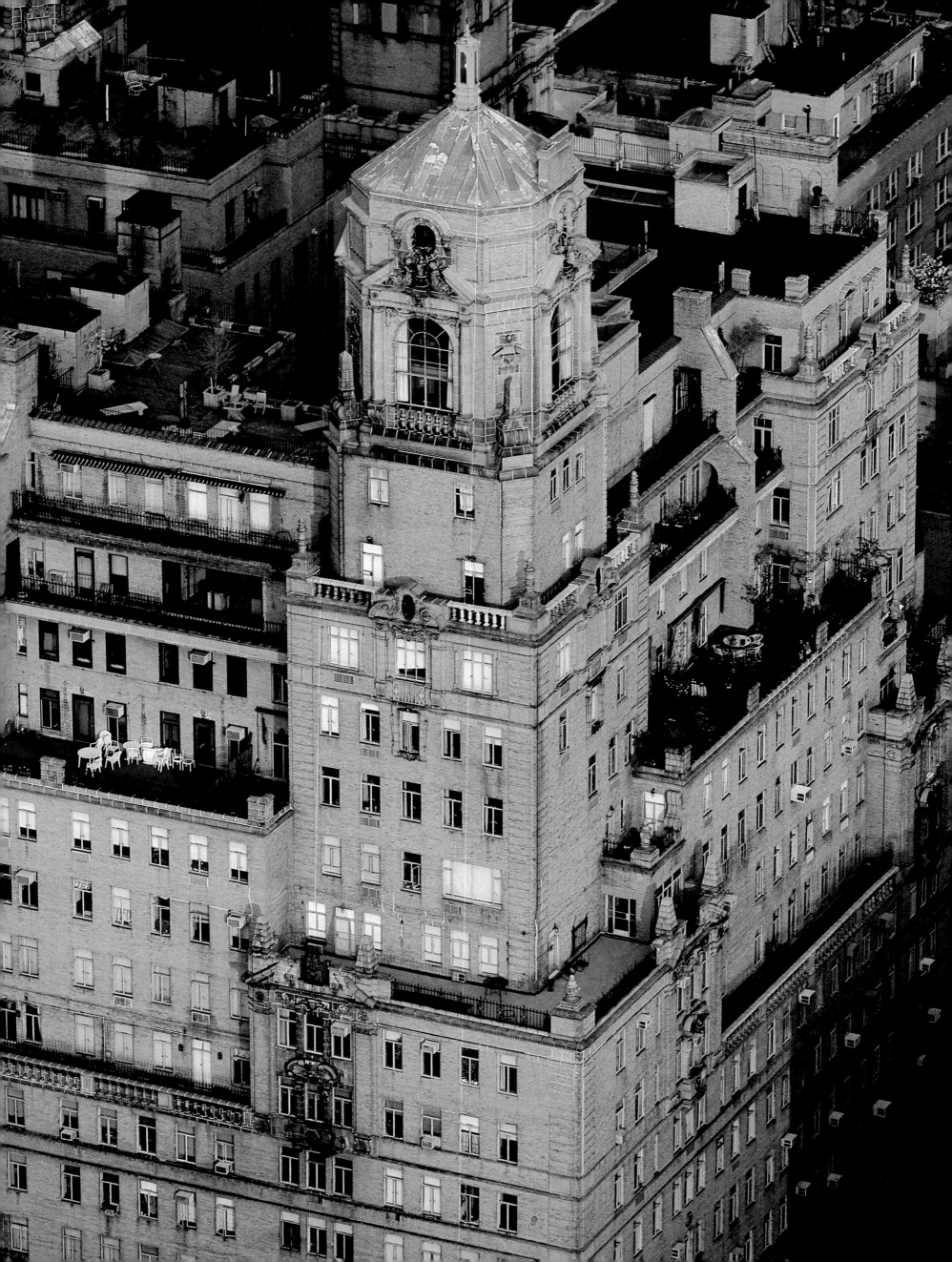

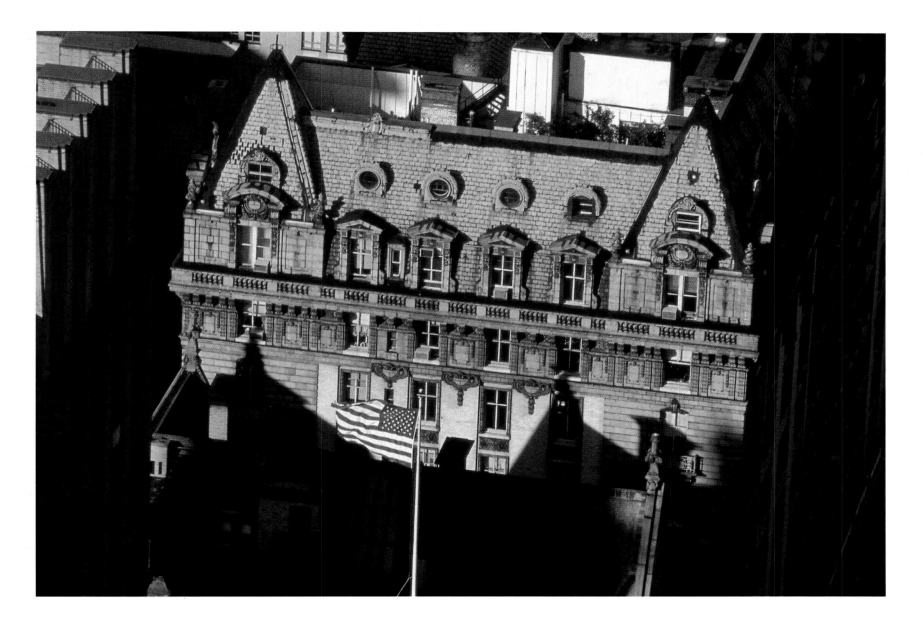

**OPPOSITE: BERESFORD APARTMENTS,
ONE WEST 81ST STREET, ON CENTRAL PARK WEST
VIEW LOOKING SOUTHWEST**

This San Simeonesque vision from the hand of Emery Roth rises on one of the few corners in Manhattan that commands two vistas. This apartment house has views over Central Park and Manhattan Square, the site of the American Museum of Natural History.

The prices for apartments that overlook the park in this co-op are more expensive the higher the floor, so residents tend to guard their views jealously. The building opened in 1929, nine years before the first centrally air-conditioned apartment house in New York was built; thus the tenants use individual air-conditioning units. The usual installation, with units resting on the bottom of the window frames, blocks views; to preserve views some tenants have the units installed in the upper parts of windows, which costs more than traditional installations.

**ABOVE: LANGHAM APARTMENTS,
135 CENTRAL PARK WEST; DAKOTA APARTMENTS
IN FOREGROUND, 1 WEST 72ND STREET
VIEW LOOKING NORTHWEST**

The bold massing of the Majestic's Art Moderne roofline sets the stage for two Central Park West buildings that are more than twenty years apart in age but at first glance seem stylistically close: the flag-waving Dakota in the foreground, on 72nd Street, and the Langham Apartments in the middle ground, between 73rd and 74th Street.

The similarity between the buildings, however, is relegated to their peaks and gables. The Dakota was built in 1884, designed in a neo–German Renaissance style by Henry J. Hardenbergh. The Dakota was described by its promoters as having "an air of lightness and airiness," which to contemporary eyes seems a strange description. Some might even view the building as "spooky," an idea no doubt reinforced by its role as the setting for the action in the movie *Rosemary's Baby.*

The Langham, which opened in 1905, was designed by Clinton & Russell in a style more in keeping with French classicism. Clinton & Russell stayed within the tradition for one of their most famous buildings, the Apthorp Apartments, but over time they changed their ideology, culminating in the Art Deco design of the Cities Service Building at 70 Pine Street (see page 12).

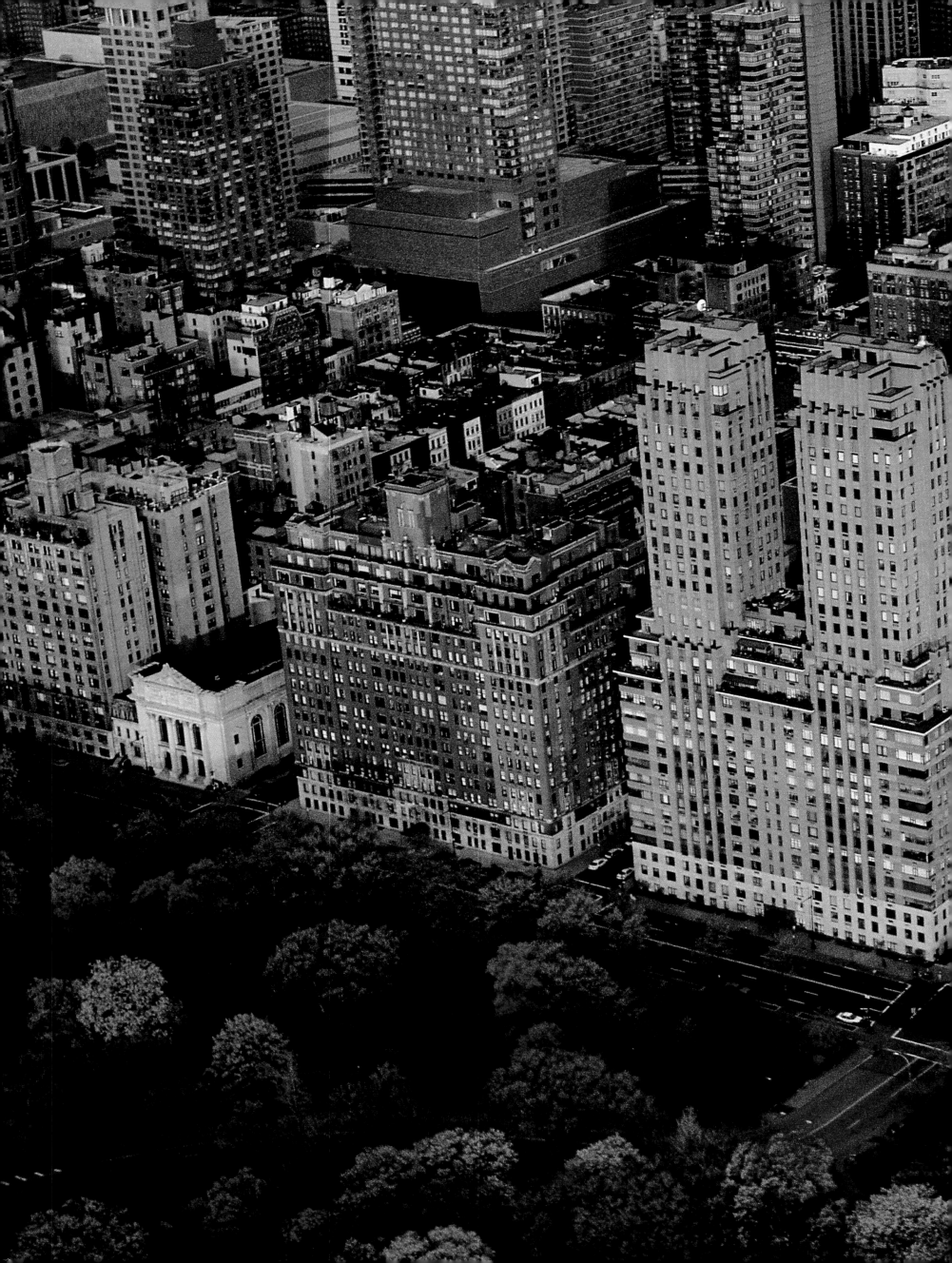

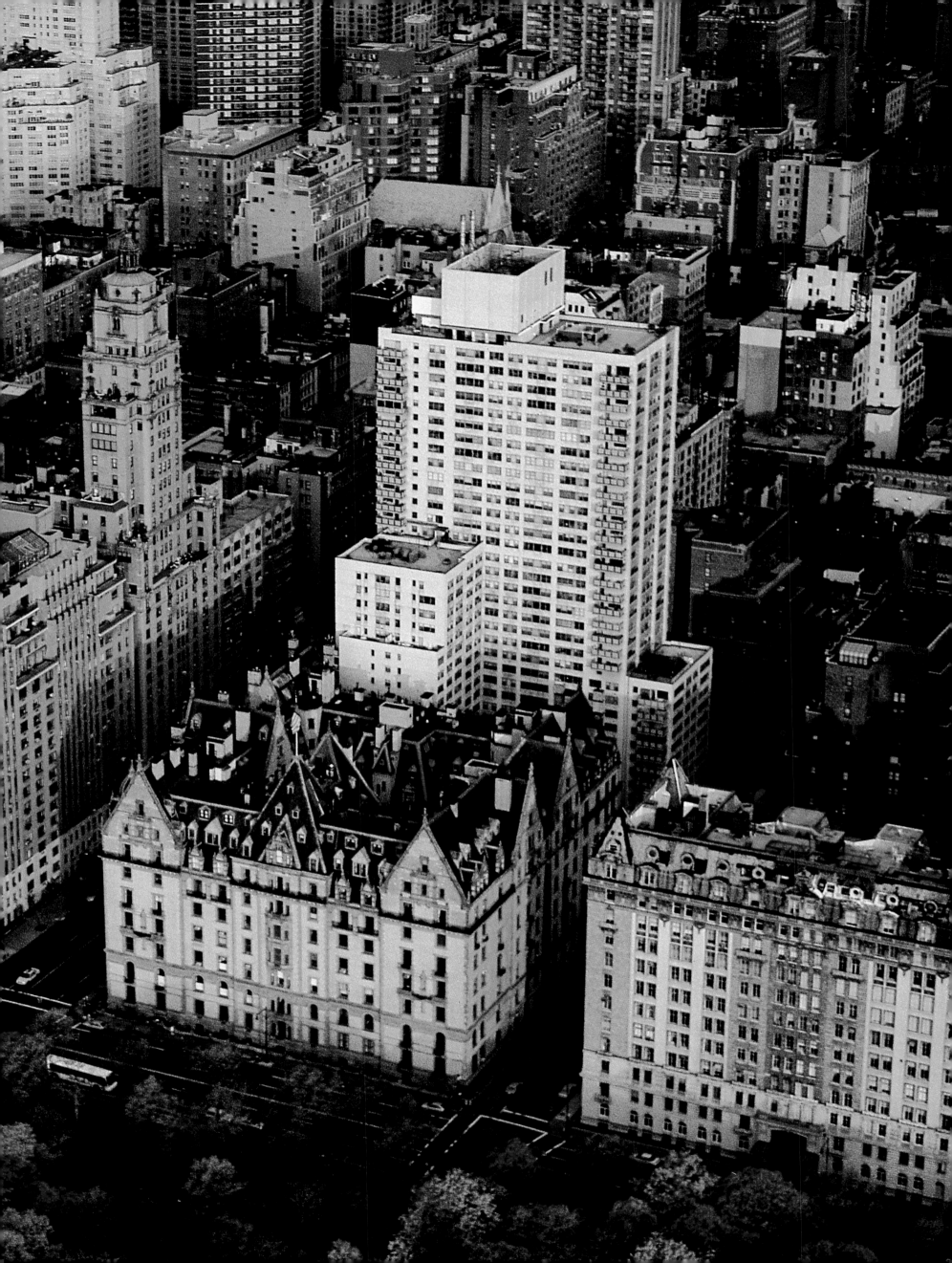

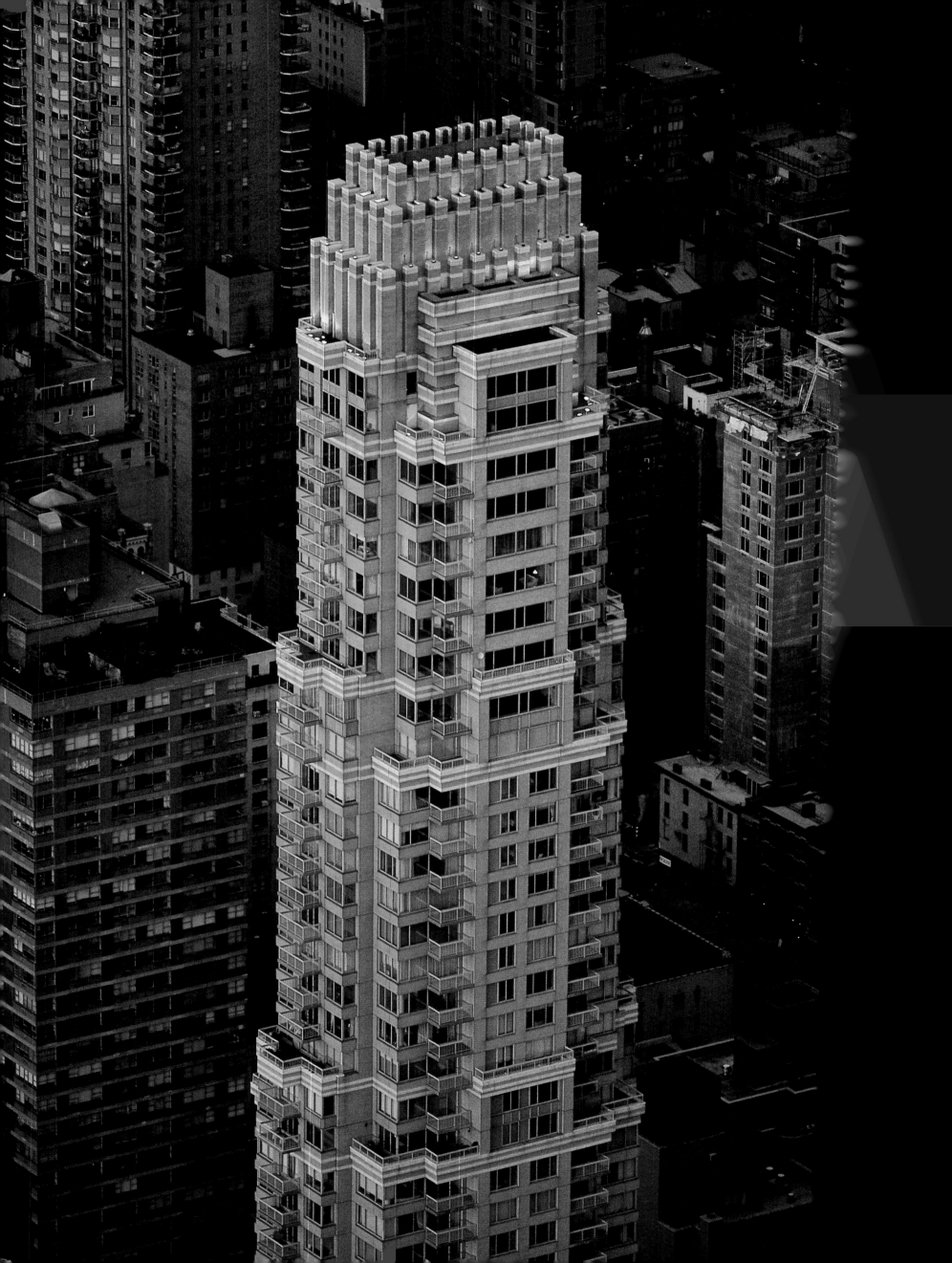

Donald Trump has an uncanny sense for the art of the deal and the ability to bend with the shifting architectural breezes. When sleek, glass-walled buildings were de rigueur, he built them; when brick-clad, neo–Art Deco buildings were the new wave, he dove in and built those too. Buildings such as architect Frank Williams's Trump Palace, a fifty-five-story condominium apartment house built in 1991, stand out in the forest of very tall towers that sprang up on the Upper East Side in the 1980s and 1990s. The massing of the building is not unlike the Empire State Building. It is all tower rising from a low base, which in this case is only one story high. It comes to the building line to maintain the wall of buildings and preserve the streetscape. Although huge, it is hardly monolithic. The setbacks are accentuated by stringcourses that encircle the building, and the corner windows are in the tradition of some of its older siblings, such as the Majestic Apartments on Central Park West. Its roofline, so reminiscent of the Chanin Building or even Trump Parc, also has its roots in the Art Moderne architecture of the late 1920s and early 1930s. It doesn't come cheap. A seven-room penthouse apartment reputedly sold in 1996 for $2.95 million.

This is not a Loire Valley château sacked by marauding forces but a grand building ruined by general indifference. Built in 1887 and partially funded by the Astor family, the building first opened as New York Cancer Hospital, the nation's first hospital to specialize in cancer. The great round pavilions, designed by the architect Charles C. Haight, allowed air to circulate freely.

The building has served various purposes since then, and its last incarnation was as the Towers Nursing Home. Today's sad, derelict building, with a sumac tree growing out of one of its windows, is still the talk of developers, who have considered incorporating it into part of a larger building scheme.

Central Park was vilified by the real-estate interests when it was first proposed in the 1850s, in part because they believed that too much of the heart of the city was being usurped for frivolous purposes. What they soon realized was that Central Park was a great urban amenity, and the blocks bordering the park quickly became the setting for some of the city's grandest mansions and apartment houses.

Perhaps the city's most famous apartment building is the Dakota, between 72nd and 73rd Street, to the right of the twin-towered Majestic. The Dakota, a great cube of a multigabled building with a central courtyard, was built in 1884, and it created a bouleversement in society. In those days the average upper-class New Yorker looked down his nose on any kind of domestic setting that was not a private home, but luxurious apartments—or French flats, as they were dismissively called by some—ultimately changed the living style for almost all wealthy New Yorkers.

The thirty-six-story, white-brick apartment house next door to the Dakota stands on the site that originally housed a subterranean electrical generating plant that supplied power to the venerable apartment house, which was erected before electricity had come to the Upper West Side.

The Lincoln Square area appears in the top left corner of the photograph. Centered at Broadway and 66th Street, this neighborhood has mushroomed in the 1980s and 1990s, with the erection of forty-, fifty-, and even sixty-story apartment houses. The neighborhood had begun to change in the 1960s, when urban renewal bulldozed away a stretch of the older city to make way for Lincoln Center for the Performing Arts. (Avery Fisher Hall, home of the New York Philharmonic, is in the top left corner, identified by four of the travertine-clad posts that frame it.)

Today's university, with about 21,000 students and 6,600 faculty members, started life in 1754 as King's College in Lower Manhattan, with eight students and one faculty member. After the American Revolution, the college changed its name to provide a more republican and democratic association, although the university still retains the crown as its symbol. By the mid–nineteenth century the school's campus was in Midtown, but in the 1890s Columbia moved to today's campus on Morningside Heights.

McKim, Mead & White, the nation's most prestigious architectural firm at the turn of the twentieth century, won the architectural competition for the overall plan of the campus. The submission was the work of Charles Follen McKim, whose scheme was for a campus in a style he dubbed "Municipal Classic," a series of interconnected courtyards, or quadrangles, with buildings defining the spaces in pure classical forms. Individual buildings would be allowed to vary the classical theme—an especially welcome idea to the school, because donors are more likely to contribute money if the building they endow can be differentiated from the rest.

Low Library, the saucer-domed building in the form of a Greek cross, set the tone for the style, and showed the wisdom of McKim's notion that the buildings should not all be stamped out of the same mold. The library, which is the university's flagship building, was donated by one of the university's presidents, Seth Low, in memory of his father.

McKim's contribution is commemorated in the plaque that was placed in front of Low Library in 1910, one year after his death. In a variation on the funerary inscription for Christopher Wren, it says: "The monuments [of an artist] look down upon us throughout the ages."

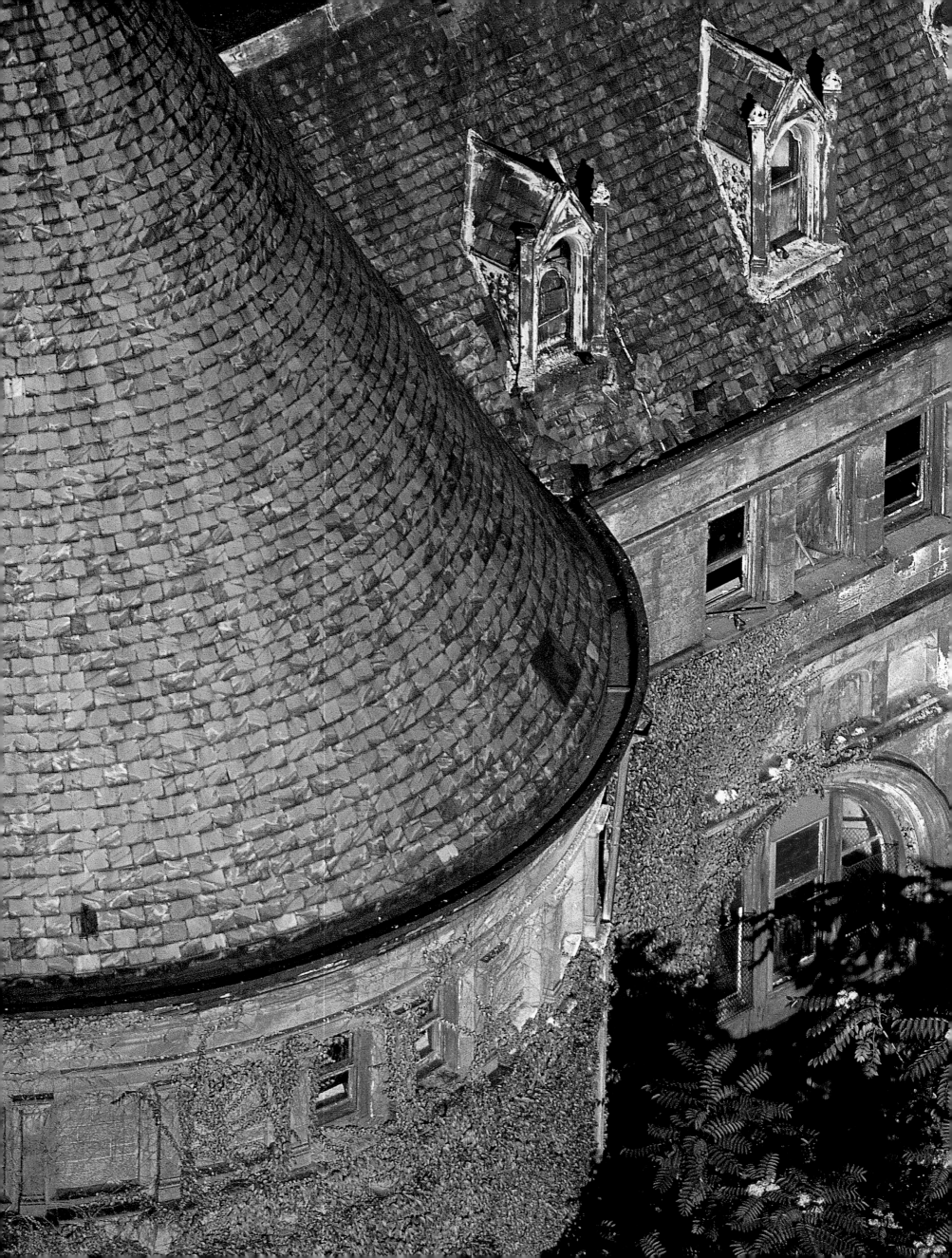

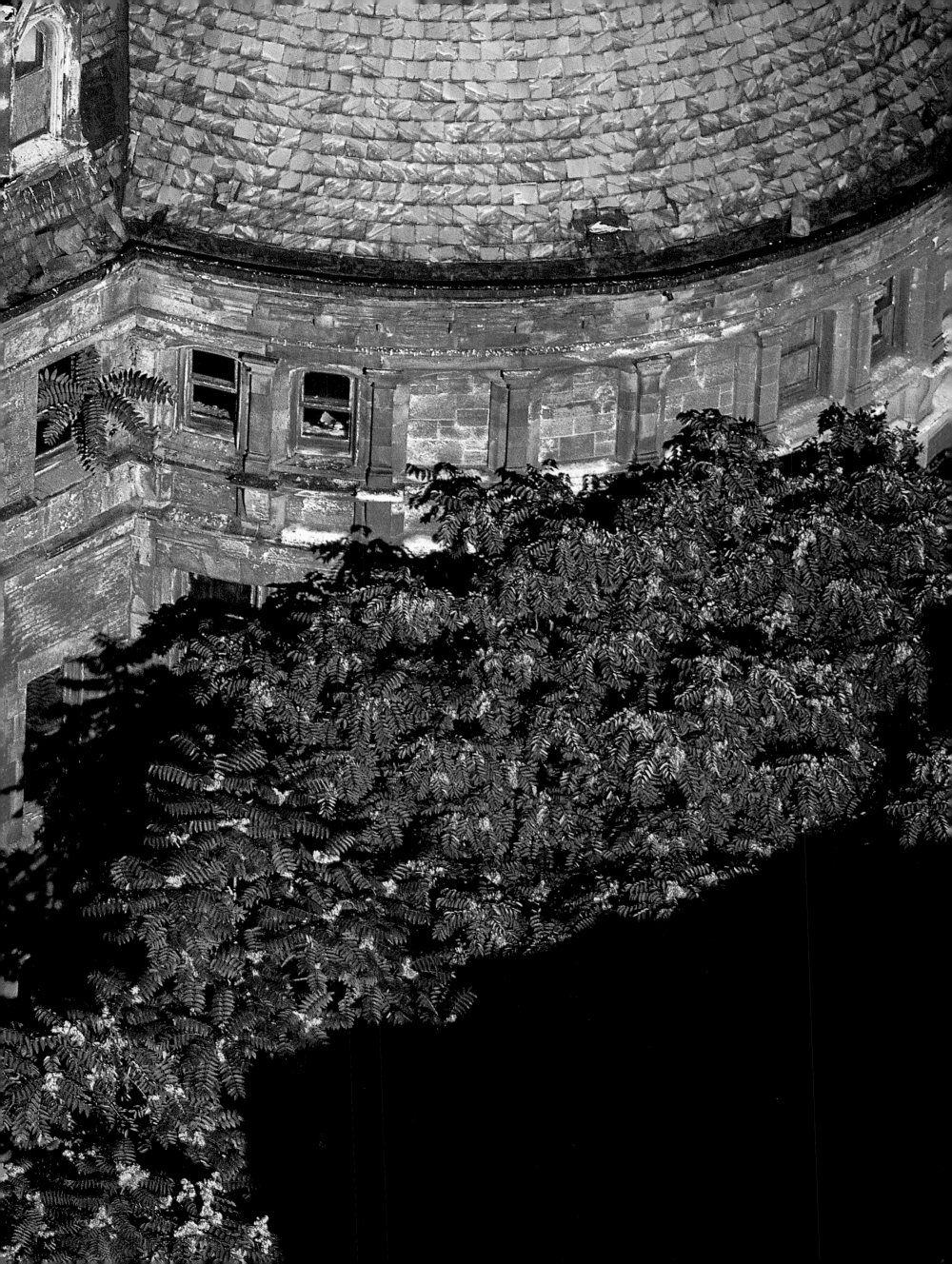

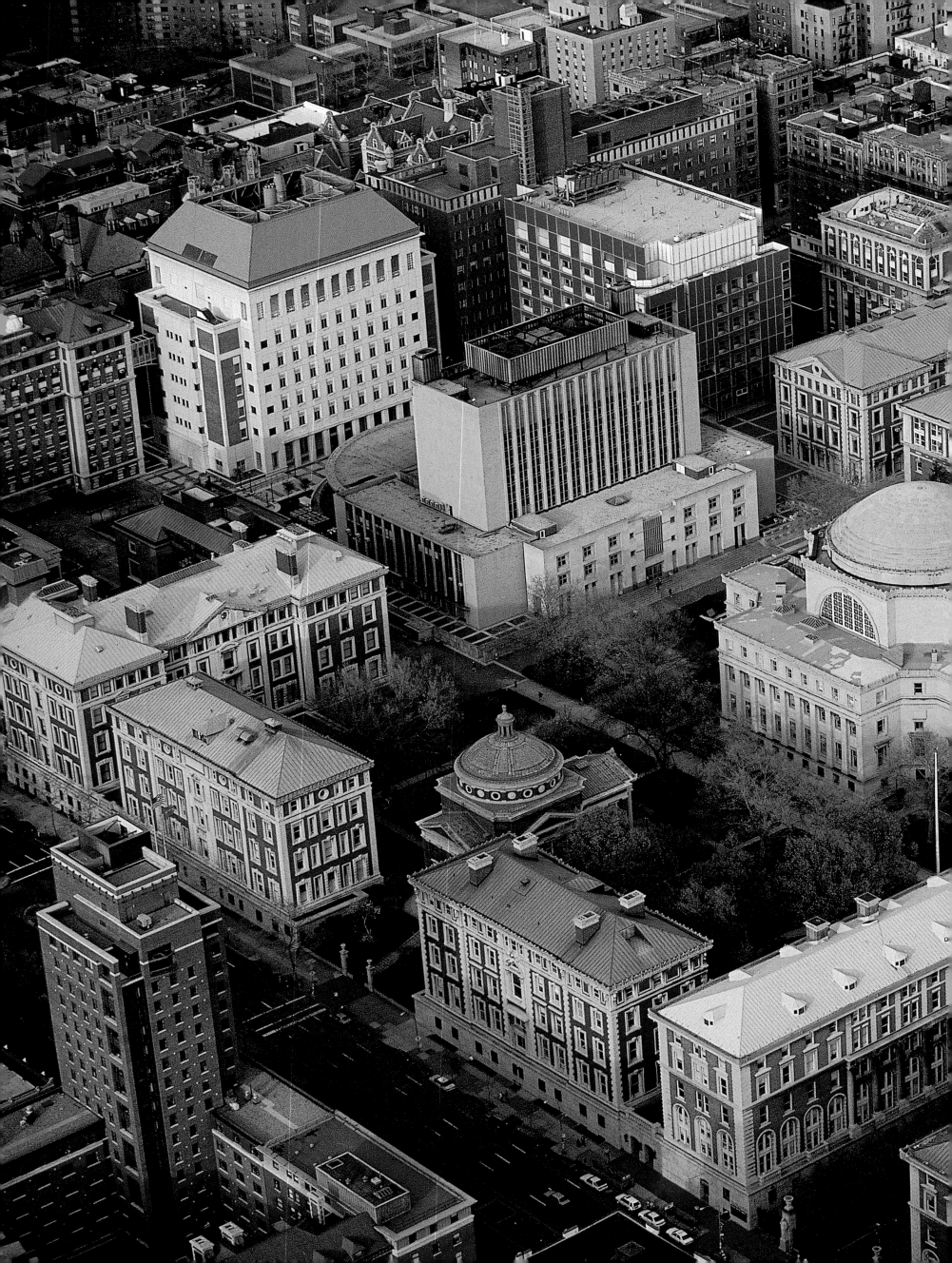

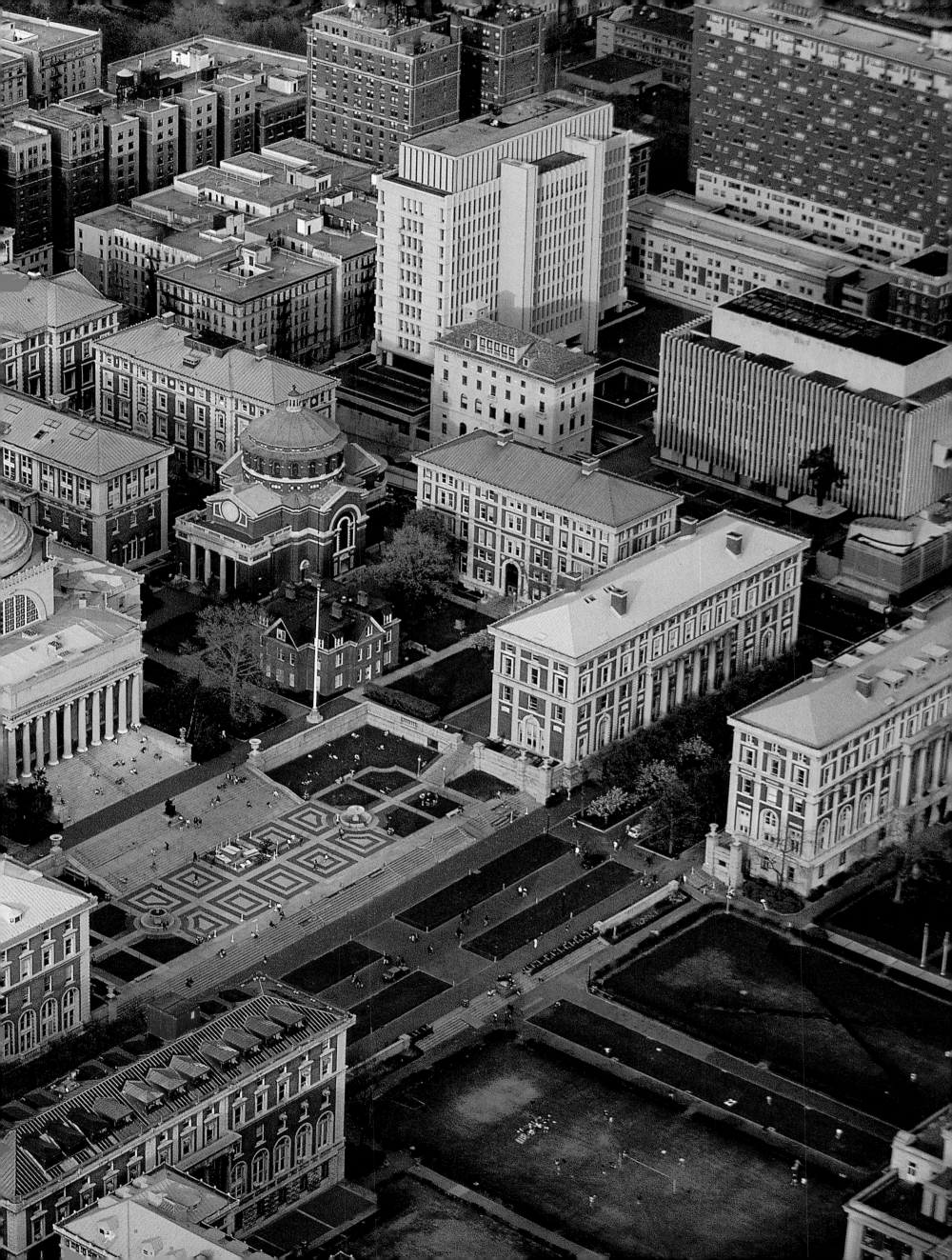

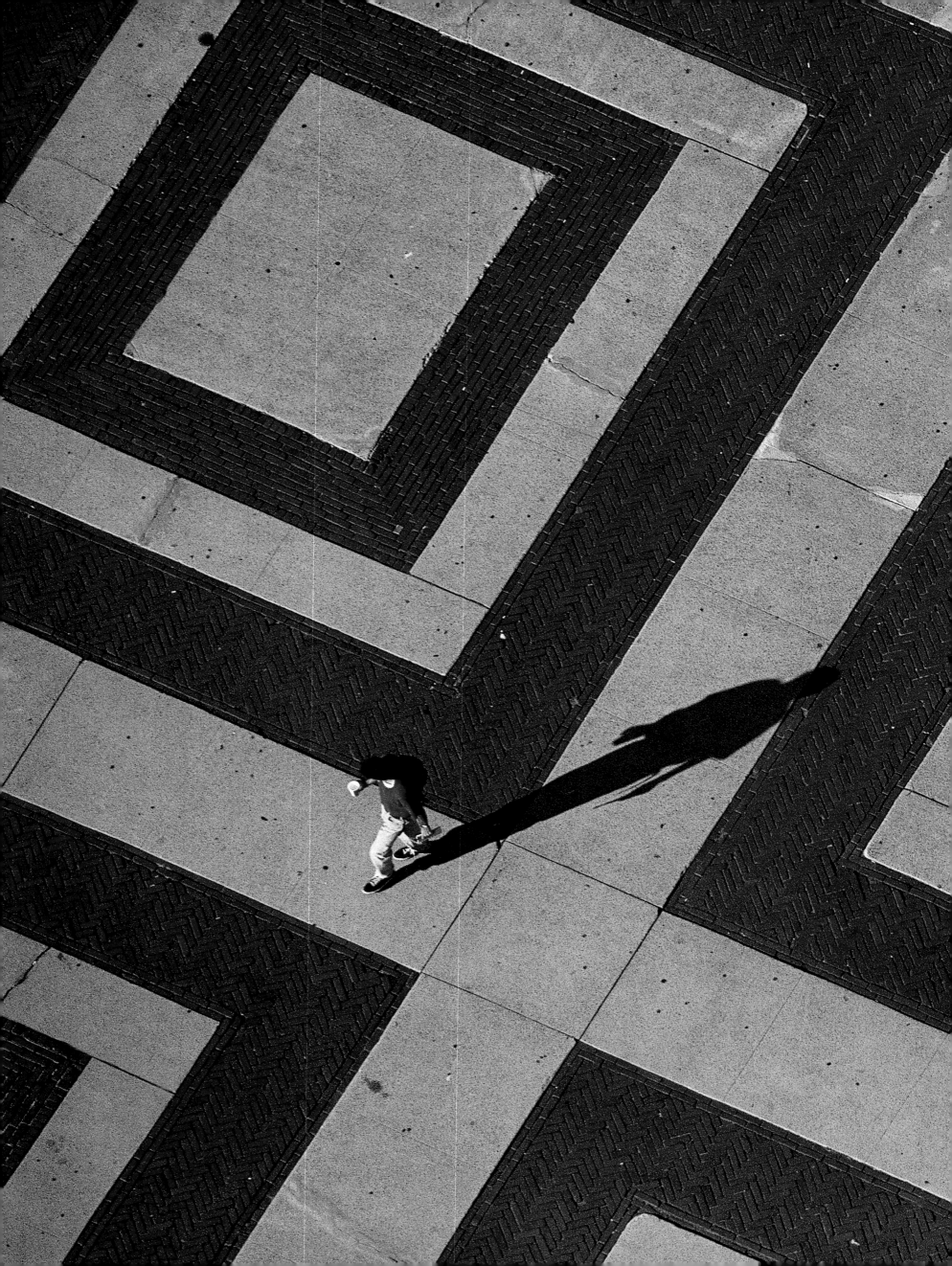

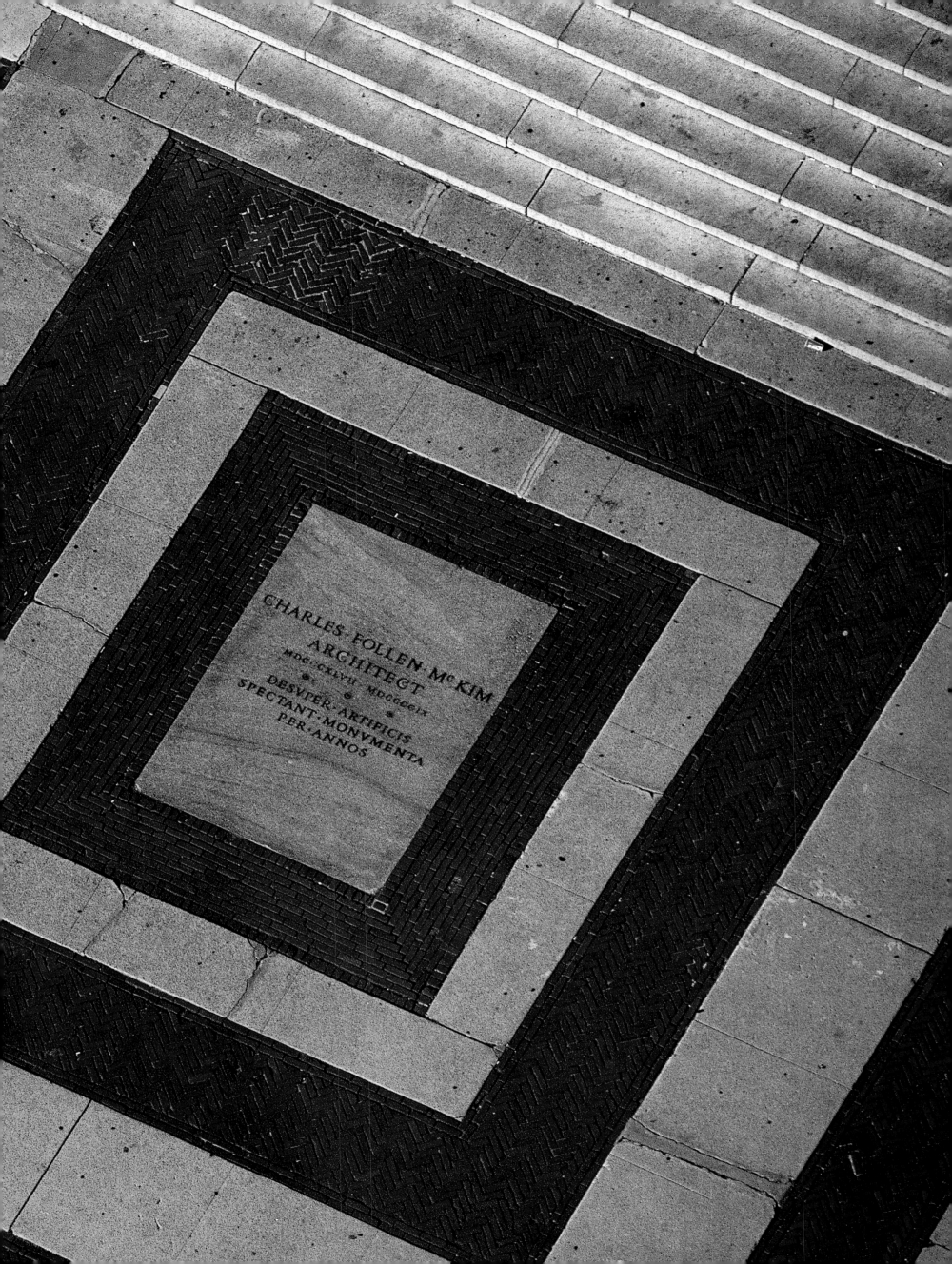

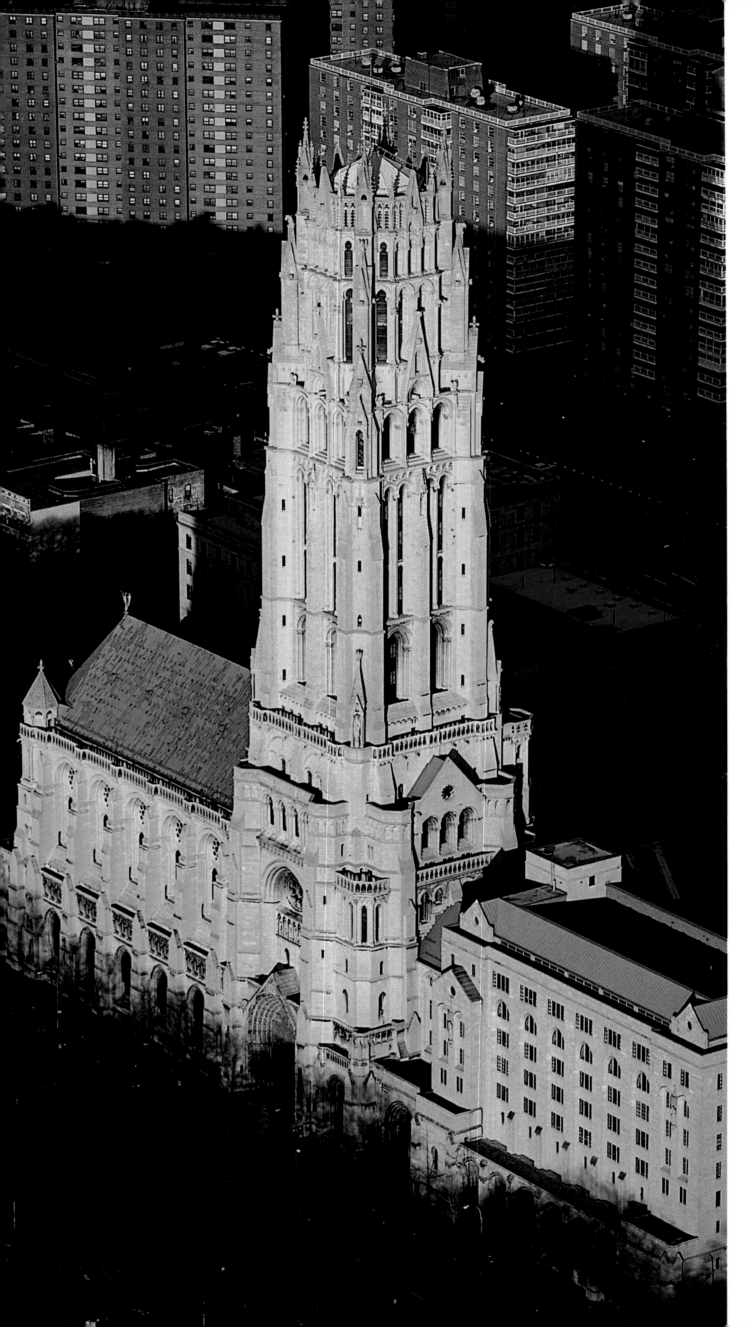

Riverside Church's most distinguishing feature is its 392-foot-high, Gothic-style tower, which is in truth a steel-framed skyscraper housing offices, classrooms, a belfry, and one of the few observatories for viewing the city that is still open.

The church itself seems stunted by the tower, but its size is deceptive—it is 215 feet long, eighty-nine feet wide, and 100 feet high, with a seating capacity of 2,500, or about that of Saint Patrick's Cathedral.

The church was designed by Allen & Collens and Henry C. Pelton, who looked to the Chartres cathedral for their inspiration. Among the reredos behind the altar you will find statues of great Americans, including George Washington, Abraham Lincoln, and John D. Rockefeller, whose son, John D. Rockefeller, Jr., put up most of the money for the church.

The Normandy Apartments, which opened in 1939, were designed by Emery Roth, who started in the Beaux-Arts school of design, moved to the ebullient eclecticism of the 1920s, and by the 1930s was shifting toward a more modern Modernism while clinging to tried-and-true neoclassicism.

The result here is a streamlined vision of the Alhambra, a glorious apartment house with rounded corners that are filled with casement windows providing spectacular views across Riverside Park and the Hudson River.

The apartment houses in the top right form part of the canyon wall of West End Avenue, which is an almost two-mile stretch of sixteen-story apartment buildings, broken occasionally by a town house or the spire of a church.

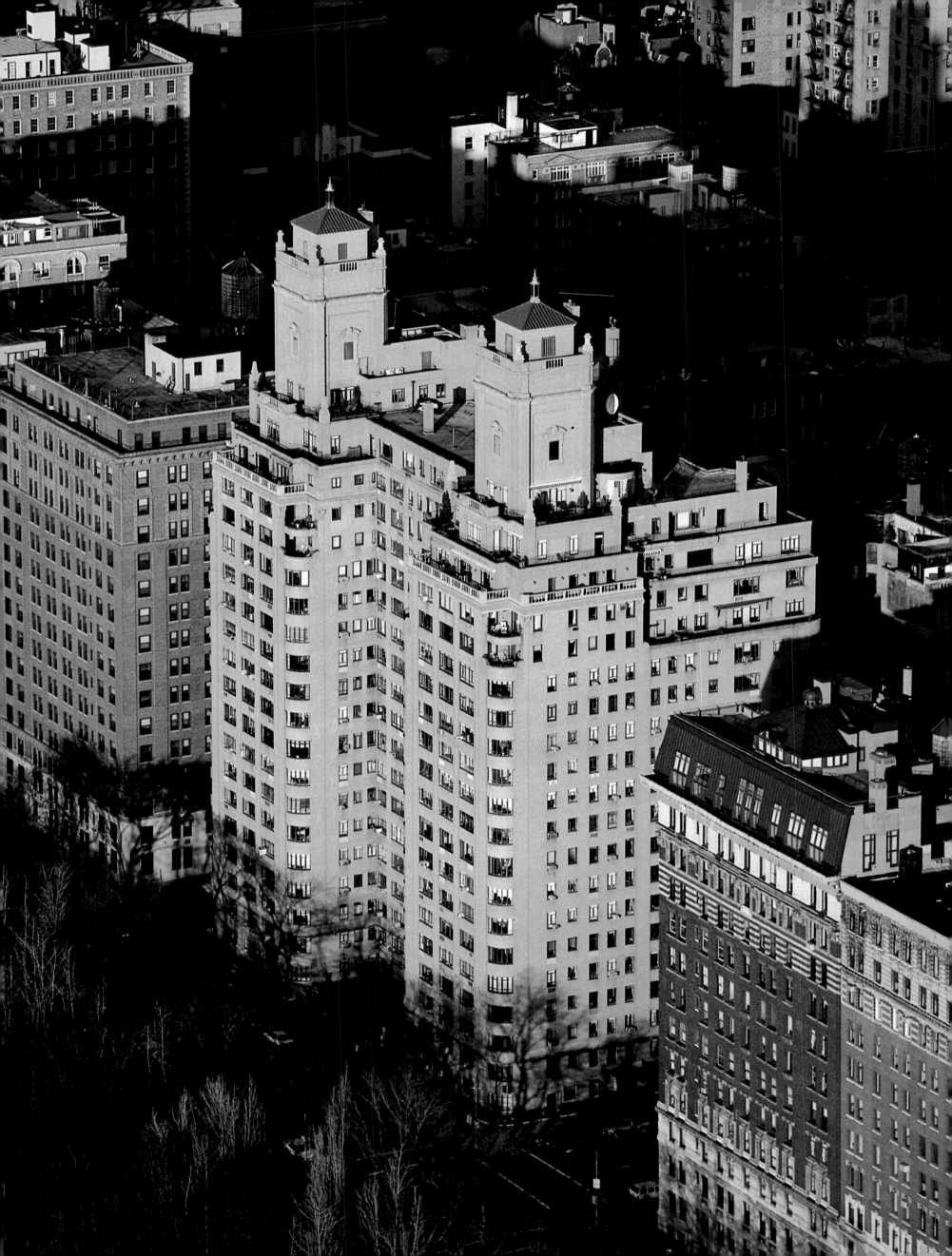

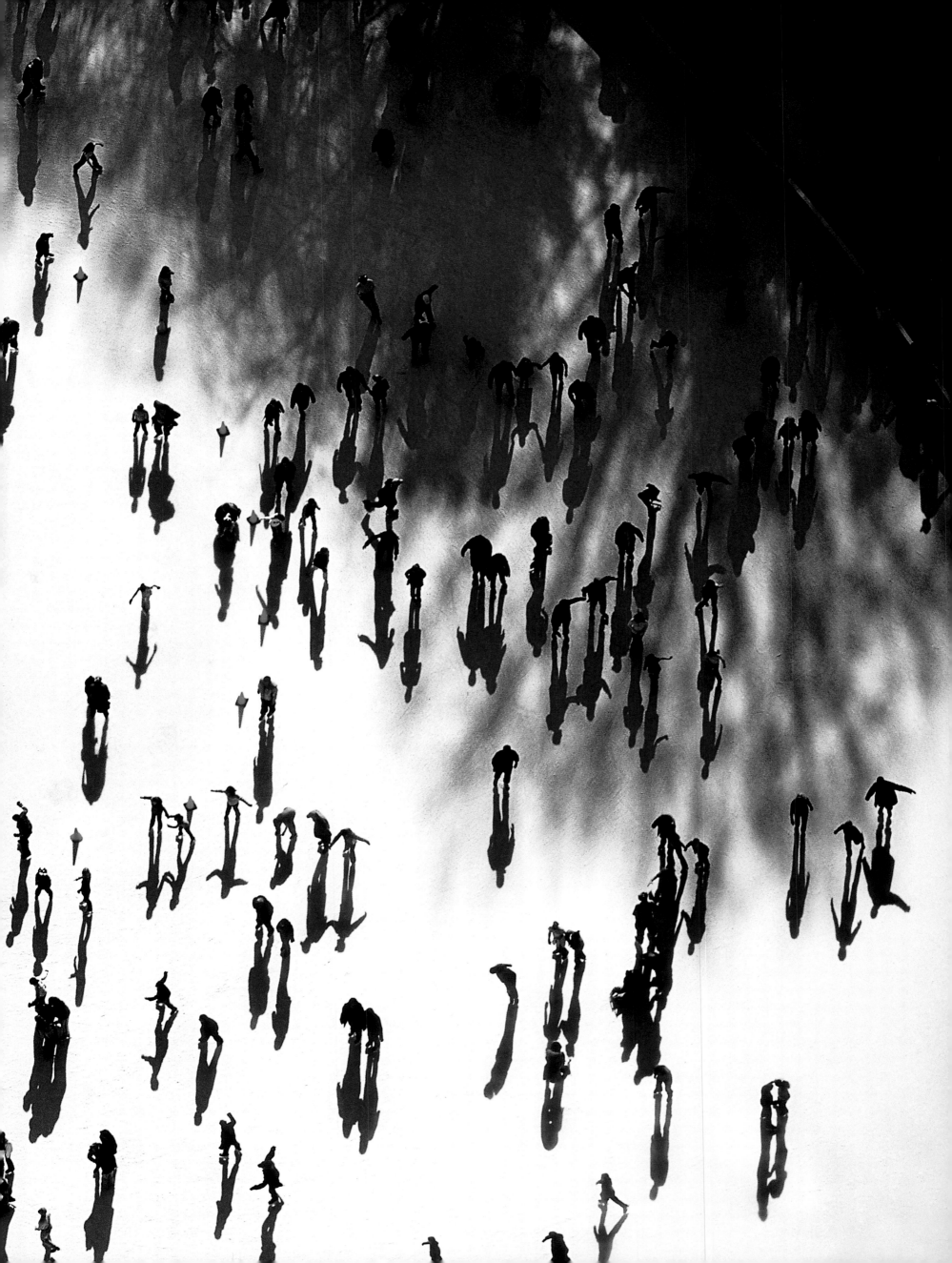

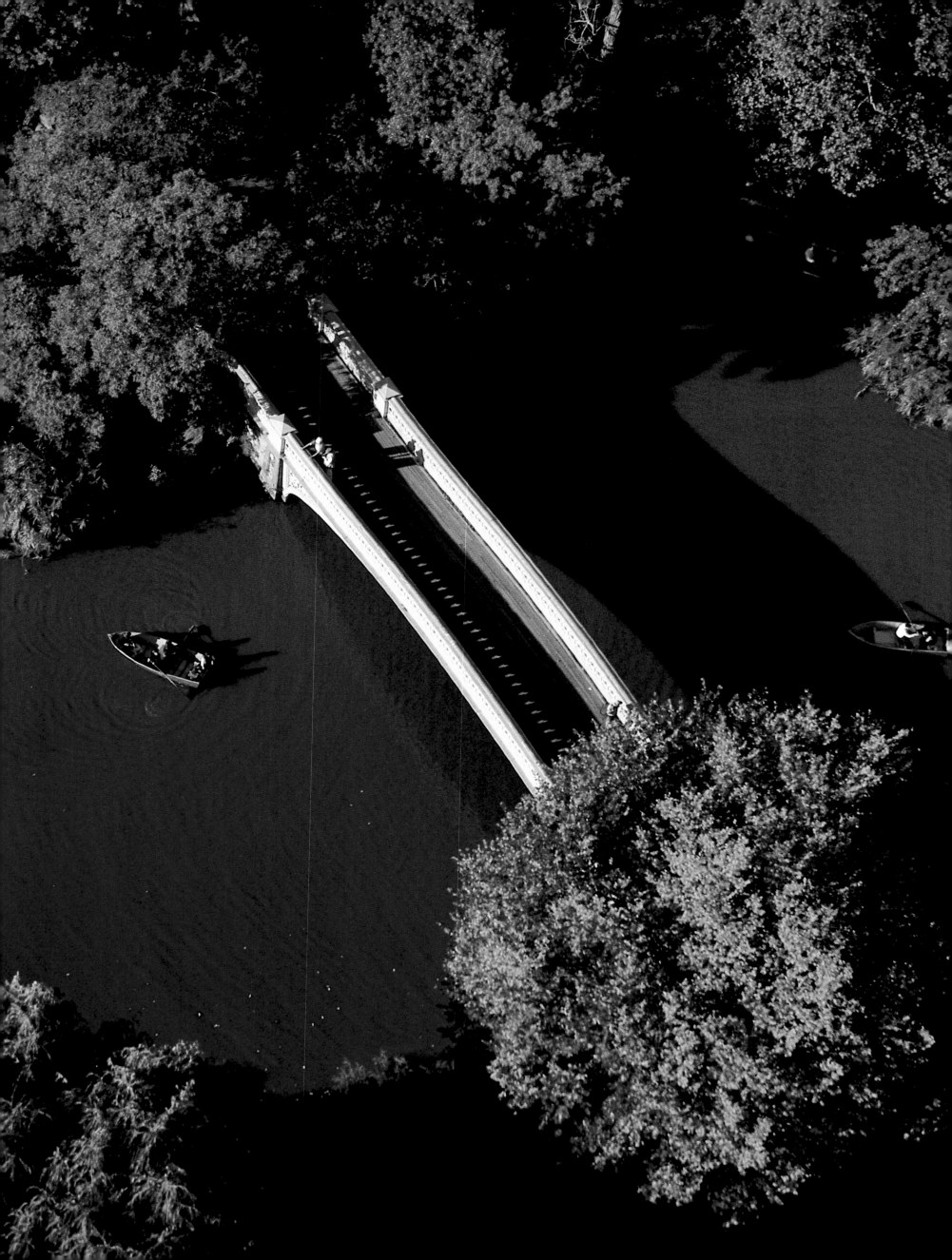

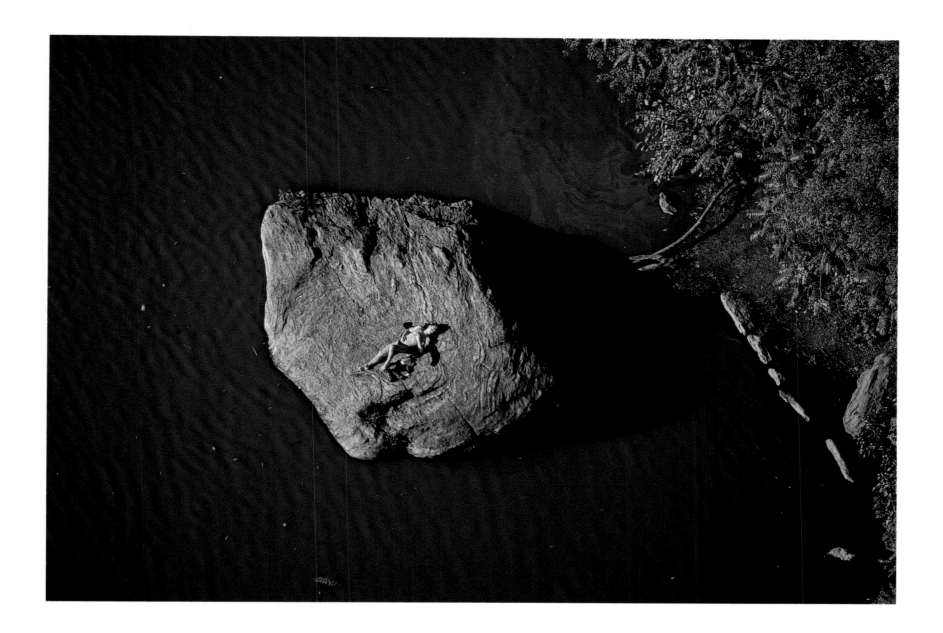

OPPOSITE AND ABOVE: **BOW BRIDGE, SPANNING THE ROWBOAT LAKE AND LINKING THE RAMBLE WITH CHERRY HILL, IN CENTRAL PARK VIEW LOOKING NORTHEAST**

Frederick Law Olmsted liked to believe that his contribution to the design of Central Park was indivisible from that of his partner Calvert Vaux, and vice versa. However, unlike Vaux, Olmsted was not a trained architect. Thus, Vaux's hand is clearly behind the park's gloriously Romantic structures such as Bow Bridge. With the reintroduction of gondolas to the lake, the Venetian image is complete.

Above, a sunbather finds privacy on a rock in the lake.

PREVIOUS SPREAD: **WOLLMAN ICE SKATING RINK, IN CENTRAL PARK, BETWEEN 62ND AND 63RD STREET**

On only six days in the winter of 1862–1863, the red ball flew atop the bell tower in Central Park to indicate that the lakes were frozen hard enough to allow ice skating. With the coming of today's Wollman Rink in 1951, and its consequent refurbishment by Donald Trump, ice skating takes place seven days a week during an elongated season.

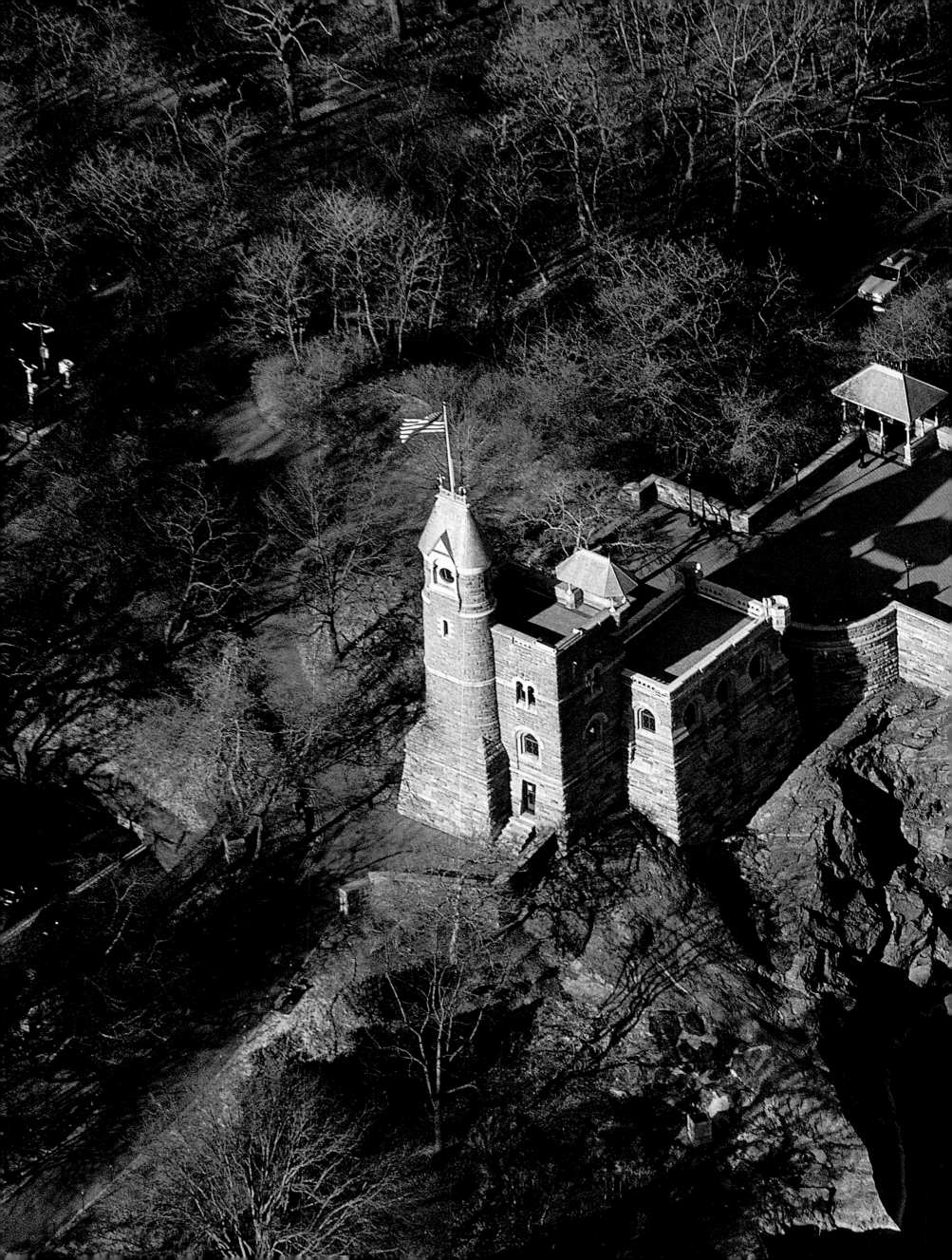

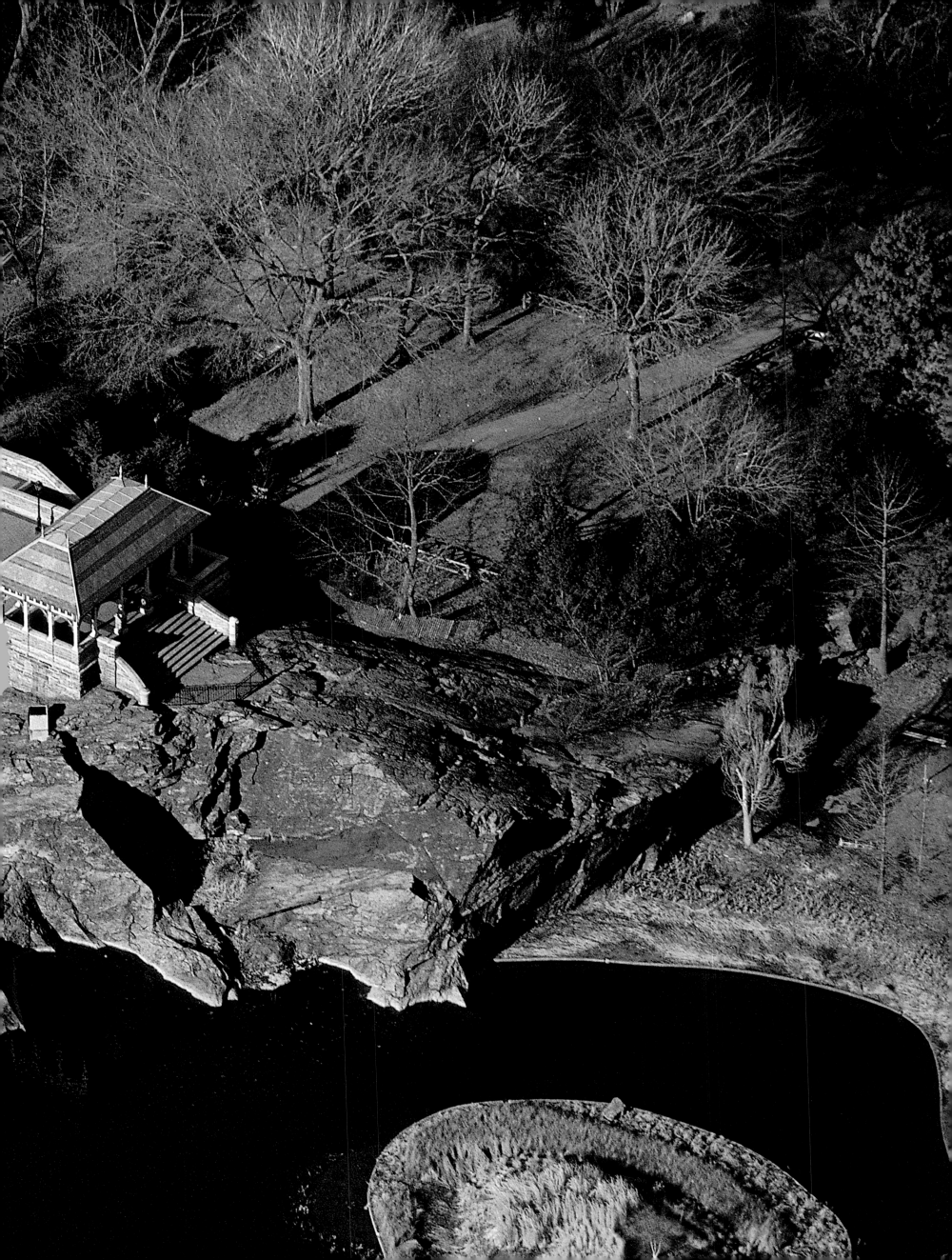

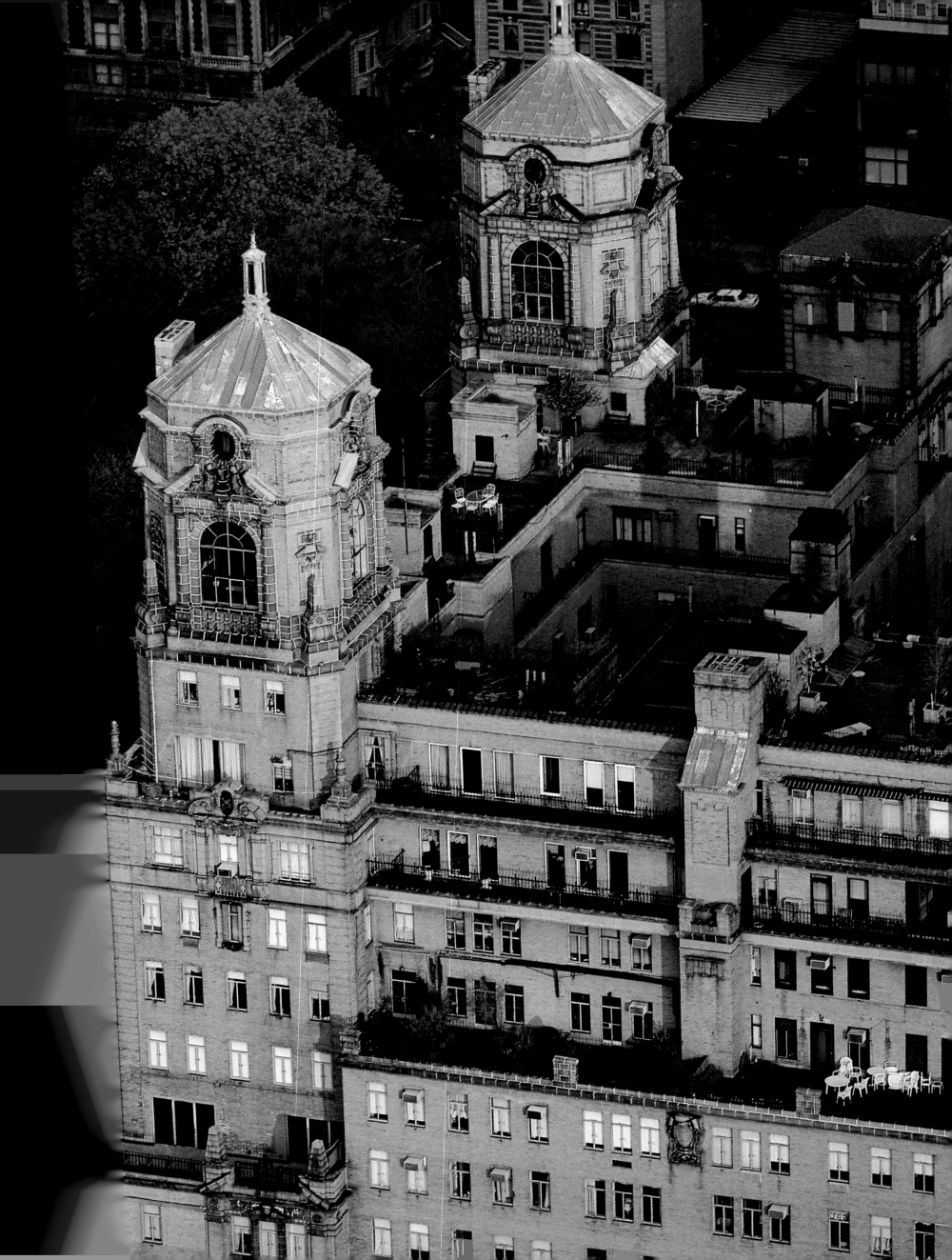

**OPPOSITE: BERESFORD APARTMENTS,
ONE WEST 81ST STREET,
ON CENTRAL PARK WEST**

For caption, see page 119.

**PREVIOUS SPREAD: BELVEDERE CASTLE,
IN CENTRAL PARK, AT 79TH STREET
VIEW LOOKING SOUTHWEST**

The Belvedere inspires little boys to scramble up the rocks at the base of the castle in the hope of storming the fortress and saving the fair damsel in distress. The Belvedere was designed to be a folly, and thus all of the romantic images it evokes are appropriate.

"Belvederes" are structures that command views, and this one is no exception. But Belvedere Castle was also designed to be seen, and the master magicians who designed it constructed a building that would appear far off in the distance no matter how close you actually are.

One of the great breakthroughs in traffic engineering is seen here in the 79th Street Transverse, one of Central Park's four sunken roads that link the West Side and the East Side. A stroller can walk the length of the park and barely notice the crosstown traffic.

**OVERLEAF: THE METROPOLITAN MUSEUM OF ART,
1000 FIFTH AVENUE, 80TH TO 84TH STREET
VIEW LOOKING SOUTHEAST**

Paris has the Louvre, London has the British Museum, and New York has the Metropolitan Museum of Art. It is, in a word, a treasure-house.

As you can see in this photograph, the museum is essentially a series of interconnected buildings, each of which makes its own stylistic statement. The Met's very first building in Central Park was designed in a Venetian Gothic style by Calvert Vaux, the architect who teamed up with Frederick Law Olmsted to design the park. The original building, which opened in 1880, is the structure within the central quadrangle nearest the park. The first major addition, by Theodore Weston, was located south of Vaux's building. By the 1890s a master plan was decided on that would situate the museum on Fifth Avenue, and Richard Morris Hunt designed the monumental building that houses today's main entrance. The style he chose was Beaux-Arts, a style he intended for all consequent buildings to follow, but by 1906 McKim, Mead & White had designed the flanking pavilions in a more subdued neoclassical style.

In the mid-1970s, when the Temple of Dendur was installed in the wing in the center of the north facade, Kevin Roche, John Dinkeloo & Associates took over the museum construction. The architects incorporated the old building walls into their new designs: one of the original walls by Vaux is now an integral part of the Lehman wing, and the south wing by Weston serves as the perfect backdrop for a statuary hall.

The tallest building facing the museum on Fifth Avenue is 1001 Fifth Avenue. The apartment house was scheduled to be a run-of-the-mill high rise, but influential neighbors pressured the developer into gussying it up. Philip Johnson and John Burgee entered the project and added, among other things, the fake mansard roof. Next door to the right is 998 Fifth Avenue; designed by McKim, Mead & White, it is one of the city's grandest apartment buildings.

**PAGES 142-143: THE SOLOMON R. GUGGENHEIM MUSEUM,
1071 FIFTH AVENUE, 88TH TO 89TH STREET
VIEW LOOKING EAST**

Despite the fact that the Solomon R. Guggenheim Museum was designed by Frank Lloyd Wright, America's most famous mid-twentieth-century architect, the building raised more than a few eyebrows when it opened in 1959. This was too brave a brave new world.

For starters, the building seemed upside down. New Yorkers were not accustomed to buildings designed like a giant helix, a logarithmic spiral that swept up and out while seemingly floating above a horizontal band; they were accustomed to buildings that stood foursquare and swept up and in, buildings that had straight sides and right angles.

As a place for viewing art, the inside was said to be even worse than the outside, and critics questioned whether it served art or art served it—or if neither served the other.

Forty years later every guidebook to the city points out the building as one of the landmarks of New York architecture, a building that boasts one of the greatest interior spaces in the city, a building that is firmly ensconced in the fabric of New York culture.

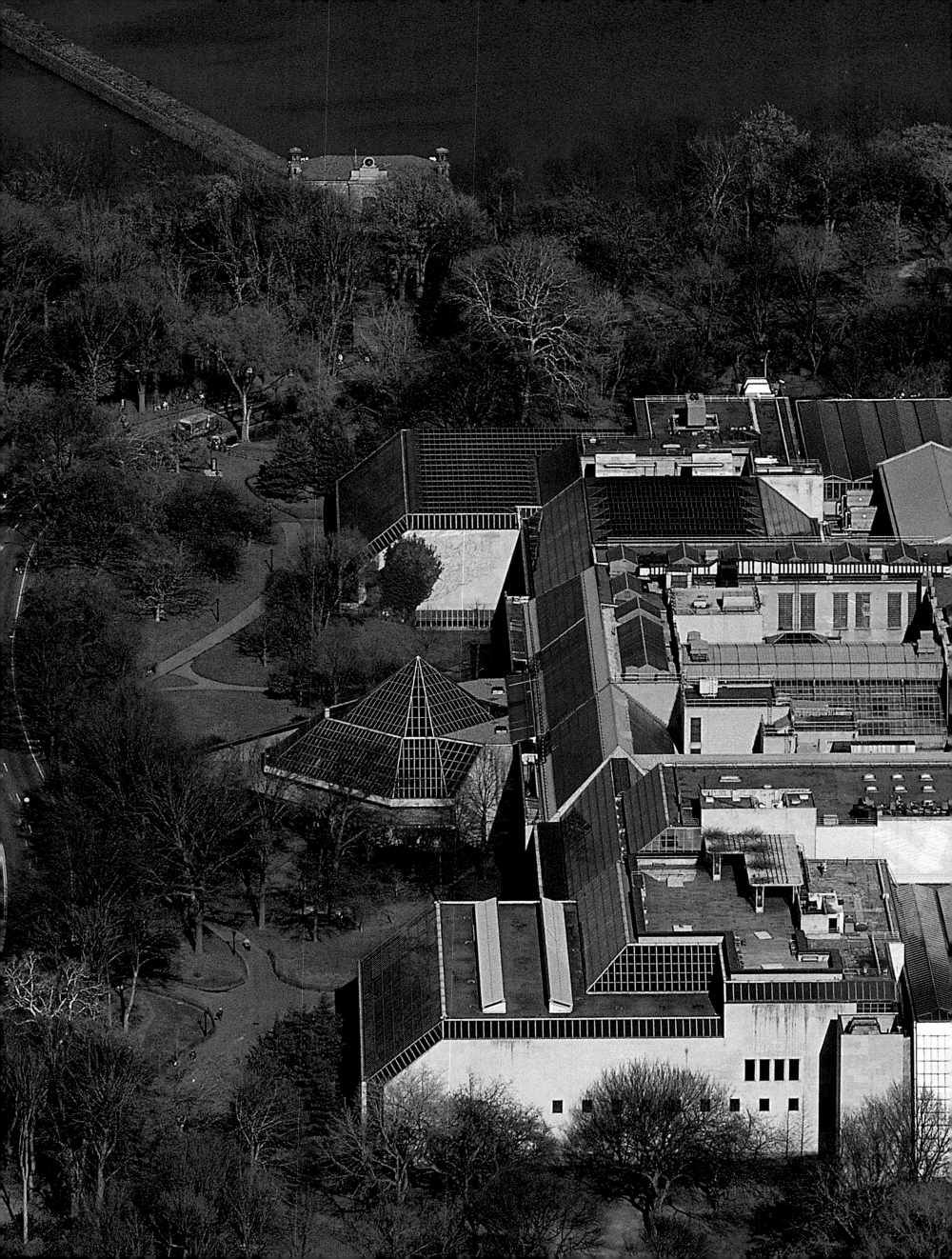

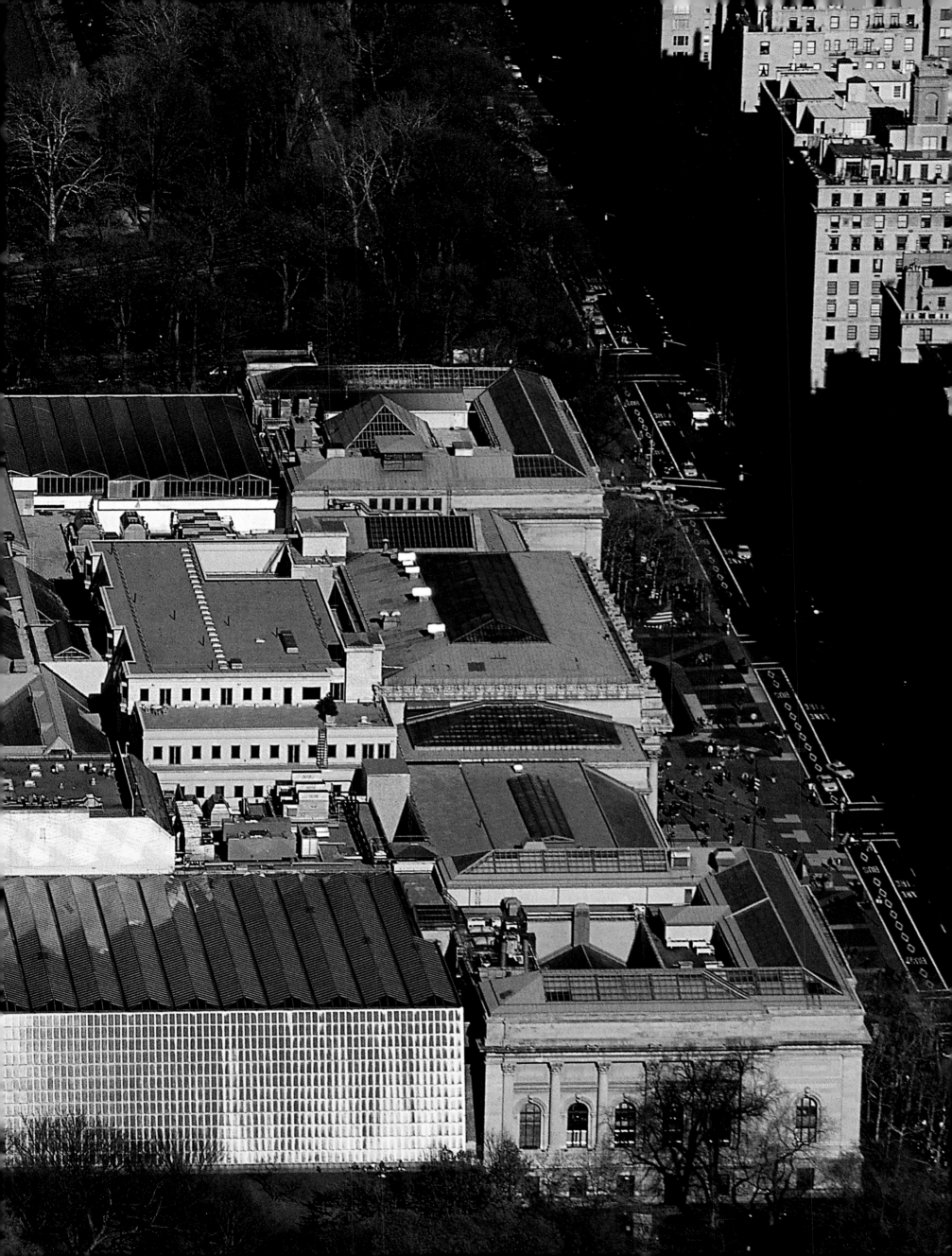

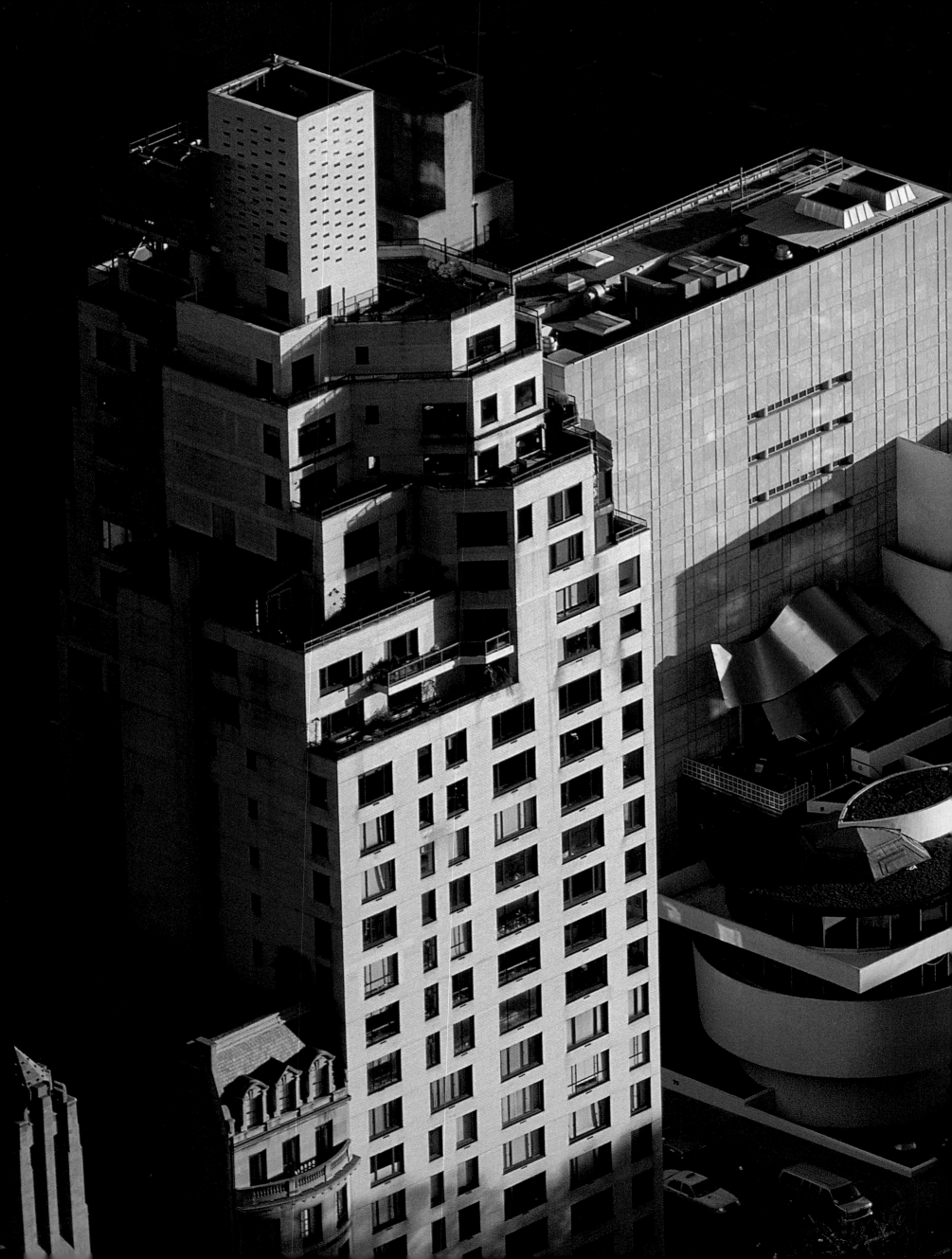

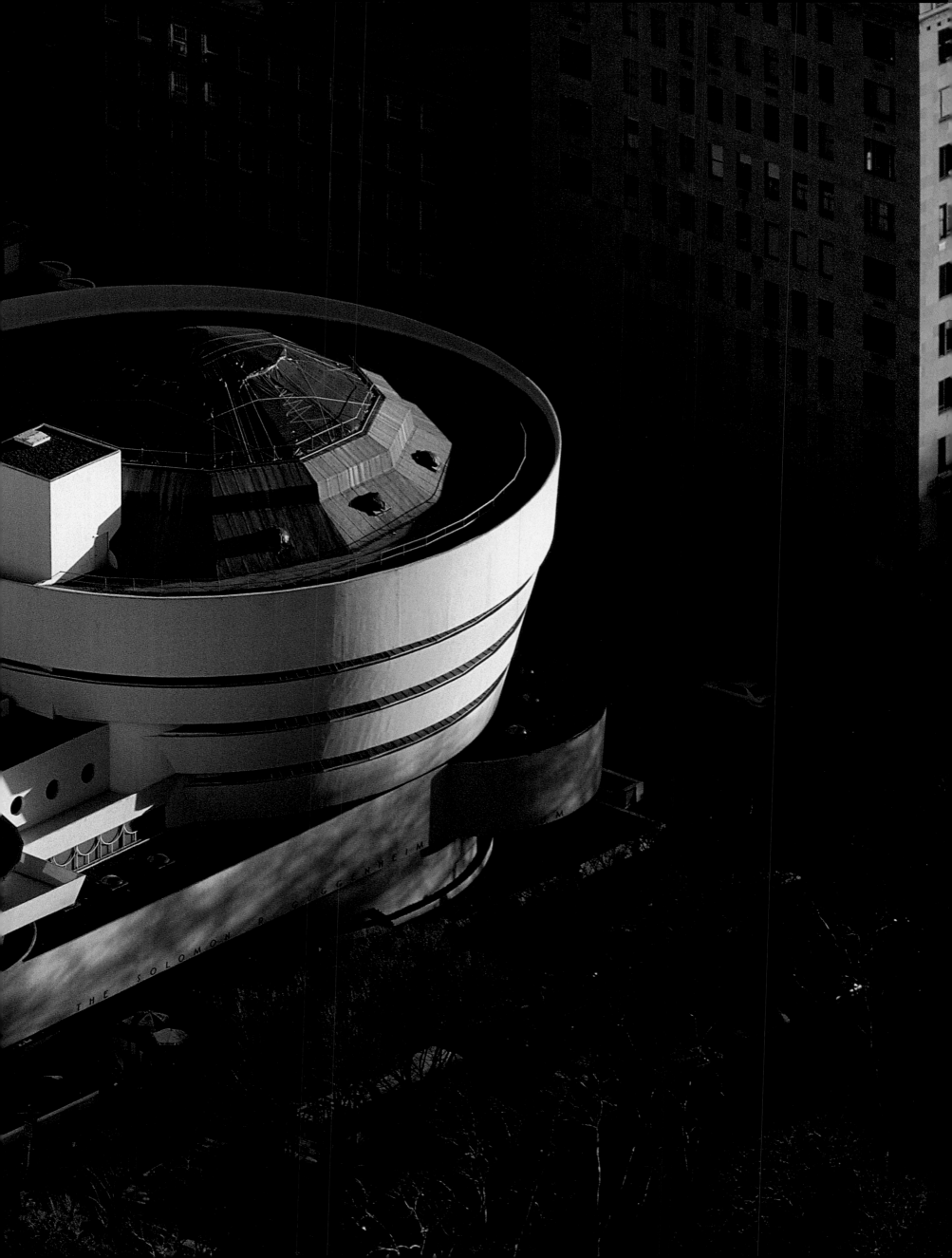

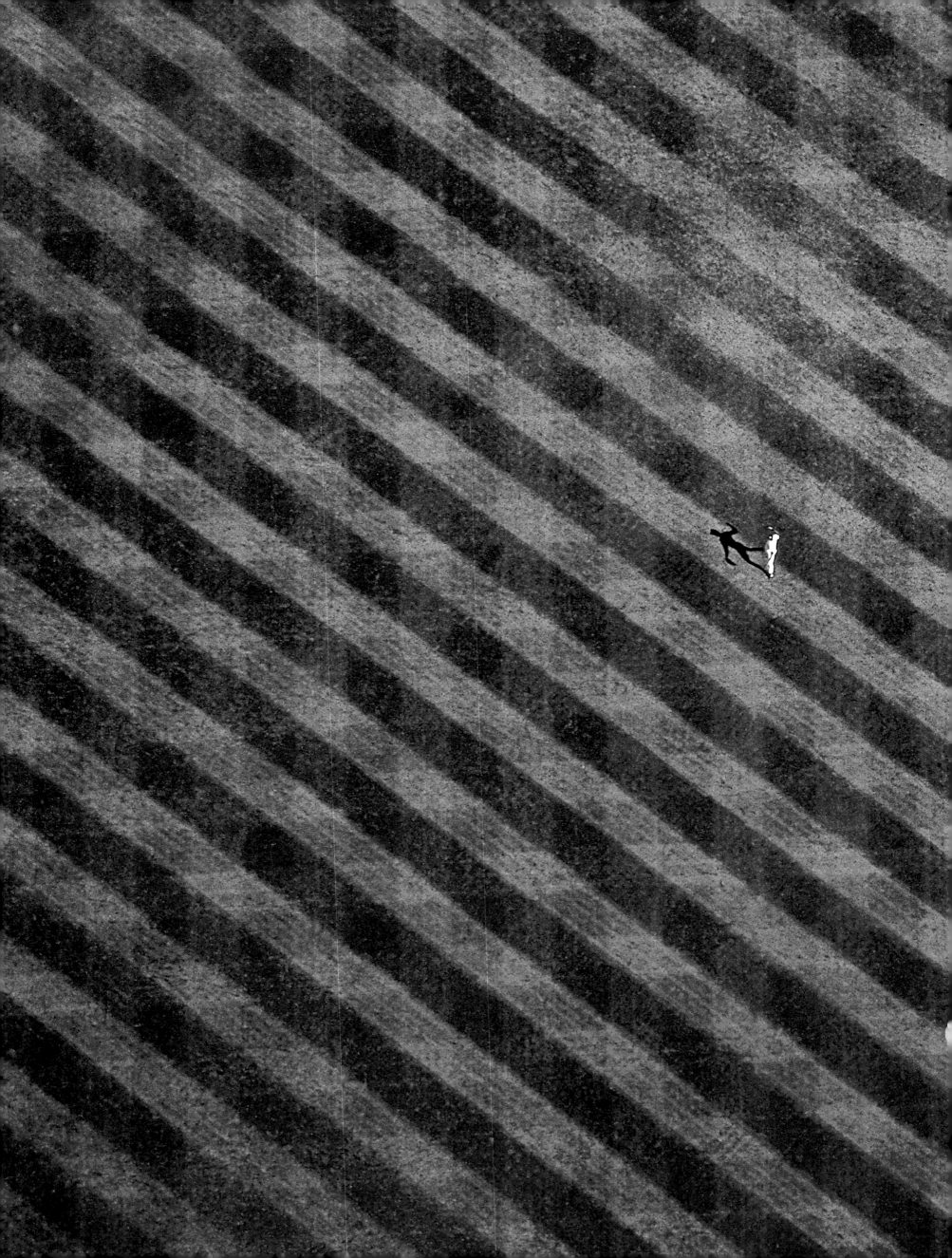

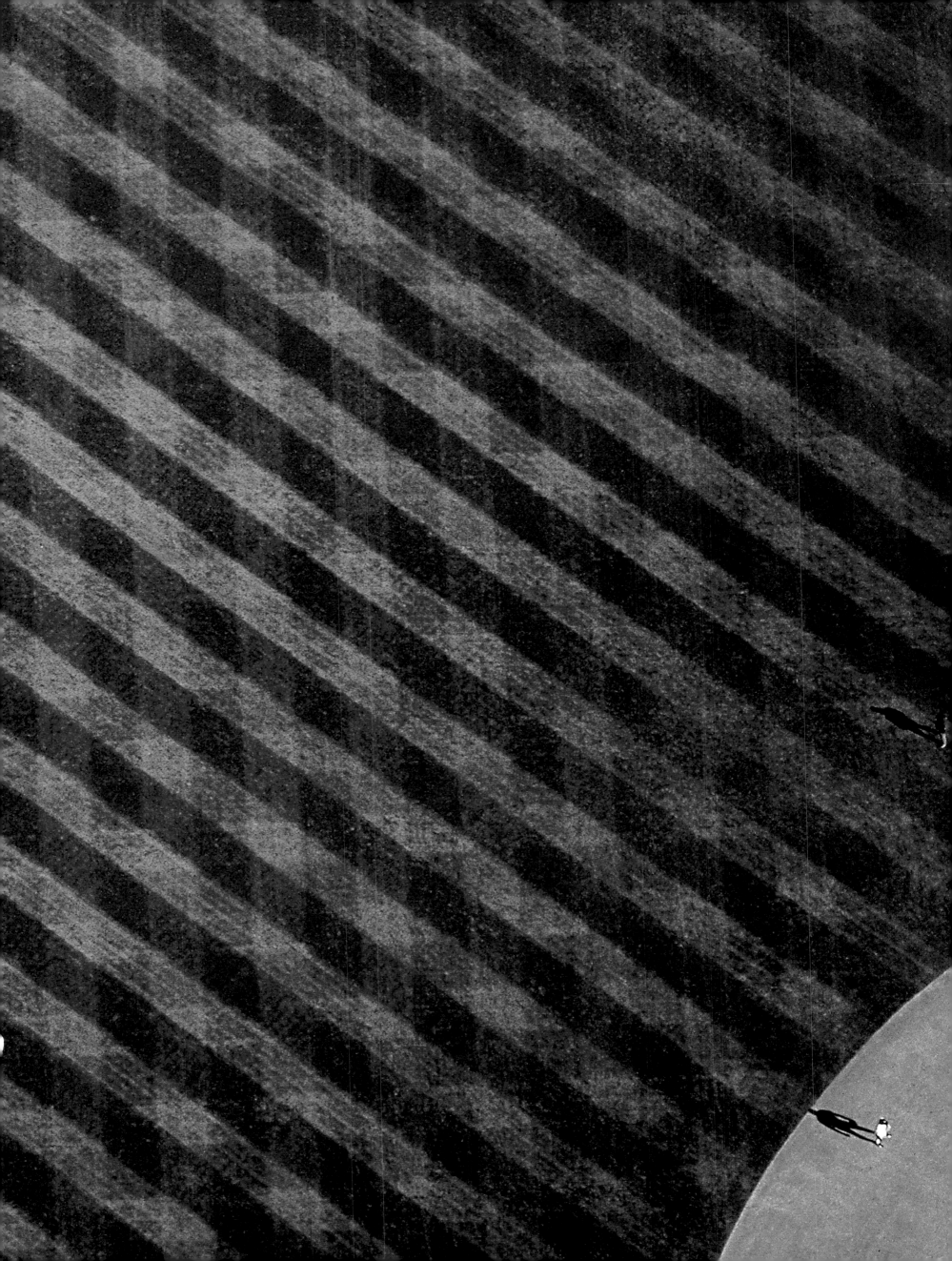

"The House that Ruth Built" celebrates its seventy-fifth anniversary in 1998. Here legends such as Babe Ruth, Lou Gehrig, and Joe DiMaggio have made the New York Yankees a great team with a famous history—and the bane of other teams, especially the Brooklyn Dodgers.

The distance from the edge of the infield in the bottom right of this photograph to the warning track in the top left is over 250 feet. The Yankee Stadium playing field is slightly lopsided—the distance between home plate and the right-center field fence is 385 feet, whereas the distance between home plate and left-center field is 399 feet. These dimensions make it easier for left-handed hitters to hit home runs than right-handed hitters, because left-handers tend to hit to right field, and right-handers tend to hit to left field. The difference used to be much greater: in the original Yankee Stadium, left-center field was at a distance of 460 feet. Thus, the right-handed DiMaggio hit more home runs on the road, whereas the left-handed Ruth hit an equal number of homers on the road and at home.

In 1976 the stadium was renovated and the outfield wall was moved in, shortening the left-center distance to 430 feet. In 1985, and again in 1988, Yankee owner George Steinbrenner moved the left-center field fence in farther. Steinbrenner said that he wanted to create room for fans to visit the monuments to past players, located behind left-center field; the real reason, however, might have been to enable right-handed Yankees (in particular, Dave Winfield) to hit more home runs.

OVERLEAF: BROOKLYN BRIDGE

The world's longest suspension bridge in 1883, the Brooklyn Bridge was billed as the "Eighth Wonder of the World." This was not merely public-relations hype and civic boosterism: the bridge across the East River, linking Manhattan and Brooklyn, was indeed a technological wonder.

The engineer John A. Roebling knew that stone in compression was ideal, so he used granite for the towers upon which the entire weight of the bridge rests. But Roebling understood that a suspension bridge with a 1,595-foot span would collapse if iron were used for the deck and stays. He needed something with the tensile strength to withstand the stresses, a material that could adjust to the different weights—the constantly changing torque—created by traffic making its way along the roadways.

Roebling did his homework and settled on steel for the decks and for the cables and stays that emanate fanlike from the towers to the decks below. It was the first use of the material for such a huge project, and a decision that predates by a decade the use of steel for skyscrapers, the building purpose for which it is most famous.

Built long before bumper-to-bumper traffic, the bridge today carries much more weight than its architect could ever have imagined. Fortunately, Roebling overengineered the bridge, and today's engineers maintain that given adequate and prudent maintenance, this bridge, this majestic and inspiring presence, should last for years to come.

When it was built in 1929, the 512-foot-high Williamsburgh Savings Bank was the tallest building on Long Island, a record the building held for sixty years. With the coming of the Citibank Building in Queens in 1989, the tower was relegated to being the tallest building in Brooklyn.

Whatever title the building holds, it is still one of the great examples of a freestanding tower that assures its tenants light and air. Of course, light is a two-edged sword in this case. Skyscrapers give light to their tenants but take from their neighbors, as the shadows in this photograph so graphically show.

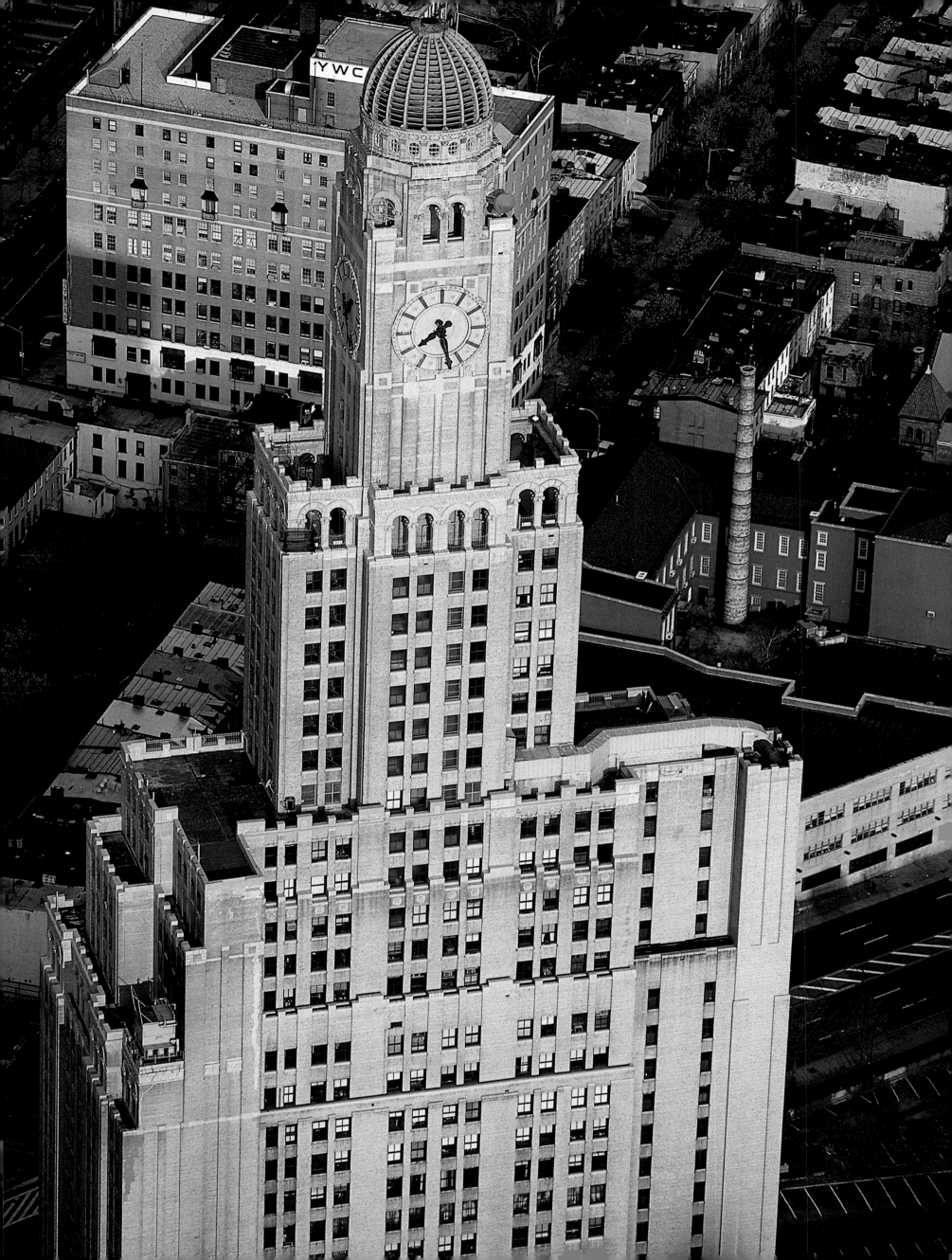

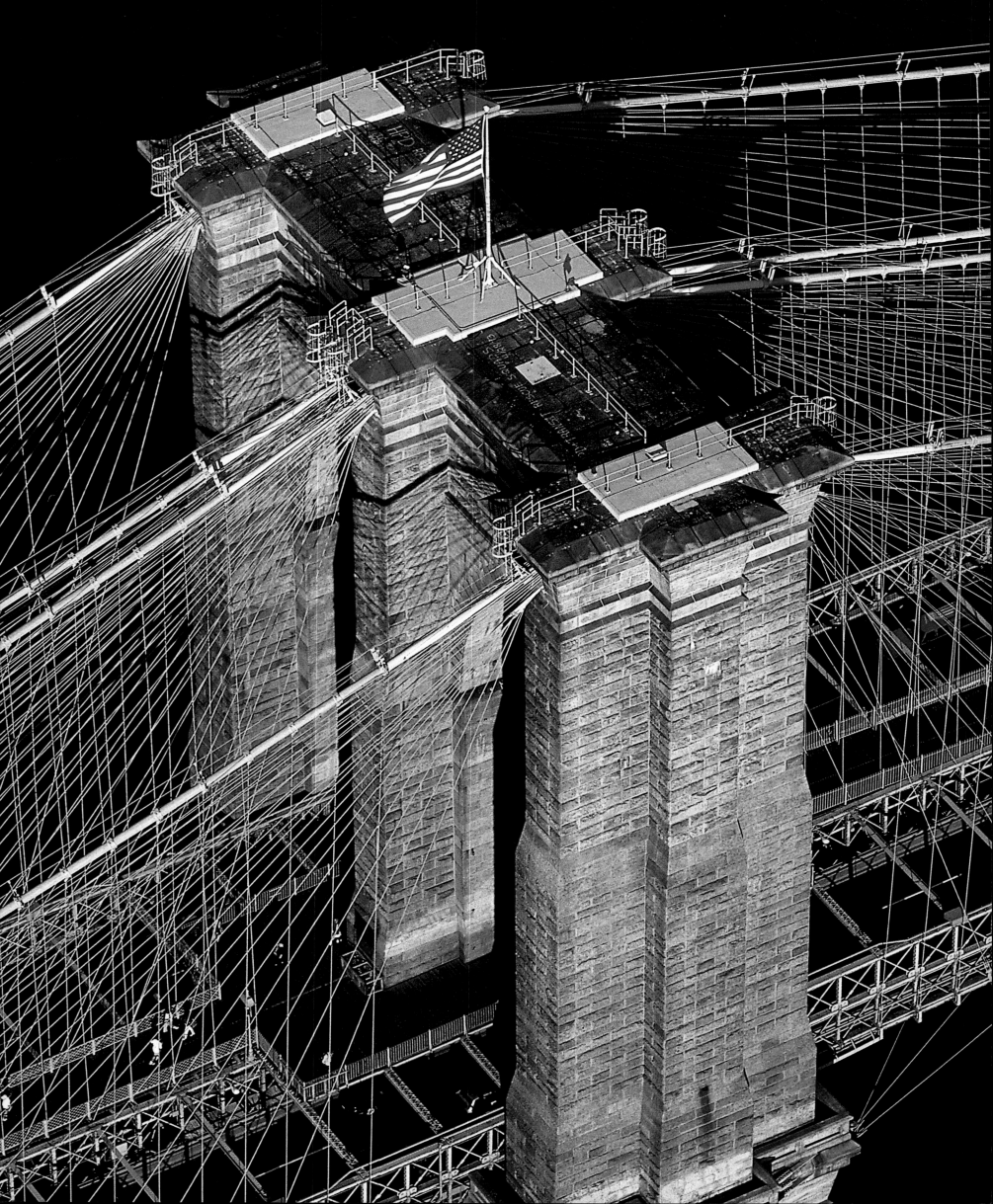

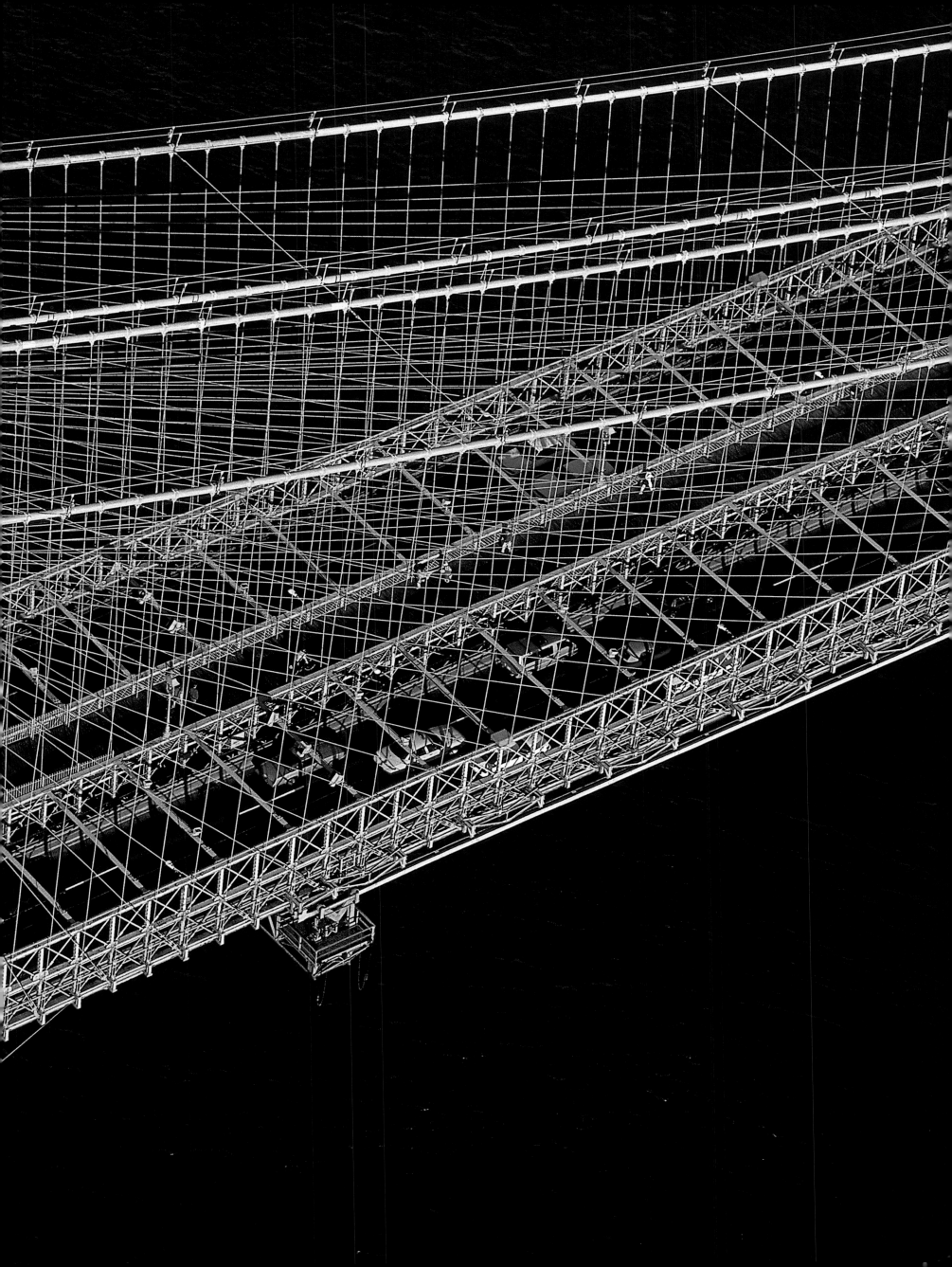

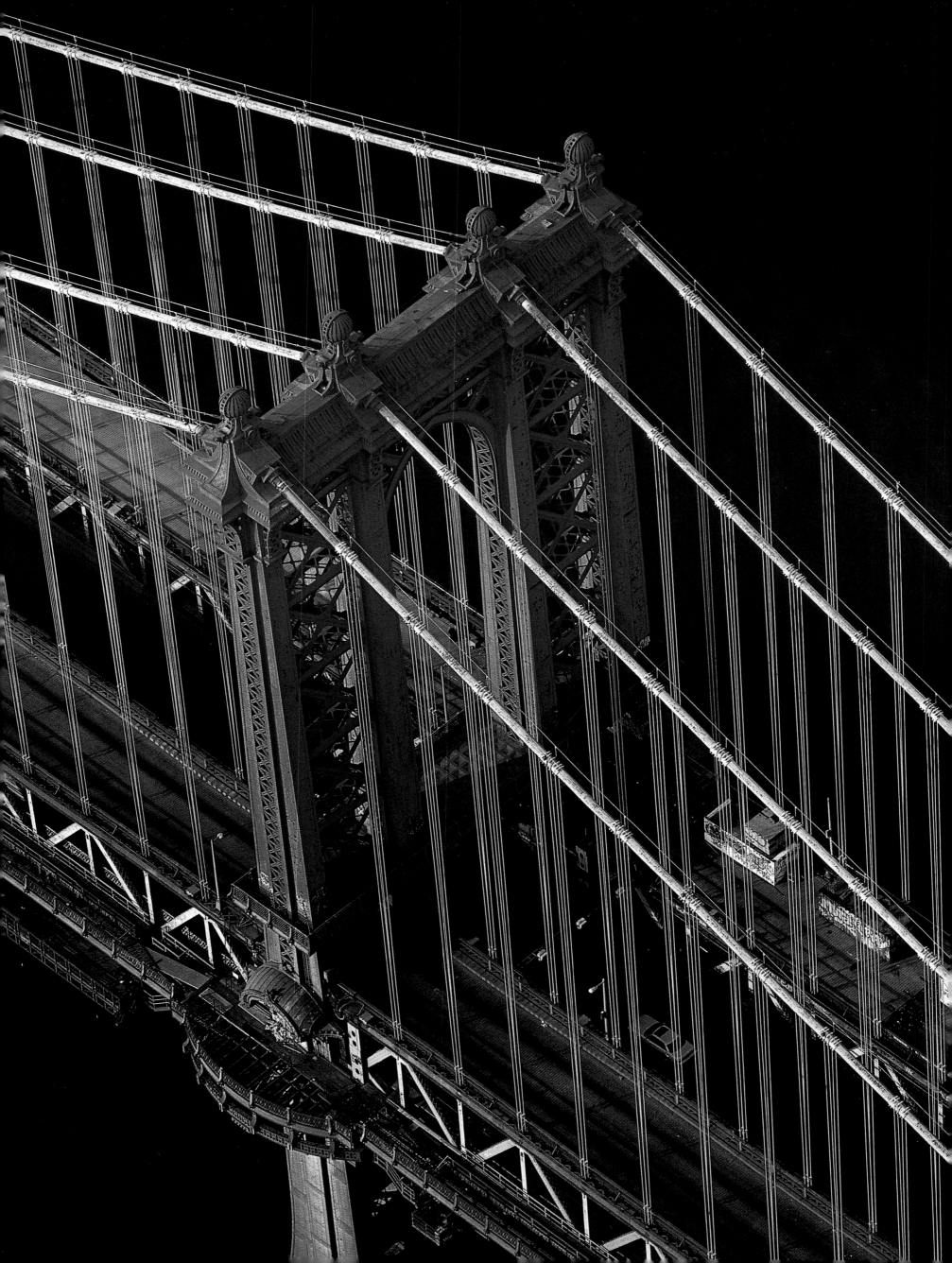

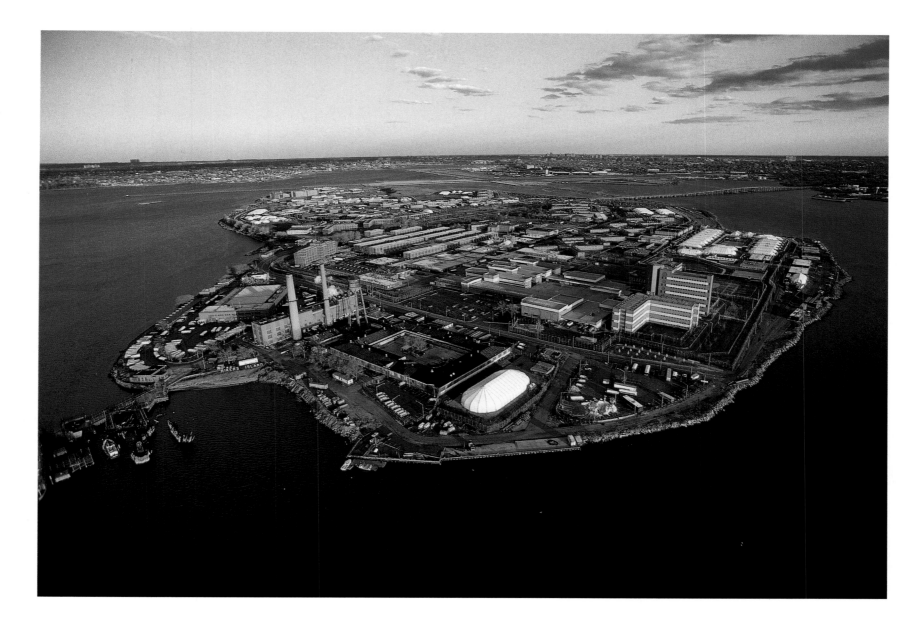

OPPOSITE: **MANHATTAN BRIDGE**

ABOVE AND OVERLEAF: **RIKERS ISLAND, IN THE EAST RIVER**

The Manhattan Bridge, which not only carries vehicles but also one of the city's most important subway lines, is one of the workhorses in the city's arterial system. But it could have fallen into the drink. The city's fiscal fiasco of the 1970s led to "deferred maintenance," ignoring the age-old truth that a stitch in time saves nine. When reconstruction began, roadways were closed and the subway system was thrown into a tizzy, but the 1909 structure, which was designed by the engineer Gustave Lindenthal, was made safe again.

This is a bare-bones bridge whose utilitarian style is in marked contrast to its Manhattan approach, a great Bernini-esque arcade whose neo-Baroque majesty is inspiring to those who slow down enough to enjoy it. The Brooklyn approach, now almost as functional in design as the bridge itself, at one time had a pair of statues by Daniel Chester French flanking the entrance, but the statues were removed, sacrificed to the cause of traffic improvement. The pair, *Manhattan* and *Brooklyn*, now grace the entrance to the Brooklyn Museum.

New York's very own penal colony. The idea of housing prison inmates on an island was not new when this prison was built in 1935—just think of Devil's Island or Alcatraz. Like those prisons, this one is surrounded by water that is treacherous. Although the land might seem within spitting distance, the prisoner who tries to make a swim for freedom is probably asking for more trouble than he is already in.

Beyond Rikers Island is LaGuardia Airport in Queens.

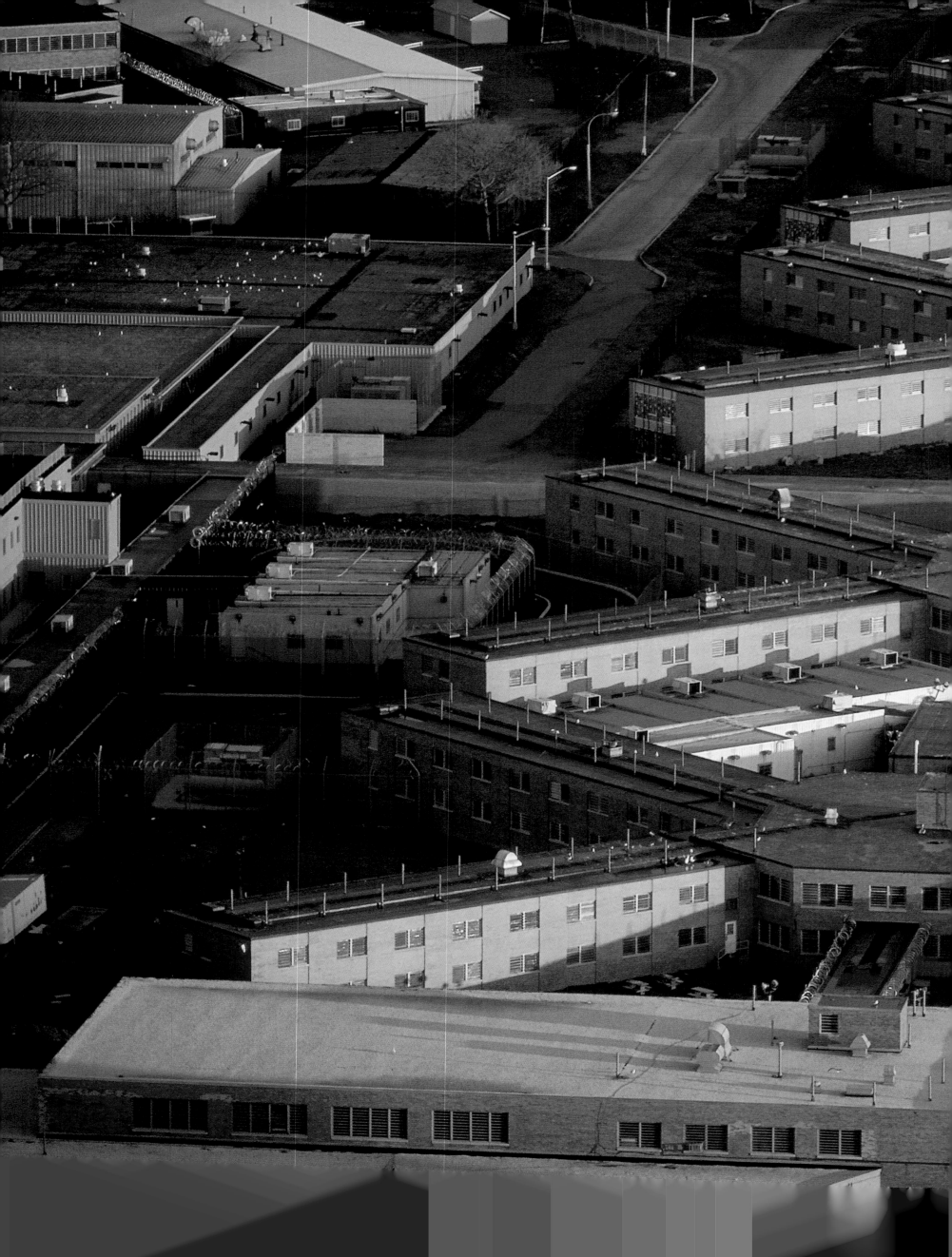

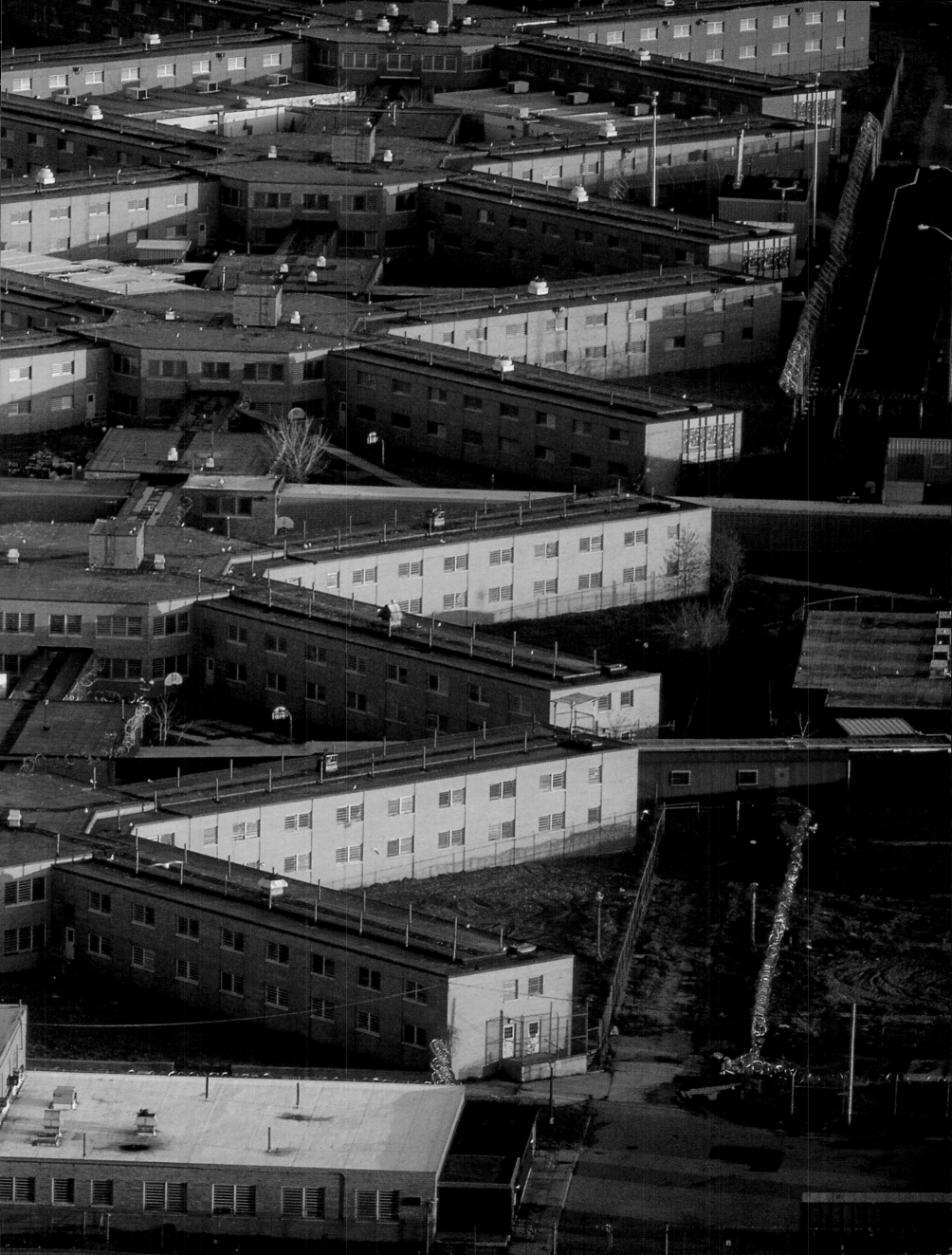

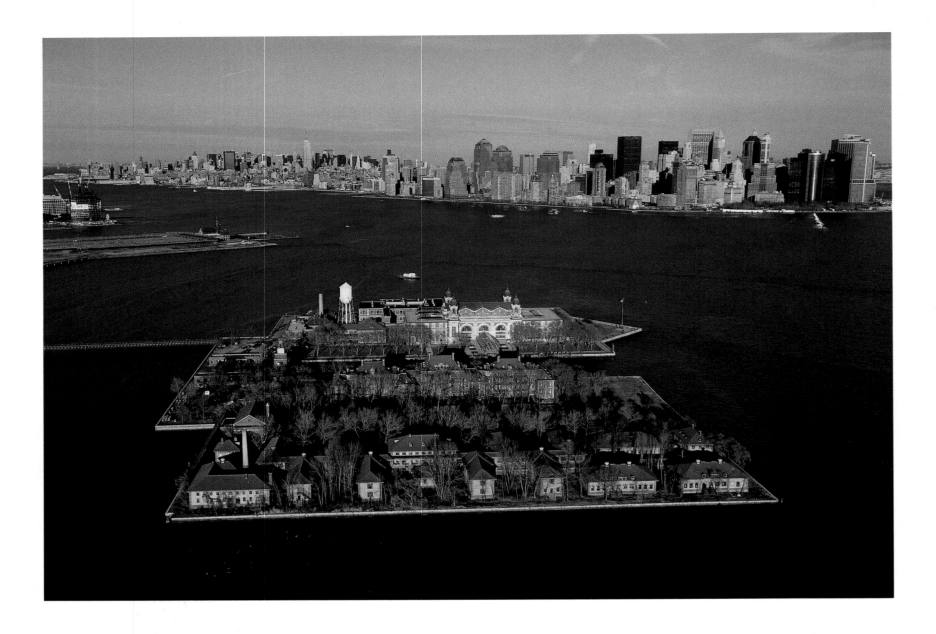

Above: Ellis Island,
in Upper New York Bay

If the Statue of Liberty is the symbol of the promised land, Ellis Island was the reality, the port of entry through which twelve million immigrants were channeled from 1892 to 1925.

The treatment of immigrants at this station flew in the face of the nation's ideal that all men are created equal. If you were traveling in first or second class, the immigration inspectors came on board your steamship, where you were treated deferentially. If you were traveling in steerage, you were herded through Ellis Island, where you ran a gauntlet of tests administered by officials who often did not speak your language.

The average steerage-class immigrant had invested his life savings in the trip to America. Usually, the investment paid off. For tens of thousands, however, the first touch with American terra firma would be their last. Ellis Island would be their isle of tears, the place where their hopes and dreams were dashed because of ill health or any number of reasons that made little sense to them, and they were sent back to their home country.

In 1954 the station was closed. The buildings now house a museum devoted to the history of immigration. The Great Hall still echoes with the sounds of hope and despair.

Opposite: Verrazano-Narrows Bridge,
Linking Staten Island and Brooklyn

This view shows the start of the twenty-six-mile New York City Marathon, which begins in Staten Island and follows a course touching upon every borough in the city, while touching the hearts of fans. With a main span of 4,260 feet, the suspension bridge that supports the runners was the world's longest suspension bridge when it opened. Designed by Othmar H. Ammann, who designed the George Washington Bridge as well, this bridge carries his indelible philosophical stamp. A man who did not believe in puffery, Ammann never tried to make a small thing bigger than it should be; instead, he made large things appear light and graceful.

Overleaf: Central Railroad of New Jersey Terminal,
Jersey City, New Jersey

This splendid terminal, designed by Peabody & Stearns, was built in 1887–89. From 1890 to 1915, its busiest years, thirty to fifty thousand commuters per day transferred between train and ferryboat, on their way to and from Manhattan. It remained in operation until 1965, when the CRRNJ declared bankruptcy.

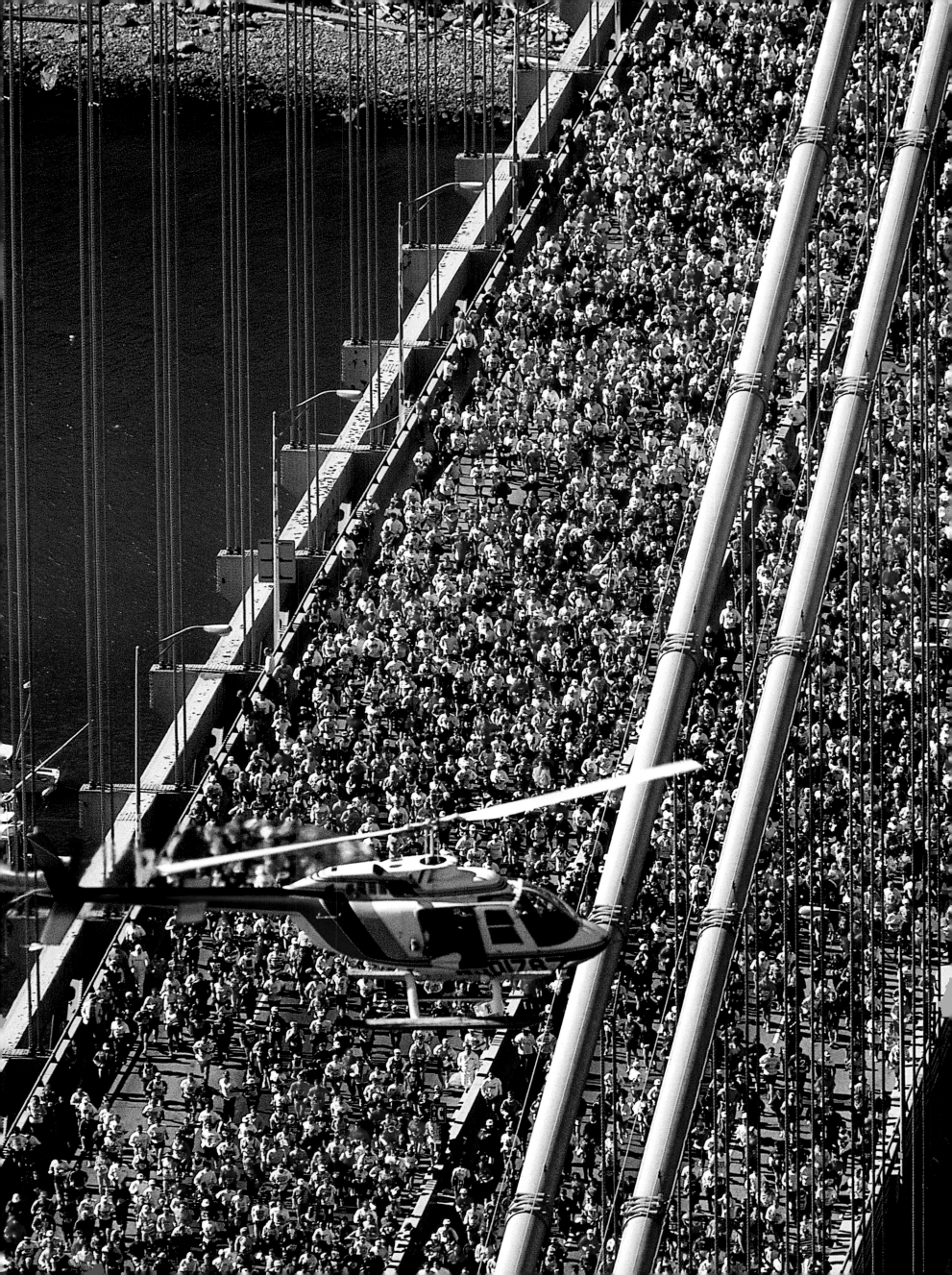

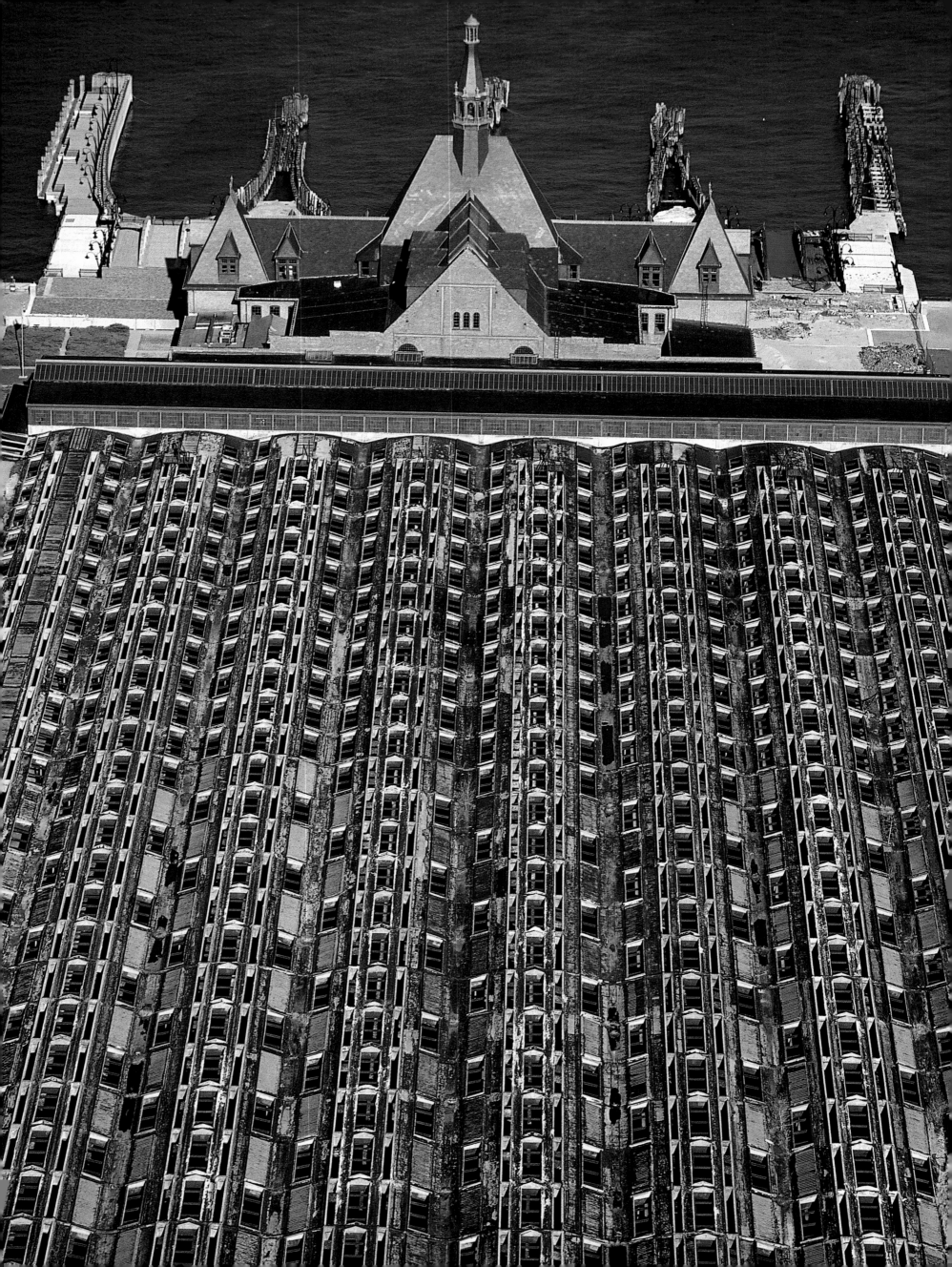

MAP AND INDEX OF SELECTED BUILDINGS

Place name is followed by page number of caption

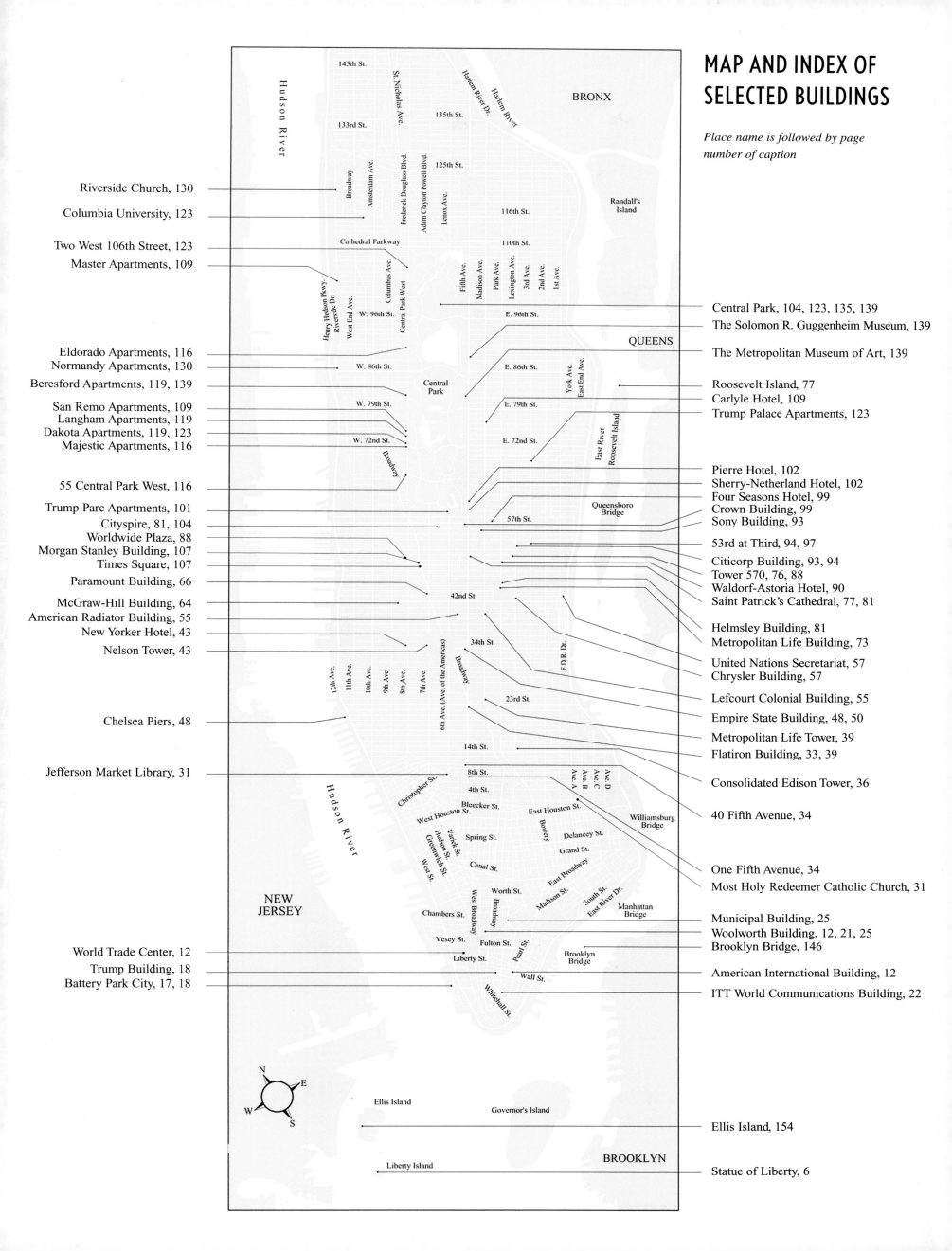

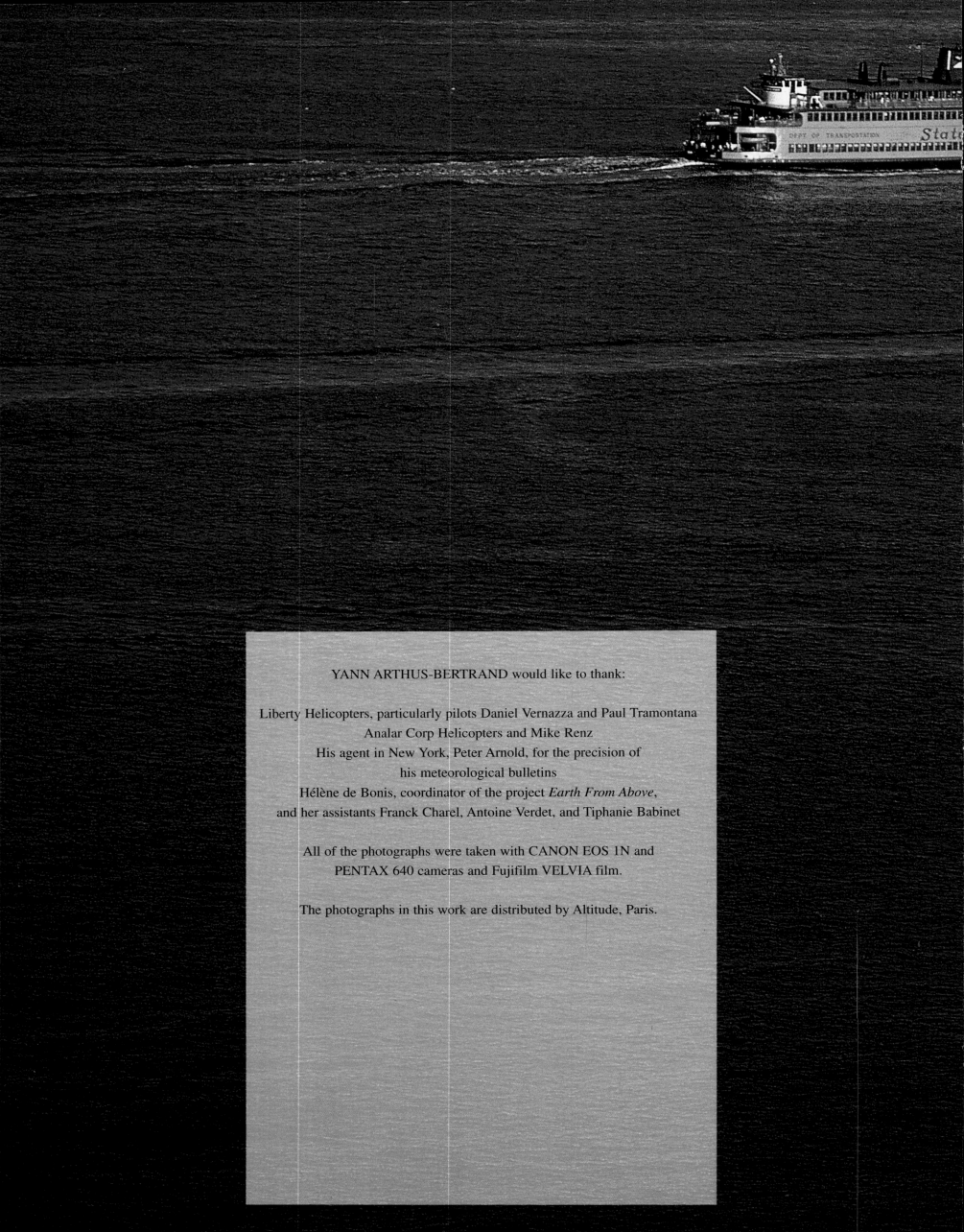

YANN ARTHUS-BERTRAND would like to thank:

Liberty Helicopters, particularly pilots Daniel Vernazza and Paul Tramontana
Analar Corp Helicopters and Mike Renz
His agent in New York, Peter Arnold, for the precision of
his meteorological bulletins
Hélène de Bonis, coordinator of the project *Earth From Above*,
and her assistants Franck Charel, Antoine Verdet, and Tiphanie Babinet

All of the photographs were taken with CANON EOS 1N and
PENTAX 640 cameras and Fujifilm VELVIA film.

The photographs in this work are distributed by Altitude, Paris.

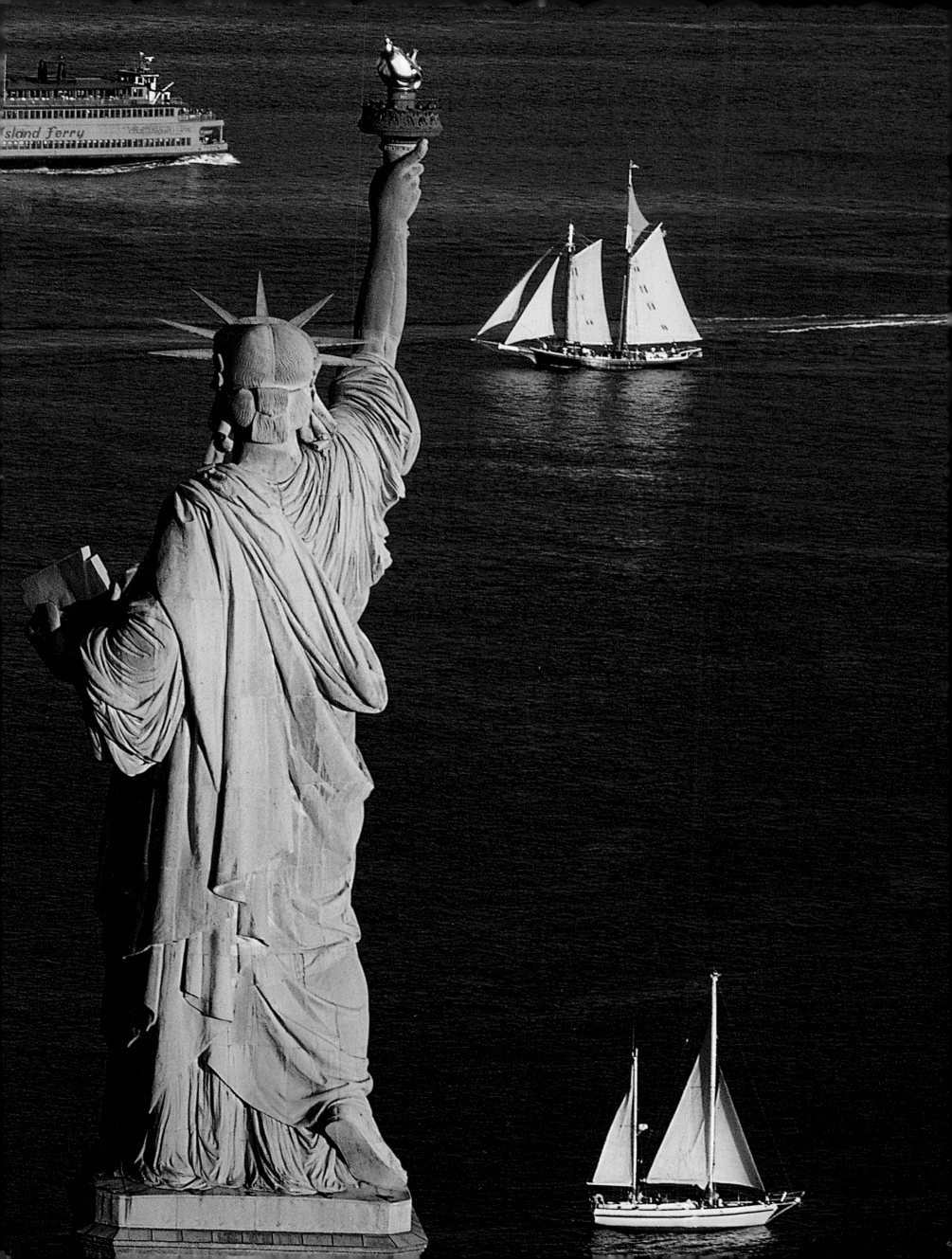

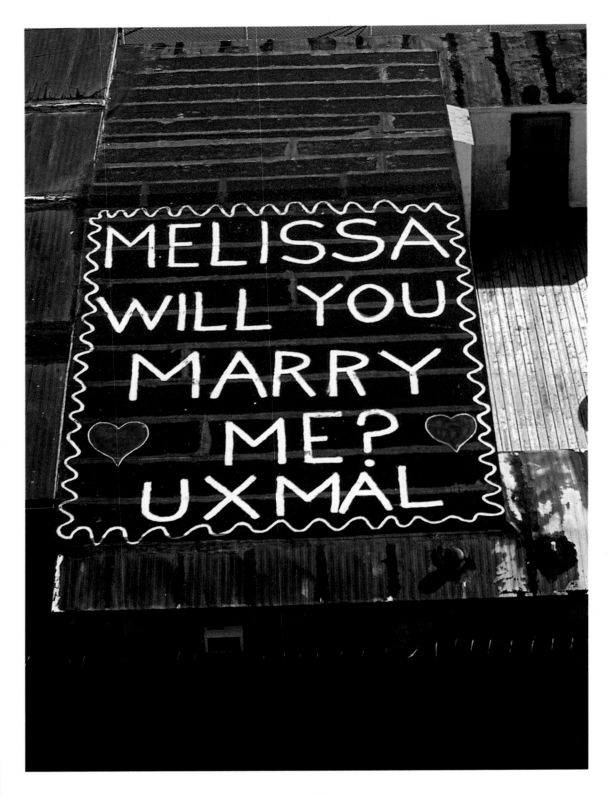

NEXT TO THE HELIPORT,
ALONG THE WEST SIDE HIGHWAY,
BETWEEN 35TH AND 40TH STREET,
AT THE HUDSON RIVER